For pluralistic pragmatism, truth grows up inside all the finite experiences. They lean on each other, but the whole of them, if such a whole there be, leans on nothing. All "homes" are in finite experience; finite experience as such is homeless.

— (William James, *Pragmatism*)

SUNY Series in Philosophy
Robert Cummings Neville, Editor

HISTORY
—MAKING—
HISTORY

*The New Historicism in
American Religious Thought*

WILLIAM DEAN

State University of New York Press

Published by
State University of New York Press, Albany

© 1988 State University of New York

For information, address State University of New York
Press, State University Plaza, Albany, N.Y. 12246

Library of Congress Cataloging-in-Publication Data

Dean, William D.
    History making history: the new historicism in American religious
thought / William Dean.
        p.   cm.—(SUNY series in philosophy)
    Includes bibliographies and index.
    ISBN 0-88706-892-8.   ISBN 0-88706-893-6 (pbk.)
    1. History (Theology—History of doctrines—20th century.
2. Historicism—History—20th century. 3. Religious thought—United
States—History—20th century.   I. Title. II. Series.
BR115.H5D4 1989   88-9745
200′.973—dc19   CIP

10   9   8   7   6   5   4   3   2   1

To my students,
as they are

CONTENTS

PREFACE

This book is prompted by an unexpected develop-
ment in recent American intellectual history. Almost one hundred years after
William James introduced it, more than forty years after scholars abandoned
it, an American historicism has arisen again. The current historicism is found
in the neopragmatism of philosophers such as Richard Rorty, Nelson Goodman, Richard Bernstein, and Hilary Putnam; in the literary historicism of
literary critics such as Frank Lentricchia; in the neopragmatic philosophies of
religion of Cornel West and Jeffrey Stout; and in the postmodern theologies
of Gordon Kaufman and Mark C. Taylor. As with the original American
historicists, they accept only historical references and deny all extrahistorical
references, including those implicit in idealism and positivism. They affirm
pragmatism, pluralism, and the constructive and value-laden power of the
imagination. They deny foundationalism, the transcendentalized subject, and
a correspondence-theory-of-truth realism. They deny both authoritarian and
subjectivistic nihilisms, and they affirm the responsibility of the subject. Most
simply, they acknowledge that historical reality is created through interpretations of the historical subject—that it is history that makes history. There is,
in short, at the end of this century a revival of a historicism which burgeoned
at the beginning of this century. This historicism is peculiarly and classically
American. Something about America once evoked it and seems still to need it.

In the pages that follow I show, first, the way this recent "new historicism"
issues to comtemporary American religious thought a new and powerful
challenge. Second, I acknowledge that today's historicists are vulnerable to many
of the current claims against them largely because they do not introduce the
classical American historicism that stands, in one way or another, behind their
own theories. The challenge by today's historicists is itself subject to challenge
because it neglects its own history. This challenge to the challengers is fair, for
it is the new historicists of today who argue that a thought must be understood
in the chain of thoughts from which it arises—and yet, they have neglected
the chain of American historicist thought that precedes their own historicism.
Specifically, they neglect the radically empirical epistemology, the radical

historicism, and the religious naturalism that their predecessors, working roughly the same way, found indispensable. Third, I describe this history of religious historicism, from James and Dewey, to the "Chicago School" theologians, to recent empirical theologians. I offer not an exhaustive chronology of the rise of religious historicism in America, but only one relatively brief interpretation of the faltering course of that history—enough to demonstrate that it is an important history, a history-making history.

The new historicism I describe is not: (1) the deterministic historicism of the Calvinists, the Marxists, and the materialists, a historicism that Karl Popper denounces in *The Poverty of Historicism* (2) the historicism of the Continental idealists and their theological children, which does see life as historical, but only in the sense that it is a moving window on what is finally absolute; or (3) the "social history," so important today in academic departments of history, the cliometric historicism that seeks verification of historical claims through the strict use of quantitative methods.

The historicism to which I refer is an American classical tradition in revolt against these historicisms. Paul Ricoeur has said, "wherever a man dreams or raves, another man arises to give an interpretation."[1] Most Western thinkers have argued that a person's dreaming and raving reflects or refracts some natural, divine, or human principle, and that the proper interpretation mirrors in some way that same deeper principle. This is what you have, these classical European thinkers said.

Over the past hundred years, a group of American philosophers, cultural thinkers, and theologians have removed themselves from this frame of reference. For them, past history mirrors no extrahistorical principle; instead, history refers only to earlier histories, which, in turn, refer to earlier histories yet. When a creature arises to interpret history, even this interpretation will be seen one day as simply history's addition to history. There is nothing deeper than the process of history making history. That, instead, is what you have, they said.

These American thinkers, themselves, made history. William James, John Dewey, George Herbert Mead, Alfred North Whitehead, the Chicago School theologians, the empirical theologians, some process theologians, and now many biblical theologians, together, established a classical tradition in American thought. It is a postpositivistic and radically empirical historicism. To the extent that it is religious, it can be called American religious empiricism, or, better, an American religious historicism.

Over and over, my interpretation returns to a motif: American religious historicism overcomes false dichotomies (falsely forced options, two-term fallacies) where it is assumed that if one option is false, the other is necessarily true. Sometimes the false dichotomy is between idealism and positivism. More important and frequent, is the false dichotomy between hope based on something beyond history and despair at the loss of that hope. American religious historicism advances a third theme, a radical empiricism that broadens the concept of experience to include the experience of values in addition to the five-sense experience of facts. It attacks the false dichotomy between idealism's access to values through intellectual intuition and positivism's access to facts through the five senses by offering a valuational empiricism. It counters the false dichotomy between extrahistorical hope and historicist despair by contending that historicism can find value, and hope, in history.

This third, American horse was to be ridden somewhere practical. James hoped to restore the individual to strenuous action; Dewey hoped to foster in society a capacity to grow in its environment. The Chicago School theologians and the empirical and process theologians wanted religion that adapts people and societies to a changing world, but allows them at the same time to retain a religious faith. They all hoped to counter what they saw to be the idealist's quiescent and on the whole irresponsible trust in suprahistorical ideals and gods as well as the positivist's despairing and on the whole irresponsible distrust of all ideals and gods. By its critics, this third horse was not refuted but disparaged, not shot but led to pasture.

In my treatment of the current revival of this American classical tradition, I want not to add to the attacks on today's new historicists, but to fortify their historicism by emphasizing the constructive possibilities implicit in three notions: first, the irony of the current American historicists (that they omit the history of their own historicism); second, the philosophical content of this omission (the radical empiricism and historicism of their historicist predecessors); and third, the theological content of this omission (an American naturalism and its attendant concept of God).

My effort to describe American religious empiricism and its historicism is a small part of an unacknowledged collaboration among more empirically oriented process theologians, deconstructionists and neopragmatics in religious studies, theologians and philosophers of religion clustered around *The American Journal of Theology and Philosophy* and the Highlands Institute for American Religious Thought, and those attending for several years the American Academy of Religion sessions on "Empiricism in American Religious Thought." Books are being written. I think especially of Nancy Frankenberry's 1987 *Religion and Radical Empiricism*. In my effort here, I accept one of the challenges of my 1986 *American Religious Empiricism*: that to be set forth properly, a historicist method must be historically grounded. That book stands to this book as an apology for a method stands to a history of a method—a history that leads, finally, beyond method.

In what follows, I write backwards, showing connections not as the omniscient scholar sees them, from past to present, but as the actual thinker feels them, from one's own present to the past. I mean never to suggest that earlier theories either cause or entirely anticipate today's theories. As I roll from our own generation to its predecessors, and from the predecessors to their own predecessors, I write not simply to learn intellectual correctives of the past, but—releasing the backward turn of the ratchet—to suggest a notion more usable today than those of fifty years ago, one hundred years ago. I write first to take a piece like Richard Rorty's 1984 "Solidarity or Objectivity?" and to push it back to John Dewey's 1934 *Art as Experience* or his 1934 *A Common Faith* or William James's 1884 *Dilemma of Determinism*—let alone to Jonathan Edwards's sermon "A Divine and Supernatural Light," preached at North-hampton in 1734. But, like so many others, I am seeking, finally, a moral and a religious style appropriate to our own harrowing times.

In this inquiry, I intend to avoid the folly of making an American experiment the exceptional, the best experiment. H. Richard Niebur recognized that "a history that was recorded forwards, as it were, must be read backwards through our history, if it is to be understood as revelation."[2] Despite all notes I may blow to the contrary, I mean always and everywhere to go easy on Niebuhr's word *revelation,* to focus on the limits implicit in his phrase *our history,* and to admit the ignorance and the relativity always attendant thereunto.

ACKNOWLEDGMENTS

In a letter to Miss Frances R. Morse written on April 12, 1900, William James intimated his personal reasons for writing *Varieties of Religious Experience:*

> The problem I have set myself is a hard one: *first*, to defend (against all the prejudices of my "class") "experience" against "philosophy" as being the real backbone of the world's religious life—I mean prayer, guidance, and all that sort of thing immediately and privately felt, as against high and noble general views of our destiny and the world's meaning; and *second*, to make the hearer or reader believe, what I myself invincibly do believe, that, although all the special manifestations of religion may have been absurd (I mean its creeds and theories), yet the life of it as a whole is mankind's most important function. A task well-nigh impossible, I fear, and in which I shall fail; but to attempt it is *my* religious act."[1]

He does seem to have failed. Nevertheless, his aspiration gives an enduring strength to the *Varieties.*

Much of that same strength resides not only in the many people about whom I write, but in those who specifically helped me as I struggled to find my way through the maze of American religious and philosophical thought. During the academic year 1984-85 I benefitted especially from counsel with Langdon Gilkey, Martin Marty, Chris Gamwell, Jerald Brauer, Bernard McGinn, Gene Reeves, and Lee Snook. This book was greatly strengthened through Nancy Frankenberry's sage and patient critical advice, and through the pungent criticism of Mark C. Taylor and Gordon Kaufman. I have received memorable clues from Delwin Brown, Paul Sponheim, Wlad Godzich, Giles Gunn, Charley Hardwick, Wes Robbins, Bernard Lee, Michael Cowan, Henry Bowden, Harley Chapman, William Hynes, Creighton Peden, and Michael Welcker, and adroit encouragement from William Eastman. Roy Phillips has established to my satisfaction that an American religious historicism, perhaps more now than before, is preachable.

I will remain indebted to the fiery support, if it can be called support, of my uncalled colleagues—especially Richard Elvee, whose breadth and depth continue to be a resource. And I am more than indebted—clearly, I am sometimes simply reinterpreted—by Patricia Dean.

Earlier and partial versions of most of the chapters that follow have lived as public lectures or as articles: Chapter 1, as lectures at Rockford College and at Western Illinois University in 1985, and as "The Challenge of the New Historicism," in *The Journal of Religion*, July 1986; Chapter 2, as lectures at The Center for Humanistic Studies at the University of Minnesota and at Iliff School of Theology in 1987, and as "Law without Logos in Ancient Israel and Late America," in *Law and Interpretation*, edited by Joel Weinsheimer, forthcoming; Chapter 3, as "The Historicism of the Chicago School of American Religious Thought," in *Religion and Philosophy in the United States of America: Proceedings of the German-American Conference at Paderborn, 1986*, ed. Peter Freese, Vol. 1; and Chapter 6, as "Naturalism and Methodologism," in *The American Journal of Theology and Philosophy*, May, 1989.

I thank the University of Chicago's Institute for the Advanced Study of Religion, which, during the academic year 1984-85, provided facilities and opportunities for beginning this book; Gustavus Adolphus College, which provided the sabbatical for that same beginning; Kathleen Brady, who compiled the index; and Therese Myers and Marilyn Semerad, whose fine editorial work contributed so importantly to this book.

Finally, the way my students contributed cannot be specified—except to say that more often than they know they made the people, events, and ideas I describe seem credible and usable and, after all, worth it all.

W.D.
February, 1988

CHAPTER 1

The Challenge of the New Historicism

In American philosophy and literary criticism, a new claim for the ultimacy of historical categories has been made. It constitutes a challenge to late twentieth century theology, which, despite its Hebrew origins, prefers Hellenistic categories, some of which mask as historicist, some of which are nakedly ahistoricist and ontological. This new American historicism is not entirely new, for variations on it—sometimes called *radical empiricism,* sometimes *pragmatism*—have been stated before by philosophers and literary critics and discussed before in theology. Nevertheless, given its own logic, the current American challenge to theology is new because it occurs at a new point in history, involves new factors and contexts, and, consequently, is materially different.

Among the current philosophers and literary critics issuing the new historicist challenge are Richard Rorty, Nelson Goodman, Hilary Putnam, Richard Bernstein, and Frank Lentricchia. They have been called neopragmatists; they are pragmatists, however, in the line of William James and John Dewey and their radical empiricism, rather than in the line of Charles Sanders Peirce and Josiah Royce and their epistemological idealism. Rorty, Goodman, Putnam, Bernstein, and Lentricchia have argued that there is not a deeper or more ideal truth behind or beneath the events of social history, despite the long tradition that says there is. Further, and more explicitly historicist, they have argued that actual truths are entirely historical creatures, conceived within history, directed at history, and grown in a historical chain, as interpretation refers to interpretation which refers to interpretation on down through the reaches of history. Recently, their form of historicism has been introduced within the philosophy of religion and theology by Cornel West, Jeffrey Stout, Mark C. Taylor, and Gordon Kaufman.

Unquestionably, theology has been heavily influenced over the past two hundred years by another, older, historicism. This historicism diverted theology

1

from the nonhistoricist modes of Augustine and Calvin, which treat history as finally a function of divine determination. The older historicism grew in nineteenth- and early twentieth-century Germany under the leadership of Kant, Schleiermacher, Hegel, Dilthey, Troeltsch, and H. Richard Niebuhr. It has argued that the world is in process, and that this process is determined largely by creatures working within history through the interaction of historical freedom and historical destiny. This historicism has consistently rested on one additional belief, however: that there is more to history than the combined forces of freedom and destiny, that history is influenced also by an extra-historical, universal, and eternal reality, usually called God, sometimes called the Absolute.

Langdon Gilkey, speaking for this old historicism in his landmark 1976 *Reaping the Whirlwind: A Christian Interpretation of History,* noted then that all the best political, scientific, and philosophical commentaries converge in empiricially pointing to a "limited 'ontology' of history."[1] He theologically develops this historicism primarily through discussions of Paul Tillich, Reinhold Niebuhr, the theologians of hope and of process, Marx, and Whitehead. Gilkey contends that all these thinkers or schools presuppose a dimension beyond that of sheer historical contingency. In other words, says Gilkey, they are all implicitly "theological," and this theological dimension is "essential."[2]

This onotological or theological historicism operates, equally but less obviously, in Martin Heidegger, Hans-Georg Gadamer, Jürgen Habermas, Wolfhart Pannenberg, and in other recent German philosophers and theologians. For, in the last analysis they want more than an entirely contingent history, depending only on the local interplay between freedom and destiny. They seek, finally, an understanding of "thought" itself (Heidegger), a universal literary hermeneutic (Gadamer), or a universal structure of intersubjectivity (Habermas), or they look to a proleptic Jesus foreshadowing the goal of universal history (Pannenberg).

But whether in Gilkey's interpretation of theories of history or in the new German hermeneutics of history, it is just this theological and ontological dimension that the new historicists would deny. And it is just this denial that constitutes the challenge for contemporary theology.

This challenge cannot be properly evaluated, however, if it is not remembered that the "new historicism" is not new, but can be traced to the classical era in American philosophy. Under the labels of radical empiricism, pluralism, and pragmatism a similar historicist challenge to theology was issued earlier by William James, John Dewey, and George Herbert Mead. In so many words, they argued that, if an idea, even a theological idea, cannot be seen either to arise from historical experience or to apply to historical experience, then the idea is meaningless. Just after the turn of the century, that challenge was accepted by several prominent University of Chicago theologians, among them George Burman Foster, Gerald Birney Smith, Shailer Mathews, and Shirley Jackson Case. In their "sociohistorical method" of religious research, these Chicago School theologians, these classical American theologians, drew the lineaments of the new historicism and applied them to biblical criticism, to religious history, and to contemporary theology. But these Chicago School theologians were quite effectively vanquished in the 1930s and 1940s by the neoorthodox theologians who advocated the older, the German historicism. Consequently, Gilkey's 1976 assessment of the current philosophies of history was basically correct; in fact, historicism was generally "theological," or ontological, in character.

In this chapter, I review the new historicism that has arisen in America since 1976. But I do so with the recognition that the "new historicism" is not only as old as the classic American philosophical and religious historicists, but in its weakest form can be traced to Socrates. (For Rorty properly associates his historicism with Socrates, when he refers to the "Socratic virtues—willingness to talk, to listen to other people, to weigh the consequences of our actions upon people.")[3] Also, I assess in a preliminary way the nature of the challenge this historicism presents to prevailing theological assumptions. Finally, I note the shortcomings of today's historicism and indicate the way America's classical new historicists in philosophy and theology can supplement significantly the challenge of the new historicism to religious studies today.

A NEW HISTORICISM AND A NEW IMAGINATION

The shift from the old historicism of Gilkey and the German hermeneuticists to the new historicism can be understood as a shift in what is meant by imagination. Both historicisms utilize an imaginative capacity to step beyond the bounds of the immediate historical context in which we live; neither historicism affirms that we are slaves to immediate history. And, for both historicisms, the imagination consults something that enables us to act in the present. However, while the old historicism argues that among the realities consulted is something universal in space and time, and thereby not entirely dependent on historical contingencies, the new historicism argues that what is consulted is simply past historical contingencies and nothing more. Furthermore, while the old historicism emphasizes that imagination replicates in history certain universal realities, the new historicism argues that imagination constructs history—sometimes rather freely, and always with the contribution of the interpreter and its community. In short, with the old historicism, the imagination is mimetic; its purpose is to reproduce in history

something extrahistorical. With the new historicism, the imagination is interpretive; its purpose is to communicate with past historical particulars—not
merely to reproduce but to interact, to initiate, to create, as one does in a
conversation.

Langdon Gilkey corrrectly refers to the mimetic imagination as *theological*,
for it is theology that has been most open (and, sometimes, most honest) about
seeking extrahistorical advice. While the old historicists often argued that history
evolved, they also contended that beneath that change there was a structure
impervious to the vicissitudes of time and perspective and that the thinker's
job was to introduce that structure into present history as faithfully as possible.
Again, this is not to deny that the old historicism is a historicism; it did certainly
participate in what Gilkey calls a "historical consciousness" in which there is
"a particular kind of awareness of history and a particular sense of how we are
immersed in it, an awareness and a sense that are in important contrast to that
of other times and places."[4] The old historicists did rebel against the classical
and medieval orders and against the governmental, ecclesiastic, and social
institutions that upheld them. They de-authorized the eternal forms of Plato
or the eternal plans of God, a procedure that may have begun in seventeenth-
century natural science more than anywhere else but that in the nineteenth
century spread from nature to the realm of history. The new determinant was
the behavior of the creature, whether random and accidental or deliberate and
free, whether in natural history or in human social history. Nevertheless, these
modern historicists themselves then took the ironic step of introducing a new
authorizing process. They authorized some underlying order or principle, this
time ostensibly not beyond history but within the workings of history. The
rationalists—from Descartes, to Spinoza, Leibniz, Hegel, Husserl, and
Einstein—authorized a structure of reason or of thought. The classical
empiricists—from Bacon, to Hobbes, Locke, Hume, Comte, Carnap, and
Ayer—authorized laws of science. The humanists—from Schleiermacher,
Schopenhauer, and Kierkegaard to some phenomenologists and
existentialists—authorized the self or one of its parts. Accordingly, for these
historicists the human task is still to exercise a variation on the mimetic
imagination, this time replicating not a reality outside history but a "historical"
principle that gives sense to the rest of history. They focused on something
supposedly in history but, finally, not something truly subject to the contingencies of history and thereby still extrahistorical. This was a "modern" historicism
that in one sense was "theological" because it claimed that history was held
together and given meaning by an abiding reality.

My task, however, is not to explain these modern historicists and their
modernist use of the "theological" but to ask what the new historicism implies

for a new and postmodern sense of the theological. What would it mean if theology were to treat the particular events of past history as that beyond which there was no recourse, and to do that because all extrahistorical imports, even the abiding realities of the modernists, have been embargoed? What would it mean if theology were to treat the historical creatures (who, in principle, could be nonhuman as well as human), rather than the abiding realities, as the makers of past history? The interpretive imagination is utterly historical: it testifies to nothing but that which works within history; it reinterprets nothing other than history; and it, and it alone, in human and in nonhuman creatures, creates history. The interpretive imagination is historical communication about historical communication, creative of historical communication. Might this imagination give to theology a somewhat different meaning?

Admittedly, the new historicism's emphasis on the creativity of the interpretive imagination has encouraged the charge that the new historicism is anarchical and subjectivistic, a charge heard more often as the proponents of the new historicism gain greater attention. And admittedly, this would seem to diminish the value of the new historicism for theological reconstruction. However, it could be said that the new historicism is not only not anarchical but also that it is both conservative and objectively grounded. Theologically rendered, the new historicism could be seen as more ecclesiastically and traditionally conservative (in the generic sense) of the religious institution and the religious tradition than the old historicism has ever been. Because it permits no recourse beyond history, not even to historical principles or to a universal savior, everything depends on the particular history that includes the religious institution and the religious tradition. The interpretive imagination is fed only by what communities and traditions and their possibilities allow; if the institution and the tradition were to be truly forgotten, then all religious possibilities would be far more severely crippled than they would be with the mimetic imagination, which always has access to noninstitutional and nontraditional realities anyway. With the new historicism, when history fails, there is no escape from the suffering and its repercussions.

The new historicists are neither academically organized nor, particularly self-conscious in the pursuit of a common program. They do share, however, an outlook that is broad and manifold. I will attempt to indicate a few salient points of their agreement and then to comment on their separate approaches to those points. These points not only connect the new historicists but also pierce the minds of many American philosophers of religion and theologians, whether they recognize it—as West, Stout, Taylor, and Kaufman do—or whether they do not.

Of course, these salient points emanate not from a set of extrahistorical principles (whose reality the new historicists would deny anyway), but more from a cultural sensibility—perhaps properly designated by one of the many uses of *postmodernism*. It is a cultural sensibility generated by a community of advocates, somewhat in the way sensibilities, attitudes, or beliefs are generated among the scientists described by Thomas Kuhn and Paul Feyerabend. The sensibility may be short-lived—it is impossible to say. In any case there have been social, psychological, and religious conditions that seemed to make this sensibility more plausible today than the modernist sensibility of the old historicists.

It is not as if the new historicists are overwhelmed by their suspicions of the modernists. The new historicist writings usually do not read like diatribes or jeremiads (although they do attempt to deflate the philosopher's presumption that "professionals" must drill through to the bedrock everyone unknowingly stands above). Rather, it is as though the new historicists are saying to the modernist old historists: it is right that you pursued the Baconian and Cartesian aspiration to find better explanations than those grounded outside history. You were correct to have attempted to de-authorize those previous grounds and replaced them with what people actually experience. But you did not come all the way; you laid extrahistorical foundations of your own. Now, in sympathy with your announced intentions, we will try once more.

The new historicist denial of universal realities amounts to a denial of the standard forms of foundationalism, of realism, and of the transcendentalized subject. One experiences only what can be experienced within historical time and space: (1) not foundations beyond history; (2) not realities that can be known, without bias, as objective correlatives; and (3) not universal subjective characteristics, inherent in all persons.

When the new historicists reject foundationalism, realism, and the transcendentalized subject, they are driven to accept: (1) a pluralism that is unlimited, and (2) pragmatism. The pluralism is unlimited because, as long as foundational realities are not experienced, there no things beyond the plurality of particulars that could be experienced. Admittedly, generalizations must be made, but they must be treated as just that—as generalizations, mere abstractions attempting to describe characteristics of the particulars of one's own world and never as things in their own right. Pragmatism enters as an answer to the confusion introduced by the absence of criteria for truth formerly provided by foundationalism, realism, and the transcendentalized subject. Pragmatism provides a formal criterion that arbitrates disputes not by reference to extrahistorical causes or correlates of ideas but by asking which ideas contribute more satisfactory historical consequences (although pragmatism when used alone always remains unclear about what "satisfactory" means).

The new historicists, then, can be seen to share these points: they reject (1) foundationalism, (2) realism, and (3) the transcendentalization of the subject; they accept (4) pluralism, and (5) pragmatism. These positions simply explicate their historicism.

A sixth and central point is the one to which the designation *interpretive imagination* refers. History grows. And any historicism must deal with that fact. *[imag. construction (G. Kaufman)]* The new historicists all, sooner or later, attribute that growth to the imaginative contribution of the historical interpreter. Unlike their historicist predecessors, the new historicists do not think that the imagination receives its ideas from something abiding within or beyond history. Rather, with a kind of postmodern Romanticism, the new historicist maintains that it is the individual who newly perceives or makes new sense of past history; this is an imaginative contribution by the interpreter and it adds to the reality that once was. But this postmodern Romanticism is checked by a kind of postmodern Enlightenment caution—although the Continental orientation of most of today's new historicists leads them to diminish this point. Still, sooner or later, all new historicists recognize that in some way the imaginative signifier's construction of reality is checked by past and future histories. History's past signified limits interpretation by determining what the "signifieds" are and, consequently, what will and will not be donated for "signification" by the present "signifier." And future history limits the interpretation through the pragmatic method by determining what interpretations will and will not work in the history that flows from the present. In other words, no individual's interpretation in the last analysis is purely individual; it is what it is partly because the individual lives within and is profoundly affected by a historical community. Nevertheless, the constructive agent in history is the imagination of the historical interpreter.

Now the new historicists do not write as I have written. Not only are they not particularly interested in treating their separate labors as part of a larger program or as a contribution to a group effort. They are uncomfortable also with the generalized ways in which I have written. Consistent with their own methods (which they happily discuss), they are inclined to focus on the historical particulars, simply to get on with interpreting other texts. Following this more consistent mode, I, too, will turn to the texts—those of the new historicists themselves.

Among the new historicists, Richard Rorty may be the most thorough. In his 1979 *Philosophy and the Mirror of Nature,* he has announced, rather than argued, that in the human mind there is no mirror of the ontological structure of the world, no glassy essence reflecting something extrahistorical.

[no reflection from a god to us only us projecting]

And with this announcement he rejected not only the idealism, that runs from ancient Greece through modern Germany, and not only the positivism and its dominant British and American exponents, but, in effect, also the old historicism that was dominant in 1976 and may still be dominant today.

Rorty has taunted the community of philosophers, telling them that they no longer can be the keepers of the sacred, extrahistorical truths. For there are no such truths, no foundations in terms of which they might make historically diverse opinions somehow commensurable, no algorithms that they might discover.[5] Add to this, Rorty says, that many of our opinions simply are incommensurable with each other, and that we have no choice but to do our best to keep talking across the ineradicable hiatus, to test our interpretations on each other in a conversation.

Speaking positively, Rorty plays on the story of the cosmologist who proposed that the world rested on the back of an elephant. When asked what the elephant rested on, the cosmologist said, "It's elephants all the way down." In his 1982 *The Consequences of Pragmatism,* Rorty suggests that "it's words all the way down," meaning that reality is composed of interpretations heaped upon interpretations.[6] It is here that the imagination enters, for interpretations do move beyond the past, and, in doing that, they do call upon the imaginative contribution of the interpreter, the construction put upon the world by each of us.[7]

Despite appearances, Rorty is a loyalist, a patriot, attempting to breathe life into the badly beaten body of pragmatism, America's best known contribution to the technical philosophy of the Western world. Finally, he comes to praise the historicism of William James and John Dewey, who have stood patiently, decade after decade, at a major turn in the road of Western thought awaiting the arrival of herds of philosophers, the Anglo-American positivists and language analysts as well as the Continental hermeneuticists.[8]

In his 1982 *Ways of Worldmaking,* Nelson Goodman, instead of saying "it's words all the way down," claims that worlds come "not from nothing, after all, but *from other worlds.* Worldmaking as we know it always starts from worlds already on hand; the making is a remaking."[9] History is made from history. We use our imagination to decompose old worlds and to compose new worlds, through weighting, ordering, supplementing, deleting, and "deforming" (i.e., correcting or distorting). Goodman recognizes that the radicalness of his book lies in its complete rejection of the idea that the frames we put on the world imitate in history the one real world lying beyond history or operative throughout all history. Furthermore, while not denying that there is an external world, or that worlds can be pragmatically judged by their capacity to fit such a world, he does reject the idea that that world can be known as it is. If he were pressed to say how the world is apart from all frames, he says he would answer, "We are confined to ways of describing whatever is described. Our universe, so to speak, consists of these ways rather than of a world or of worlds."[10] "We are not speaking in terms of multiple possible alternatives to a single actual world but of multiple actual worlds."[11] "I am afraid," Goodman says at the opening of his concluding chapter, "that my remark above about conflicting truths and multiple actual worlds may be passed over as purely rhetorical."[12] But, he says, that would be a mistake.

While Rorty and Goodman were generating a new historicism within philosophy. Frank Lentricchia was reaching a similar historicist position within literary criticism. Lentricchia's new historicism was set forth initially in his 1980 *After the New Criticism,* where, in a long chapter on poststructuralism, he faulted the "Yale Critics" (J. Hillis Miller, Geoffrey Hartman, and Paul de Man) not for their poststructuralism, but for their formalism.[13] The Yale Critics were correct in rejecting the structuralists, who sought to explain literature by reference to a logical code lying beneath the text. They were correct in affirming, with Jacques Derrida, that literature was never to be seen as a form of "speaking," where "speaking" is the act of giving voice to the presence of being as it shows through the text or the reader. They correctly followed Derrida in affirming that literature was a form of "writing," where "writing" is the interpretation of earlier "writings," which are interpretations of still earlier "writings." Lentricchia applauded the newly fashionable Yale Derrideans for *Taylor* their acceptance of Derrida's picture of reality as "a chain of texts" —an image squaring almost perfectly with Rorty's "words all the way down" and Goodman's "worlds from other worlds." Lentricchia objected, however, to what he regarded as their formalism and their consequent flight from history, both of which result from their attraction only to the negativity of Derrida, to Derrida's attacks on logocentrism as the central commitment of Western thought. Denying logocentrism but affirming little else, the Yale Critics see writing and the interpretation of texts, Lentricchia said, as nothing more than "free play in the blue."[14] *?* This is a formalism because the text and the play with texts are made to be sufficient unto themselves, to have no significant connection to anything else. It is this irrelevance to history that had made the earlier New Critics unacceptable;[15] in this respect the Yale Critics represent no important advance on just those critics they had hoped to supersede.

For good measure, Lentricchia argues that the Yale Critics are ahistorical in a second way. When they are not being formalists, they are mere subjectivists, giving all power to the reader's solitary act of interpretation. But this, too, is to escape history; to fail to recognize the way the reader, as well as the text, is contextual is to ignore history.[16]

Although at places Derrida can be seen as a formalist himself,[17] Lentricchia chooses to emphasize Derrida's historicism and to define and extend that historicism through an examination of the historicism of Michel Foucault. Derrida's task, says Lentricchia, is to follow "the ineffaceable historicity of discourse," the "trace-structure" of the chain of texts, showing the way texts reinterpret earlier texts that reinterpret still earlier texts. The point of Derrida's deconstruction of the ontological presence of being is to reconstruct the historicity of texts (where "texts" are understood to include social artifacts, such as games and wars, as well as literary artifacts). The starkness of this position becomes apparent when it is realized that there is nothing further to consult beyond the history of texts and the history of those who interpret texts, and who, in interpreting, "write" new texts. (In the same vein, Wlad Godzich defends the potential for social responsibility within the deconstructionist approach, particularly as it is equipped to criticize the social irresponsibility of religious and political institutions.)[18]

Hilary Putnam's 1981 *Reason, Truth and History* is distinctive in its efforts to save the new historicism from the dangers of relativism. It is not that Putnam in this book rejects historicism. He affirms, after all, that a fact is a fact only because a "truth" says it is a fact; and that a truth is true only because it is "rational" to believe; and that what is rational to believe is rational only because it conforms to a "value" we hold; and that, finally, we hold a value only because we belong to a "history."[19] It is apparent, then, that our world is enlarged not by the mimetic imagination of truths beyond history but by the interpretive imagination's interaction with history. The people who attempt to stand outside history to develop "a more 'rational' notion of rationality" create a monstrosity, for they, in fact, take notions from their history while *relativism* pretending to establish them on nonhistorical grounds (Putnam cites Nietzsche's effort to oppose his own morality to that of the tradition).[20] Nevertheless, Putnam is worried about the destructive potential of relativism within historicism.

Putnam is convinced that our problems with relativism are rooted in our earlier "ideal theory of rationality, a theory which would give necessary and sufficient conditions for a belief to be rational in the relevant circumstances in any possible world."[21] When we became convinced that that ideal theory of rationality was an unfullfillable wish (that, in fact, it may have been borrowed from what is now an obsolete view of science), we fled unnecessarily (like jilted lovers) to two quite unacceptable forms of relativism. First, from the positivist tradition we took a "criterial" form of relativism, where we had nothing beyond local institutional, or conventional norms. Second, from the philosophies of science being written by Thomas Kuhn and Paul Feyerabend we took a relativism that allowed us to have simultaneously held but incommensurable postions. Putnam pursues what he calls *transcendental arguments,* or arguments presupposing a rationality that is not ideal but that is wider than the rationality of these two forms of relativism; and he uses these arguments to demonstrate that each of the two relativisms is internally inconsistent.[22]

Richard Bernstein's 1983 *Beyond Objectivism and Relativism* concentrates on securing the new historicism in the history of Western philosophy. In this effort, two images dominate—one temporal and the other methodological. First, we live in a period beyond the period dominated by what Bernstein calls "the Cartesian anxiety," where it was thought that if an inquiry failed to establish something clearly, distinctly, and rigorously, then it was a failed inquiry. Agreeing with Putnam, he contends that no longer do we need to think that, if something is not estabished objectivistically, then it is merely relativistic and, for that reason, meaningless. Our period is characterized by a position beyond objectivism and relativism, where objectivism and relativism are being replaced by *phronesis,* where discourse seeks primarily to contribute to the practice of the community.

Bernstein's second image is "the metaphor of the cable," an image that describes his own method. Bernstein cites Charles Sanders Peirce, who contends that philosophy ought "to trust rather to the multitude and variety of its arguments than to the conclusiveness of any one. Its reasoning should not form a chain which is no stronger than its weakest link, but a cable whose fibers may be ever so slender, provided they are sufficiently numerous and intimately connected."[23] Accordingly, Bernstein describes the way the Continental hermeneutics of Hans-Georg Gadamer and Jürgen Habermas; the philosophy of science of Thomas Kuhn, Paul Feyerabend, Imre Lakatos, and Peter Winch; the political philosophy of Hannah Arendt; and the neopragmatism of Richard Rorty form a new cable of philosophic opinion. In the combined work of these figures, objectivism and relativism are replaced by the acceptance of a practical and communal knowledge, which tests the truth of a position by asking whether and how it might apply to the practice—that is, to the history—of the community.

Of course, such communal and historical knowledge is impossible if forces at work in contemporary society prevent any meaningful communities. While Bernstein must contend for the possibility of community, he acknowledges that we can no longer, like Marx or Hegel, rest in the revolutionary or theoretical assurance that some "logic of history" will prevail, rationally guiding communities and their dialogue. "If anything, we have or should have learned how much the contemporary world conspires against it and undermines it. And yet," Bernstein adds, "it is still a *telos,* a *telos* deeply rooted in our human project."[24]

Bernstein does not say how, standing beyond objectivism and relativism, we might once again talk about a telos working in our midst. Nevertheless, with this he has moved from what appears to be a quite secular form of postpositivism to the threshold of a religious communalism.

Furthermore, each of those people we have discussed holds open such a hope for a valued community. Rorty would like to combine "private fulfillment, self-realization, with public morality, a concern with justice."[25] Goodman maintains that what is right is what fits into the practice of a community.[26] Putnam's penultimate paragraph concludes with the pastoral advice that "we are not trapped in individual solipsistic hells, but invited to engage in a truly human dialogue; one which combines collectivity with individual responsibility."[27]

Within this pragmatic framework Lentricchia, Cornel West, and Jeffrey Stout extend the political dimensions of community in ways that are implicitly or explicitly religious. They seek to extend the community from that of the polite, leisured conversation of the university intellectual to the practical conversation of society at large as it struggles to build a more viable and just life. It could be argued that apart from this extension the theologian may receive the new historicism as an interesting method, but not as something practically usable in religious communities and in society.

In his 1983 *Criticism and Social Change*, Lentricchia objects to the deconstructionists' unwillingness, Paul de Man's in particular, to recognize the political importance of education, to their unwillingness to see "society as a funtion of education."[28] Lentricchia's book, he says, was "triggered"[29] by Hayden White, a historicist among historians,[30] but it is largely an exposition of the historicism of the literary critic Kenneth Burke.[31] Lentricchia argues for a practical, material, and social understanding of the historical sources and effects of knowledge. He wants, in effect, to add to the value-free programs of pragmatism and deconstructionism the social values of Antonio Gramsci, who has provided a noncoercive and cultural version of Marxism.

Lentricchia extends the interpretive imagination beyond the intellectual interpretation of the past to include the social interpretation of the past, a social interpretation accomplished in order to contribute to the social change of the future. Lentricchia argues that Rorty's image of the conversation unknowingly reflects the bourgeois individualism of the culture in which it is gaining acceptance.[32] Conversation is about "university humanists," seeking "the free pursuit of personal growth anchored in material security."[33] Whereas Burke attempts to justify conversation in terms of its broad political and economic consequences in addition to its more personal satisfactions. Lentricchia thereby amplifies historicism so that, unwittingly, it includes the kind of history discussed by the Hebrew prophet, the Christian moralist, or the religious person attempting to relate religious interpretation to social history.

In his 1982 *Prophesy Deliverance*, Cornel West takes a similar step but with an eye to religion rather than to literary criticism. Earlier, in *Boundary 2*, West had argued that Rorty, Goodman, Kuhn, Roy Sellars, and W. V. Quine are correct in their rejection of realism, the myth of the given, and the transcendentalized subject but that, finally, they were creatures of various bygone cultural attitudes (he cites the "old aristocratic preoccupation" of Goodman, the "ideology of professionalism" in Kuhn, and the "nostalgic appeal" made by Rorty). Finally, West says, postmodern American philosophy fails to offer a constructive program, "a new gospel of the future," and leaves us "hanging in a limbo."[34] Later, in the *Union Seminary Quarterly Review*, West draws similar conclusions about Rorty's *Philosophy and the Mirror of Nature*:

> To tell a tale about the historical character of philosophy while eschewing the political content, role and function of philosophy in various historical periods is to promote an ahistorical approach in the name of history. To deconstruct the privileged notions of objectivity, universality and transcendentality without acknowledging and accenting the oppressive deeds done under the aegis of these notions is to write a thin (i.e., intellectual and homogeneous) history; that is, a history which fervently attacks epistemological privilege but remains relatively silent about political, economic, racial and sexual privilege.[35]

In place of this thin history, West calls for a "thick history," one which includes the social and heterogeneous accounts, including the economic, political, cultural, and the personal. In *Prophesy Deliverance*, West moves on to develop his own thick history of Afro-American Christianity. He begins by maintaining that the primary objective of Afro-American philosophy is to offer "a demystifying hermeneutic of the Afro-American experience which enhances the cause of human freedom."[36] He ends by suggesting that Gramscian Marxism offers the most adequate political analysis and practical procedure for the present situation.

West is constantly attentive to the social sources of history—specifically, to the social sources of American racism and to the varieties of social response that Afro-Americans have proposed. He sets the social problem: "*The present dilemma of the Afro-American liberation movement is to find its way between the Scylla of bourgeois liberalism and the Charybdis of right-wing Marxism.*" And he proposes the social solution: "Revolutionary Christian perspective and praxis pave this middle pathway."[37]

West moves toward a theological analysis in two ways. First, and unlike Lentricchia, West does not treat Marxism as a source of those values missing in pragmatism and deconstructionism. While West uses Marxism as a tool of analysis, he derives his social objectives from *"the Christian principle of the self-realization of individuality within community."*[38] Second, West applies those Christian objectives to the specific historical community of Afro-Americans and does so with the intention of changing that group's social history.

West's new historicism is "not concerned with 'foundations' or transcendental 'grounds'," but is, instead, concerned with "a genre of writing, a textuality, a mode of discourse that interprets, describes, and evaluates Afro-American life in order comprehensively to understand and effectively to transform it."[39] He calls, then, not for a mimetic imagination, but for an interpretive imagination.

In 1985, West set his own project within the history of American philosophy of religion. According to West, that history effectively begins in the first four decades of this century in the "Golden Age of philosophy of religion in modern Euro-American thought,"[40] which runs from James to E. S. Brightman; it is eclipsed by logical positivism; when the resurgence of American philosophy does occur with the writings of W. V. Quine, Nelson Goodman, and Wilfred Sellars, these philosophers and their successors, like Rorty and Bernstein, ignore the philosophy of religion. American theologians do nothing to counter this because they are so distracted by the combined influences of logical positivism and the antiphilosophical stance of Karl Barth. Now, however, historical action has been theologically rediscovered in the writings of the liberation theologians and in the liberationist writings of process theologians Schubert Ogden and John B. Cobb, Jr. West sees his own historicism as combining neo-Gramscian social criticism and Christian prophetic criticism with a historicism "akin to that of Rorty and Bernstein—and especially that of Jeffrey Stout."[41]

Jeffrey Stout's 1981 *The Flight from Authority* begins the long and difficult task of showing the general implications of the new historicism for religious ethics. He seeks to explain how it happened that in the modern West we moved from the notion that moral theory depends on religious theory to the notion that moral theory is autonomous, independent of religious theory. His explanation of this development is historical. His way of reintroducing a non-autonomous, religious morality depends on the new historicism and on the interpretive imagination.

The autonomy of morals has its roots in the early sixteenth century, when the Western world first became broadly preoccupied with a flight from authority. The intellectual "probability" once provided by the intellectual authorities was vitiated because they had become divided; the response was to flee the now unreliable authorities and to resolve the new and radical skepticism by finding new grounds for certainty. Descartes responded to this crisis by choosing new foundations in human thought and experience. With his and related "flights from authority" began the modernist effort to found morals on people's own thought and experience rather than to follow the medieval practice of basing everything on the opinions of the intellectual and establishment leaders.

Stout's eventual solution is to return to the seventeenth century, to adopt the Port-Royal Jansenist's (including Blaise Pascal's) alternative version of "probability," which talked in today's sense of the likeliness of an occurrence rather than in the medieval sense of the security offered by authorities. Moving then from the pragmatism of Willard Quine to what Stout calls "the new historicism" of Ian Hacking, Thomas Kuhn, Alasdair MacIntyre, and Richard Rorty, Stout concludes that the only possible answer to the modernist's question is a postmodernist historicist answer. Moral theory by itself cannot resolve the modern skeptical quest for certainty, it cannot offer a certainty based on a neutral, foundationalist *scientia*. Rather, moral theory must be based on the probabilities of history, specifically on one's private and cultural religious history as seen from one's personal and communal location. The reasons to which I appeal, says Stout, "are determined by my situation."[42] Beyond that, to some *relativism* more general, neutral, and noninterpretive stance, one cannot go.

THE NEW HISTORICISM AND AN AGENDA FOR THEOLOGY

If the new historicism continues to hold up in American thought, it will affect American theology profoundly. The new historicism claims that what figures in one's history will figure in one's current thought and action; and this would seem to apply even to the effect of the history of the new historicism on theology. Already, both West and Stout appear to have responded philosophically to the religious implications of the new historicism.

Two theologians, Gordon Kaufman and Mark C. Taylor, have extended already the implications of historicism to traditional questions of theology. While in the closing chapter I introduce a more extensive treatment of these historicist theologians, I note here that they, unlike the philosophers of religion Stout and West, embark on theological questions, such as the meaning of God, the authority of scipture, the contemporaneous nature of religious faith, and the nature of Christology. Each has written two theological books that clearly are historicist: Kaufman's 1981 *The Theological Imagination* and his 1985 *Theology for a Nuclear Age* and Taylor's 1982 *Deconstructing Theology* and his 1984 *Erring: A Postmodern A/theology*. Kaufman's notion of "imaginative construction" is virtually the theological embodiment of what I am calling the *interpretive imagination*. I see Kaufman as a Continental neo-Kantian moving ever-closer to an American naturalism, thereby carrying the potential for combining the best of the historicisms of both continents. Taylor's notion of "erring," the wandering by which the knower deconstructs the past and constructs a new future, also functions in most ways as an equivalent of what I have called the interpretive imagination. Taylor's 1986 *Deconstruction in Context* both beautifully outlines the tradition behind the deconstructionism and explains Taylor as its exponent. The two-centuries-old heritage behind deconstructionism is to Taylor what a more focused neo-Kantianism was to Kaufman. For both Kaufman and Taylor, theology is a historical discipline in the sense that it builds itself entirely within history and out of a history of thought, and it is a constructive discipline in the sense that the imagination's interpretation of that past history creates new theological truth. In the work of both theologians, there is the clear promise of an important historicist theological movement.

These two cases not excepted, the general significance of the new historicism for American theology can be approached by reference to two implications of the interpretive imagination. According to the interpretive imagination (1) a past history (signified) is known, but (2) it is known only through the relativity of the signifier's sense of significance. These two epistemological features of the new historicism set it apart from modernism and align it with postmodern ways of speaking. The first implication suggests the positive character of a newly historicist theology; the second implication suggests what a historicist theology must live without.

First, while many philosophers of the modern era have been skeptical of our knowledge of a real past, the new historicist typically has not been. The skepticism of the modernist is evident in Descartes's rationalism, in David Hume's empiricism, in Kant's struggle with solipsism, in Husserl's phenomenology, in existentialism, and in the more formalist and subjectivist side of deconstructionism. As Roger Scruton has said, when Hume combined Descartes's concentration on epistemology with his own empirical skepticism, he broke down "our common sense claims to objective knowledge. The consequent retreat into the confines of the first person was accompanied by no thread of reasoning that would enable him to emerge from there."[43] In Christian theology, the combined influences of Hume and Kant contributed, in turn, to Barthian, neo-orthodox, existentialist, and Wittgensteinian fideism, which usually both retreated from history and the historical Jesus and emphasized the dogmatic, affectional, or linguistic contours of faith and the Word.

Against this modernist skepticism, proponents of the interpretive imagination, as well as proponents of the mimetic imagination, have claimed to know something about the historical past. They may not know the historical past with the objectivism of the realists—that is, with a God's eye view of it, or with the objectivity suggested by the correspondence theory of truth. But the historicists still presume an objectivity that says there is a historical past that can be known and they have found nothing particularly startling about that. The new historicism, with its interpretive imagination, has rejected an imprisonment in the subjective ego and a flight from history. Admittedly, the new historicism has accepted a dependence on particular histories and a resulting uncertainty about history in general, just those tendencies that would lead an old historicist like Paul Tillich to find in it a counsel of despair, an abandonment of thought to relativity and to meaninglessness. But the new historicists would see Tillich's criticism as resulting from a forced dichotomy between theonomous truths independent of the contingencies of history and a meaningless relativity. They would strive for a third position, "beyond objectivism and relativism," that would permit meaningful reflection on an aspect of history from a historical standpoint.

A new historicist theology would apply the interpretive imagination to a particular religious history. Here the Christian theologian would look not just at any religious history, but at the history of Christian scriptures, institutions, and thought. And the Christian theologian would look at that history not from an isolated interpretive standpoint, but from a standpoint in conversation with other Christian standpoints also naturally concerned with that religious history. The same conditions would apply to a Hebrew, a Native American, a Buddhist, or any other religious thinker. The Christian, all the same, would look at a specific material history in which a God and a people were thought to interact. While the Christian historicist would interpret that history in conversation with other Christians, he or she would reinterpret that history, reshaping tradition to meet the nuance and need of his or her own cultural situation. The effect is not to alter merely the form of the Christian message, as though leaving some eternal substance intact, but to work apart from such finally dualistic distinctions and to acknowledge the continual creation of fundamentally new Christianities.

This positive historicist program in theology would be guided not only by the workings of the interpretive imagination but by the two more positive points of the new historicism stated earlier: a pluralism that is unlimited and a pragmatism that arbitrates. The pluralism of a new historicist theology would permit the open acceptance of one's own religious past as one historical option among many options. This, in turn, would eliminate both the traditional and awkward apologia for the absoluteness of one's own religion and the despair wherein any nonabsolutistic acceptance of one's own religion becomes sheer relativism, sheer meaninglessness. But recognizing the limits to what can be claimed about historical knowledge, the new historicist religious thinker would embark on a pragmatic critique of theological meaning and truth. There, theological ideas would be tested through conversation and historical action. This pragmatic and local test is the most that can be expected; absolute criteria for theological meaning and truth—criteria valid for any history—would be beyond the pale.

The second major implication of the interpretive imagination for an American theology is more negative: a new historicist theology is confined to the relativity of the signifier's sense of significance and must live without references to something extrahistorical. This point is highlighted by another comparison with the tradition of modernist skepticism. In a massive irony, the modernist tradition in philosophy, despite its skepticism about knowledge of the objective world, claimed to know more than the interpretive imagination now permits itself to claim. Driven by the Cartesian anxiety, the modernists introduced a new authorizing process. As we indicated earlier, they found universal, rational, scientific, and subjectivist principles that give meaning to history. This, in turn, gave to the modernists an altogether unexpected confidence.

By comparison, a new historicist theology can know no extrahistorical principles, but only a contingent interpretation of the contingencies of history, and must live with the resulting lack of confidence. While the theology of the new historicism—that is, a theology of the interpretive imagination—shares with the theology of the mimetic imagination a belief in something beyond the immediate present, it does not share with it a belief in a law or an ultimate reality consistent through historical change. For a new historicist theology change in history would be attributable not to the ingression of the eternal into the temporal but to the contingencies of history—specifically, to the contribution of the knower's interpretation, which occurs in history, refers to history, and occurs in interaction with a God who is wholly historical.

The new historicist theology would incorporate the three more negative points described earlier: the denial of extrahistorical foundations, the denial of the realism of the correspondence view of truth, and the denial of the transcendentalized subject. This challenges three aspects of most Western theology: its foundations in a God beyond history, its correspondence view of God language, and its account of the essential characteristics of faith.

First, and most obvious, a new historicist theology would challenge theology's typical use of metaphysics—that is, that it knows the most basic, universal, and eternal elements of all that is. It would claim that theology must be conducted by reference, rather, to the web of natural and human history. The interpretive imagination that lies behind the new historicism would suggest that religious faith does not imitate anything universal in time and space, but grows out of the creatural interpretation of history and of a God which can be understood in historicist terms.

Second, although the new historicist theology would claim a knowledge of history, it would challenge that Christian realism that treats God and Christ as though they could be known as a positivist knows facts—basically unencumbered by the recognition that the signified is, with certain qualifications, what the signifier interprets it to be. Obviously, fundamentalistic supernaturalism and miraculous verifications of religious ideas would be denied. Denied also would be much of the old historicism, particularly the historicism of the German crisis theologians, what Tillich regarded as their cryptopositivism, their theological realism concerning the acts of a divine "being," a being known as it is, apart from the bias of historical perspective.

Third, and with regard to the theological left rather than the theological right, the new historicist theology would challenge the transcendentalization of the subject implicit in the effort to detect theological truth by analyzing the configuration of a persons's faith. This applies most directly to some theological uses of Tillich's own existentialist "ultimate concern," of Schleiermacher's "absolute dependence," or of Bultmann's notion of existential freedom, for the truth of faith in these forms does not depend, finally, on historical considerations.[44]

AMERICAN THEOLOGY AND THE CHALLENGE TO THE NEW HISTORICISM

While it should be recognized that today's new historicists challenge current theology, to leave the indictment in their hands would be to subserve theology to a recent line of thinkers who are not notable for their religious sensitivity.

The neopragmatists arise not from the religiously alert classical American pragmatists, but from the recrudescent American philosophy found in the writings of W. V. Quine, Nelson Goodman, and others. Quine and Goodman, while connected with the original American pragmatists through C. I. Lewis, arose within (and were largely responsible for retiring) the positivistic and analytic worlds. Their work was not primarily sustained by the original pragmatism, and they had little interest in the religious claims so central to James, Dewey, and Whitehead.

Equally, the deconstructionists issue from a line of Continental thinkers who were increasingly alienated from religion. This line of thinkers originally had believed that philosophy was the quest to replace plurality with unity and to give the self a sense of the identity with that unity. Religion made sense only to the extent that it aided in that quest. Now the quest for oneness has become incredible and the manyness of all that is has been admitted; equally, the self must abandon its quest for identity and accept its difference from all that is, particularly as the self is separated from the other by time. Hence, religion is primarily a creature of a dead quest and must itself be abandoned. The writings of Mark C. Taylor and his deconstructionist colleagues in religion[45] should be seen as courageous efforts to find a paradoxical religious meaning despite this "irreligious" turn of events; but they are so wed to this history that their theological construction sometimes can appear merely rhetorical, a hungry and purely spiritual gesture unfed by the new resources that might allow them to construct something new out of this history of disillusionment.

It would be ironic, to say the least, to allow the recent and often theologically ignorant, new historicist philosophy and literary criticism to determine religious thought today. Consequently, while recent new historicism may present to contemporary theology certain inescapable challenges and necessary causes, it cannot provide the resources for a new historicist theology. There are real and important theological lacunas in today's new historicism. These can be seen, I will argue, through a reacquaintance with the history of distinctly American philosophical and religious thinkers who culturally precede but usually fail to philosophically influence this new historicism.

My points are simple. First, if a historicism is truly historicist, it must understand not only the statements of others by reference to their historical chain of interpretations, but it must also understand itself the same way. While today's new historicism was set in the same national culture that fifty to one hundred years before had formed an earlier new historicism, the proponents of today's new historicism sometimes lack the historicist consistency to see themselves clearly in the light of their own formative history. Second, the examination of the original new historicists will identify omissions in today's historicism, omissions that tend repeatedly to be caused by forced dichotomies, finding only two options in situations that involve at least three options. So intent to reject the Hellenistic, idealist, or positivist claim that this world is erected on foundations outside the flux of history, today's historicists have neglected to develop their own affirmation that this world is built from historical actions alone. So intent to reject the metaphysics of their predecessors, they have left the impression that they are mere relativists, mere subjectivists, virtual nihilists. Using the same tactics, they often seem to say to theologians, If classical theology died with metaphysics, then there must be no theology at all. Richard Bernstein properly decries this logical error in his *Beyond Objectivism and Relativism*. His point is that postmodernism is a third option which damns the tendency inappropriately to say, if not "a," then necessarily "b". However,

Bernstein concentrates not on the religious-nonreligious dichotomy, but on an epistemological dichotomy, as in, If not objectivism, then relativism. My objective, however, is not to leave the new historicists with an indictment, but to move on to a more fully developed third and positive option, one that will include space for religious truth.

In Chapter 2, "American Historicism and Religious Historicism," I argue that today's new historicism has both American and religious antecedents, usually unrecognized. I do not establish a causal connection here between earlier American and religious thought and today's new historicism. But I assume, perhaps rashly, that whether a connection is recognized or even operative, the antecedent at least ought to be one basis for re-visioning today's new historicism. Given the myth of new historicism, fundamental elements within a formative culture tell important tales about what should and should not survive in the culture. (In this and other chapters, I will concentrate my analysis on Richard Rorty, rather than treat all of the philosophical and literary critical new historicists together. While this abbreviation neglects the real differences between Rorty, Bernstein, Goodman, Putnam, and Lentricchia, it makes managable what otherwise would be an unmanageably complex discussion. Furthermore, Rorty is a good case study here, for the particular questions I do apply to him can be applied to the other four new historicists with virtually equal propriety.)

In Chapter 3, "The Chicago School," I argue that during the first four decades of this century the University of Chicago's Chicago School of theology stated and practiced a method that, in most essentials, embodied today's new historicism as it pertains to the study of religion. Furthermore, when the Chicago School reinterpreted biblical and dogmatic history, it demonstrated a kind of appreciation for historical antecedents missing in today's new historicism.

In Chapter 4, "The Hidden Empiricism," I argue that the new historicists exercise several normative commitments they fail to acknowledge and cannot acknowledge because they have no epistemological way of taking them seriously. I suggest that they presume an experiential acquaintance with values for which they cannot account.

In Chapter 5, "The Radical Historicists," I demonstrate the way two theologians, Bernard Meland and Bernard Loomer, and two American pragmatists, William James and John Dewey, had described a "radical empiricism" that can account for values in historical experience without violating pragmatism or historicism.

In Chapter 6, "Beyond Method: Toward a Concept of God," I argue that today's new historicists in one respect still adhere to the modernism to which they, as postmodernists, object. Still captivated by a Cartesian anxiety about how to think rightly, they neglect questions of what there is to be thought. The classical American pragmatists in philosophy and theology moved beyond this anxiety when they turned to the "what" of naturalism in place of the "how" of methodologism. This, in turn, led them to speak about the reality of God in the natural context.

There are, in short, unresolved problems in the new historicism, problems that religious scholars may be uniquely equipped to answer. The uniquely explicit ways in which Western theologians typically depend on history—in their case, the history of religious institutions, scriptures, and doctrines—gives them a unique capacity to ask, How is the new historicism itself unwittingly a product of history? To what extent is that history American, and to what extent is it religious? Furthermore, religious scholars are deeply schooled in uncovering and analyzing implicit values, ultimate concerns, religious motives, historical meanings, and vague and indistinct affections and assumptions. As a consequence, often they are better equipped than their academic collegues to meaningfully pursue questions such as: What values lurk within the new historicist outlook? What epistemological and cosmological assumptions are suggested by those values? And how might these assumptions themselves require something approximating a notion of God?

All this said, I insist that this account is not in the most ambitious sense an argument, for where arguments are full there is an implicit trust that reason can finally arbitrate questions of a lived history. Such a high estimate of reason is not finally justifiable in historicism. If this account is persuasive, it is persuasive only as a fuller understanding of history is persuasive. That and no more.

CHAPTER 2

American Historicism and Religious Historicism

If, in fact, we live in "a chain of texts" (Derrida), where it's "words all the way down" (Rorty), where we create "worlds from other worlds" (Goodman), then the theory, itself, implicit in those phrases also lives out of a sequence of historical antecedents. While the recent new historicists have been free in reminding others of their historical confinement, they have not been notably outspoken in reminding themselves. If, in fact, we must let go of skyhooks and walk like earth creatures on our own local planes of history, then so must the theory that tells us to. But, strangely, the recent American new historicists who pronounce that same theory survey Western thought like the God they reject, first citing Germany, then France, occasionally their own national culture. Have these historicists abandoned their shy sister historicisms—that of the sociologists of knowledge (such as Peter Berger and Thomas Luckmann) or the philosohers of science (such as Thomas Kuhn and Paul Feyerabend)—who contend that how we think is a function of the local culture we inhabit? Did they not grow up in the American culture? Were they not children of the culture that through pragmatism and its historicism clearly anticipated their own historicism? Can they mean that their historicism sprang, instead, from Europe or, better, that it is today just the sort of history-free animal they had condemned to extinction? Have they hung a bounty on all others so they could roam the universal planes without competition?

Of course not. In fact, it would be hard to find two philosophers more steeped in American thought than Richard Rorty and Richard Bernstein. Nevertheless, when they look to their American position, they, like people with X-ray vision, often claim to see Europe instead. In his *Consequences of Pragmatism*, Rorty claims that Continental idealism is the parent of American literary criticism's textualist historicism and that Hegel is the parent of America's pragmatic historicism. The textualists, the deconstructionist Yale Critics in particular, Rorty says, are "spiritual descendants of the idealists, the species

23

having adapted to a changed environment."[1] The pragmatists owe to Hegel's "temporalization of rationality" the single most important step" in arriving at their distrust of "Philosophy."[2] Bernstein argues in *Beyond Objectivism and Relativism* that the new, the saving, the third option (the neohistoricist, the neopragmatist, the hermeneutical option), can be traced to a Kant-Husserl-Heidegger-Gadamer-Derrida axis of thought—thus, in effect, ignoring the fact that American pragmatists before all but Kant were originally sounding the same third theme. Although Rorty and Bernstein often stress the importance of the classical American pragmatists, here they read them out of the geneological tree. In these books they are dim about the American lineage, from Jonathan Edwards to Charles Sanders Peirce to William James to John Dewey to George Herbert Mead to Alfred North Whitehead.

At the surface of the scholarship, Rorty and Bernstein are correct: American new historicists do cite German hermeneuticists and French deconstructionists. It does appear that the Continental emphasis on the constructive power of interpretation did lead them to believe that history makes history, that it was this European reading which set them off.

But this will not quite do. Even Continental historicism argues that local experience is definitive, that interpretations address one's own tradition, not other people's traditions. Consequently, it is a problem that in their geneologies the current American new historicist thinkers neglect their own American traditions: their childhoods, neighborhoods, churches, social and ethnic groups, colleges, restaurants and drinking establishments, newspapers, and native feelings. If the American historicists' picture of the world itself comes from their lived history, if it is not general but specific, if it is not simply Western but American . . . well then, it comes from *their* history, not the German's or the Frenchperson's history. If America has an intellectual tradition of historicism, then it should be the major source of American new historicism.

It is not simply that in their geneologies Rorty, Bernstein, and other tracers of the new historicism sometimes throw a pitch that is a off. Far more important, the consequence may be uncatchably wild. As these pragmatic historicists tell us repeatedly, interpretation leads to practice; if the interpretation is off, it creates a practice which does not work and, thereby, is not true. It follows, then, that if an interpretation is alien, its use will be alien—among other things, to the American culture that invented pragmatism, radical empiricism, and the particular pluralism and historicism that follow from radical empiricism and pragmatism.

On the other hand, an appropriately American historicism, centering on American culture, would have a greater chance of suggesting practices that work in and are true for America.

Of course, the issue is not national pride, but appropriate action. I mean not to defend earlier forms of American exceptionalism: where, first, with the Puritan exodus myth America is God's new Israel, Europe is Egypt, the watery Atlantic is the desert of wandering, and the new world is the promised land where God, finally, will fulfill promises to humanity; or where, later, with the republican freeholder myth of Frederick Jackson Turner, American is a unique democracy repeatedly renewed by the frontier experience, and where one's relation with nature allows the Eternal to speak, unimpeded by the paper capitalism of commercial Europe; or where, later, with the evolutionary progressivism of Charles Beard, America is the vanguard of a world-saving industrialist democracy;[3] or where, later, with the Cold War, America is God's people on a crusade to free slaves of Communist oppression. I do not mean, following the archetype so well described by Sacvan Bercovitch,[4] to issue a new American jeremiad, arguing that if only we overcome this postmodern and Continental declension from the promise of America's Golden Age philosophers and theologians, then the prophesied Golden Age of philosophy and theology will be upon us. No one in his or her right mind could seriously propose a new form of exceptionalism, after the damage it has already wrecked on Native Americans, the Third World, and Vietnam. Furthermore, exceptionalism has lost its foundations. The monistic worldview underlying exceptionalist arguments has been replaced, on the whole, with a pluralistic worldview denying any nation an absolute identity, allowing an identity only relative to a nation's own history, and confusing any talk of a nation's manifest destiny in the community of nations.

Nevertheless, America's historicist theory had better be a theory appropriate to its culture; otherwise, the historicism might do more damage than good. Particularly, if an American historicism smells Continental, then so will an American theology after it has been revised by a Continental historicism. Certainly, there is nothing wrong with the Continental camphor itself; nevertheless, it may lure American religious thought in ways inappropriate to American styles, mores, characters, and feelings.

Now this all would be to beg the question if two points are not confronted in greater depth initially: Can historicism in fact be seen also as American, rather than only Continental? Further, Can an American historicism in fact be treated as religious? Certainly, recent new historicist writings would suggest that it is more convenient, at least, to treat historicism as Continental. Equally, Rorty, Goodman, Putnam, and Bernstein by their omission of a religious dimension suggest that the Hellenistic yearning for the extrahistorical is so typical of religion that a nonreligious historicism would make more sense than a religious historicism. In what immediately follows I attempt not to chronicle the American lineage of the new historicism, nor to chronicle the religious historicism that depends on that new American historicism. But in order eventually to offer something approximating such a lineage, I begin here the elementary task of establishing that historicism can be distinctively American, and that it can be religious—even religious in a distinctively American way. I do this not inductively, but only by illustration. I suggest that beneath the surface of Richard Rorty's writing, a distinctively pluralistic emphasis echoes the classical American thought of James and Dewey. Further, I suggest that what is distinctively American in religious historicism is not found in the historicism of Wolfhart Pannenberg, Europe's leading religious historicist, and is found in the recent biblical methods of tradition history, sociological criticism, and deconstructionist criticism. I conclude, however, by noting that the religious expression of American religious historicism is incompletely expressed in these biblical methods.

THE NEW HISTORICISM AS AMERICAN

Richard Bernstein and Cornel West illustrate two different approaches to geneologies of American historicism. In *Beyond Objectivism and Relativism*, Richard Bernstein tags historicism as hermeneutics and traces hermeneutics to Germany, while in *Prophesy Deliverance!*, Cornel West tags historicism as pragmatism and traces pragmatism to its American roots and, indirectly, to Afro-American Christianity. Bernstein follows hermeneutics from Schleiermacher's interest in the interpretation of Biblical texts, to Dilthey, Heidegger, Bultmann, and Gadamer, taking his cue from when and where the term *hermeneutics* is used.[5] In Bernstein's telling, German hermeneutics enters the stream of Anglo-American analytic philosophy only in 1979 when Richard Rorty in his *Philosophy and the Mirror of Nature* "dared to suggest that the lessons of hermeneutics might be essential for the understanding of philosophy itself."[6] Although Bernstein contends that his account of hermeneutics is presented "from an Anglo-American perspective."[7]it depicts a tradition growing to maturity in Germany and now barely off the boat. Cornel West, by contrast, begins his *Prophesy Deliverance!* by citing Afro-American Christian thought and the James-Dewey-Mead heritage of pragmatism. In setting forth his own historicism, West eschews extrahistorical " 'foundations' or transcendental 'grounds' " and consistently sees his method as inseparable from its American origins.[8]

Admittedly, Bernstein's weaving of Continental hermeneutics into recent American new historicism is instructive for the transatlantic similarities it demonstrates and for its powerful suggestion of a coming new transatlantic consensus. Bernstein is particularly effective in his concluding chapter where he ties the work of Jürgen Habermas, Richard Rorty, and Hannah Arendt to the hermeneutics of Hans-Georg Gadamer. It is true that all these thinkers have rejected conventionally extrahistorical (universal and eternal) and subjectivist sources and criteria for truth, and they all do avoid the traditions of idealism, positivism, existentialism, and variations on those approaches. Most important, they seek to build a community of dialogue as the best preparation for social action.

Furthermore, Bernstein is not oblivious to the tensions within his own linkage of Continental hermeneutics and American new historicism. Bernstein does acknowledge that Rorty has introduced "what at first might appear to be a devastating critique" of Habermas and Gadamer.[9] Bernstein describes the way Rorty objects to Habermas's theory of communicative action, a theory that Bernstein himself characterizes as an effort to uncover "the universal conditions that are presupposed in all communicative action."[10] Rorty argues that Habermas's theory springs into life when "Habermas goes transcendental and offers principles."[11] Rorty insists that historicism properly considered is largely a struggle against just the kind of move Habermas makes when he seeks to find something commensurable, shared by all contributors to a dialogue. Bernstein cites several of Rorty's rather oblique comments about Gadamer to show how Rorty finds Gadmer also to be positing a universal method. Nevertheless, Bernstein is convinced by the homologies between the Continental hermeneuticists and the American new historicists, not the differences. From this it follows naturally that a kind of transatlantic conversation follows.

I think, however, that it is Rorty who succeeds in demonstrating that his more typically American historicism (whatever its lapses into Continental geneologies) is finally irreconcilable with the hermeneuticism of the three Continentals—which is not to say that he cannot converse with them. This difference can be demonstrated best by a comment on Gadamer, and by an account of Rorty's occasional interpretations of Gadamer.

First, the tension within Gadamer's *Truth and Method* should be noted. Gadamer closes that book with the following sentences: "The fact that in the knowing involved in them [the human sciences] the knower's own being is involved marks, certainly, the limitation of 'method,' but not that of science. Rather, what the tool of method does not achieve must—and effectively can—be achieved by a discipline of questioning and research, a discipline that guarantees truth."[12] Ironically, this closes a book which has attempted both to reject the objectifying and science-modeled "method" of attaining knowledge and has attempted to defend the hermeneutical discipline of discovering "truth," a discipline modeled on the analogy of the free "play" between the interpreter and the interpreted. For Gadamer, play is neither an objective reality apart from the players, nor the creation of the player's subjectivity, but the relation between the players. Hence, "it is, rather, the game itself that plays, in that it draws the players into itself and thus itself becomes the actual subjectum of the playing."[13] Equally, hermeneutics is meant to be about neither an independent text nor the subjectivity of the interpreter of the text, but about the relationship between the text and the interpreter. Nevertheless, in contrast to all that, the book's closing sentence hints that Gadamer's real meaning may be more methodic after all.

Rorty associates Gadamer with the formalism of "weak textualism."[14] A weak textualist is one who treats a text not as something which can be used for the interpreter's own purposes (the position of the strong textualists), but as something which can be entered, which can show its own vocabulary and its own formal structure, and which can be decoded so that it can be rightly understood. Gadamer, like the weak textualists, treats the relation between the interpreted and the interpreter as something which can be *properly* understood, something about which the truth can be given to the world.[15] It appears, in other words, that Rorty is treating Gadamer's project of analyzing the linguistics of human discourse as analogous to the literary critic's "new criticism." He sees Gadamer's hermeneutical aim, at bottom, as an aim to treat the world of human discourse, even the world of play, as something one can get right, so that the truth can be guaranteed. Ironically, then, Gadamer's *Truth and Method* would become not the denial of method it claims to be, but the affirmation of a new universal method. But again, for Rorty hermeneutics (or historicism) is, more than anything else, an attack on all such universal schemes for getting things right. For Rorty, hermeneutics, properly understood, is a form of strong textualism seeking only to obtain the desired consequences, not to get the text right. Rorty's critique of Gadamer, in other words, at least diminishes the consensus Bernstein seeks to establish.

Rorty may best explain his objections to a close transatlantic alliance when he offers a pragmatic reason for preferring a pragmatic historicism free of the code-cracking or any of the universalizations he believes he detects in Habermas or Gadamer. In a chapter in *Consequences of Pragmatism*, "Overcoming the Tradition: Heidegger and Dewey," Rorty asks the question, Would Dewey oppose Heidegger's faint and modest hope that "Thought," as opposed to all conventional forms of ontology, might one day be recaptured by philosophy to provide guides for living? Yes, Rorty answers, Dewey would oppose that Heideggerian hope. And why? Because, says Rorty, "Heidegger's hope turns us away from the relations between beings and beings."[16] Rorty, following William James's notion that "truth is one species of the good,"[17] finds pragmatism laden with a kind of morality. Rorty objects to Heidegger's hope because it militates against community and its tradition.[18] The search for transtraditional justification turns us away from relations between people or situations or creatures of whatever sort. It turns us to principles instead. And this is a moral error for a person who wants to participate in the moral conversation which begins with Socrates's effort "to weigh the consequences of our actions upon other people."[19] Heidegger, in hoping for a properly understood Thought, has preserved "all that was worst in the tradition which he hoped to oversome.[20]

Rorty amplifies his moral objections to transtraditonal aspirations in his 1983 "Solidarity or Objectivity?" which opens with a distinction between the "two principal ways in which reflective human beings try, by placing their lives in a larger context, to give sense to those lives."[21] The first way, the way of "solidarity," is the way of those who find sense in their lives by contributing to a community, either to a community in which they actually live or to an imaginary community filled with heroes or heroines. The second way, the way Rorty wants to call "objectivity," is the way of those who find sense in their lives by connecting with an "immediate" nonhuman reality—immediate in the sense that it comes unmediated, "that it does not derive from a relation between such a reality and their tribe, or their nation, or their imagined band of comrades." Solidarity helps people understand by offering a connection with a community. Objectivity, on the other hand, abandons solidarity, distances the individual person from a surrounding actual or imaginary community, and seeks to gain the Truth without reference to a community, "without reference to any particular human beings." Elaborating on the objectivists as Truth-seekers, Rorty gives the following accont:

> It was perhaps the growing awareness by the Greeks of the sheer diversity of human communities which stimulated the emergence of this ideal. A fear of parochialism, of being confined within the horizons of the group into which one happens to be born, a need to see it with the eyes of a stranger, helps produce the skeptical and ironic tone characteristic of Euripides and Socrates. Herodotus's willingness to take the barbarians seriously enough to describe their customs in detail may have been a necessary prelude to Plato's claim that the way to transcend skepticism is to envisage a common goal of humanity—a goal set by human nature rather than by Greek culture.[22]

To illustrate solidarity, Rorty cites James. Those who are keyed to solidarity "view truth as, in William James's phrase, what it is good for *us* to believe. So they do not need an account of a relation between beliefs and objects called 'correspondence,' nor an account of human cognitive abilities which ensures that our species is capable of entering into that relation."[23] For them, truth is not something for its own sake, but for a group of people. For them, ethnocentricity and provincialism are virtues, and in place of metaphysics, solidarity is the "*only* comfort."

Rorty finally may exhaust himself through repeated attacks on the "objectivitists." His praise of solidarity is abstract, and he falls short of working out specific, practical social recommendations for particular communities, a shortcoming Bernstein, Cornel West, and Frank Lentricchia have criticized— assuming, apparently, that Rorty was equipped to make practical recommendations.[24]

The fact remains that Rorty seems to have put his finger on the types of practice typical of American historicism and of Continental historicism. Solidarity can be distinguished from objectivity by distinguishing what Rorty calls a hermeneutics of attitude from a hermeneutics of method. The hermeneutics that is an attitude asks us "to abandon the notion of discourse proceeding within a preexisting set of constraints, and instead open ourselves to the course of conversation"; it abjures "the Kantian notion that there is something called 'a structure of rationality' which the philosopher discovers and within which we have a moral duty to remain."[25] The hermeneutics that is a method is illustrated by Dilthey's "useless" attempt to set forth a hermeneutical "method of the human sciences."[26]

For the contemporary student of theology Rorty's comments on attitude can be extended. It was in the name of attitude that Kierkegaard objected to Hegel's "absentmindedness"; that is, to Hegel's willingness to be so distracted by his interest in "the idea" that he forgot he was an existing person in relations with a living realities. It was in the name of attitude that Jesus was said to have objected to the Pharisees, whom certain passages of the New Testament treat as so preoccupied with the legalisms dictating what went into their mouths that they neglected what came out and how that might affect others.[27] Or, returning to Rorty, it is in the name of attitude that Rorty protests the hermeneutical "quest for the holy which turns us away from the relations between beings and beings."

There is a severity in Rorty. It is a willingness to live without the comforts of an extrahistocial metaphysics. It is a willingness in a Socratic fashion merely "to talk, to listen to other people, to weigh the consequences of our actions upon other people." This is why Rorty treats pragmatism not as a conceptual but as a moral position. It abandons hope of finding something extrahistorical in our starting points. If we give up this hope, Rorty goes on to say,

> we shall lose what Nietzsche called 'metaphysical comfort', but we may gain a renewed sense of community. Our identification with our community—our society, our political tradition, our intellectual heritage—is heightened when we

see this community as ours rather than nature's, shaped rather than found, one among many which men have made. In the end, the pragmatists tell us, what matters is our loyalty to other human beings clinging together against the dark, not our hope of getting things right. James, in arguing against realists and idealists that 'the trail of the human serpent is over all,' was reminding us that our glory is in our participation in fallible and transitory human projects, not in our obedience to permanent nonhuman constraints.[28]

Rorty became convinced that those who seek metaphysical comfort are bewildered by the person who abandons such comforts and see such a person "as an ironic, sneering aesthete who refuses to take the choice between communities seriously, a mere 'relativist'."[29] From his side, Rorty praises "ethnocentricity." We have no choice but to "privilege our own group, even though there can be no noncircular justification for doing so . . . We Western liberal intellectuals should accept the fact that we have to start from where we are, and that this means that there are lots of views which we simply cannot take seriously." Rorty accepts this "lonely provincialism, this admission that we are just the historical moment that we are, not the representatives of something ahistorical."[30] He notes the inconsistency of this position with two metaphysical comforts: first, the comfort in claiming that humans have rights nonhuman creatures do not possess, for all such claims are based finally on the belief that the human species alone is linked to some extrahistorical reality which gives us a select dignity; second, the comfort in knowing that our best achievements will be remembered always. The pragmatist, Rorty says, "wants solidarity to be our *only* comfort, and to be seen not to require metaphysical support."[31] (However, it is not as though Rorty lives without a metaphysics of his own, not one which offers the comforts of static truths beyond history, but one which must give its own sense of moral virtue, nevertheless).[32]

Variations on Rorty's notion of solidarity are typical of the American new historicist tradition and distinguish it from the Continental hermeneutical tradition. One variation is found in Bernstein's more personal conclusion to *Beyond Objectivism and Relativism,* where he treats pragmatism as a movement aiming above all at the creation of the dialogic community. It is to this good community that pragmatism finally gives itself. Hilary Putnam, as we noted earlier, concludes his *Reason, Truth and History* with virtually the same encomium for community. He excoriates the solipsism of those who would work outside the social fabric of history, as well as the mere relativism of those who affirm the empty form of "only the dialogue." For Putnam, the ideal aim of historicism is for collectivity combined with responsibility.[33] For Nelson Goodman, rightness of judgment is found when something fits practice; and practice is historical and social, and never purely individual.[34] Frank Lentricchia affirms that the task of the intellectual is to create truths with consequences for the community—an affirmation that carries *Criticism and Social Change* to a Marxist hope.

The difference between Continental hermeneutics and current American new historicism, however, is one only of degree. But it is significant; and this significance can be appreciated best by a reference to the cultural and intellectual histories that lie behind the two approaches. Continental, particularly German, hermeneutics tends to rely on a method to give a uniform answer to questions of meaning, while American new historicism tends to rest content with a piecemeal analysis. Behind Continental thought there is a lingering idealism that is monistic; behind American thought there is a pluralism. Descartes looms over Continental thought; on the Continent, his problematic—to overcome the bad habit of false opinions and to find the intellectual approach that at last will get it right—seems nearly inescapable. It permeates Kant's effort to overcome skepticism through defining at last the categories of all subjective thought. It is an indispensable backdrop for Hegel's effort to establish a correlation between human rationality and the structure of history. It explains Dilthey's effort to be not merely a historicist, but to derive a lawful science of historicism. It finally shows in Husserl's phenomenological procedure, which becomes more than a procedure; which becomes, instead, a transcendental and structured subjectivism. It is never quite thrown over by Heidegger, who, despite abandoning the transcendental self-conception arising out of *Being and Time,* hopes to forge hermeneutics into Thought. And at the end, it jumps out of Gadamer, who—despite his rejection of British empiricism and scientific method, despite his forthright rejections of logocentrism in Hegel and in other forms of idealism—still hopes to find a method for guaranteeing truth in the human sciences.

America's Descartes is its plurality of immigrants. America is not an English nation, as the nineteenth-century immigration established. America is not a Puritan nation, as recent research into the non-Puritan South (where most early American Christians lived) is now demonstrating. America has no history of a nationally established church and in this is virtually unique among Western nations. Waves of immigration in the nineteenth century made America the most culturally heterogeneous nation in the modern world (more heterogeneous even than Yugoslavia). With such cultural diversity, it was unlikely that the effort to get it right could ever constitute the national drive in American culture that it did in German culture. Of course, the Puritans hoped to get it right, and the disciples of British and, then, German philosophy and theology hoped to get it right; but in neither instance is the particular case the national condition. When Americans spoke with a distinct voice, they spoke as people willing to live with pluralities and without the Cartesian thread that tied everything together. As Martin Marty has noted, Americans liked what William James called "a sort of republican banquet . . . where all the qualities of being respect one another's personal sacredness, yet sit at the common table of space and time."[35] This American tolerance, Marty notes, is neither religious indifference nor irrationality, but a counterintollerance that appreciates the nonindifference of others as well as of oneself.

Speaking for this American pluralism, William James distinguishes two forms of pantheism:

> a monistic form which I called philosophy of the absolute, and a pluralistic form which I called radical empiricism, the former conceiving that the divine exists authentically only when the world is experienced all at once in its absolute totality, whereas radical empiricism allows that the absolute sum-total of things may never be actually experienced or realized in that shape at all, and that a disseminated, distributed, or incompletely unified appearance is the only form that reality may yet have achieved.[36]

The business of the world in its deepest sense, James felt, is undertaken not when the world is known in its absolute totality, but when the particulars are experienced in all their unexplained particularity. James not only accepts this pluralism even when speaking religiously, but introduces the new tactic of pragmatism for coping with the new difficulties it makes for finding some sort of truth in a nonunified world.

In this, John Dewey was to concur. "Every existence is an event," he said, and not to be confused with something noneventful.[37] Our primary task, Dewey urged, is to investigate the possibilities inherent in separate events and environments. He despaired of "*the* genteel tradition" that flows from Aristotle and Kant and fixes its trust in the general, the uniform, the constant.[38] He rejected the idealists and positivists, who mistake their legitimately imagined generalities for the world itself—and who then convince themselves that what is particular, irrational, changing, is simply not real.

It is this same denial of the ultimate reality of the general itself and this same insistence on the particulars in all their incorrigible plurality that lie beneath Rorty's insistence on letting nothing come between oneself and the dialogic community. It is this loyalty to the perishing event (often, a person) that must be addressed by an appropriately American historicism. And it is this plurality, this loyalty, and the historicism that flows from them, which lead to a peculiarly American religious historicism.

THE NEW HISTORICISM AS RELIGIOUS

The neopragmatists have not been notable for their emphasis on religion within a new historicist outlook. For the philosophers particularly, the neglect

of religion suggests that religion simply should be abandoned along with all
reference to extrahistorical truths.

Initially, in order to suggest that the new historicism can be religious, and
that this religiousness might be distinctively American, I use two indicators.
First, beginning with the second question, I argue that there can be a religious
historicism distinctive to America by showing how the most complete expression
of religious historicism on the Continent, the historicist theology of Wolfhart
Pannenberg, is alien to the American new historicism. Second, to argue that
an American historicism can be religious, I point to three methods in late
twentieth-century Hebrew Bible criticism, methods that are both new historicist
and religious: tradition history, sociological analysis, and deconstructionism.

Pannenberg has launched a major alternative to Christian idealism,
positivism, and fideism, and has offered a historicist hermeneutic for Christian
theology. Particularly in *Offenbarung Als Geschichte*, Pannenberg announces
a new theological emphasis on history, dependent in large part on the new quest
for the historical Jesus. In his "Preface to the American Edition" of *Revelation
as History*, Pannenberg indicates his sympathy with the mode of thought
informing American historicism when he says, "Instead of authoritarian style
of theological thought, the open, rationality of the Enlightenment is preferred,
but combined with a concern for the substance of the Christian tradition."[39]

Because of his historicism, Pannenberg rejects two authoritarian theological
alternatives: first, the seventeenth-century orthodox concept of revelation, which
identifies revelation with an inspired Bible and supernatural truths; second,
the notion of revelation as the direct self-disclosure of God. Pannenberg
contends that Karl Barth's emphasis on the direct self-disclosure of God in the
revelation through the Incarnation reflects more than anything else a Christian
adaptation of Hegelian idealism.[40] In *Jesus—God and Man*, Pannenberg calls
arguments from God's direct self-disclosure Christologies "from above."[41] Not
only is there no biblical evidence for the notion of revelation as direct divine
self-disclosure, Pannenberg argues, but the notion is antithetical to biblical
religion. The notion of direct self-disclosure requires that there be only one
instance of such a revelation, because God cannot be totally revealed in basically
different instances.[42] But the notion that God is revealed in a single instance
of revelation contradicts the decisive Israelite belief that God is indirectly
revealed in a multiplicity of divine acts in history.[43] This ignores even Jesus's
dependencies on Israel and its scripture. Furthermore, Christologies from above,
whether they be idealistic or pietistic, whether they depend on Hegel,
Kierkegaard, Schleiermacher, Ritschl, Martin Kähler, Wilhelm Hermann, Paul
Althaus, or Rudolf Bultmann, leave unanswered the basic, modern question:
How, depending so heavily on your subjective experience, do you know you

are not the victim of a self-delusion?[44] A Christology from above ignores the human requirement that "we always think from the context of a historically determined human situation," rather than from the divine context which alone could let us know that Jesus directly discloses God's essence.[45]

Pannenberg prefers, then, a historical approach to revelation. He wants to discuss revelation as God's acts in universal history, and to do this, he must speak of God's indirect self-disclosure through the many events of history and of a Christology "from below." Pannenberg's general contention, then, is that we must look to history and to history alone as the source of our knowledge of God. When Pannenberg starts with history, he joins forces with those biblical scholars of the new quest for the historical Jesus, such as Gerhard Ebeling, Ernst Käsemann, Ernst Fuchs, Günther Bornkamm, and Hans Conzelmann.

Starting with history gives Pannenberg a problem, however, which, in turn, leads him to take a stand at odds with the historicism of the American tradition. If no single revelation can directly disclose God, Pannenberg argues, then the totality of history alone would give us the full and complete revelation of God. But currently "universal history is simply too boundless and unremitting in its progress" to yield such a complete revelation.[46] The totality of history cannot be known until its end, until the uncertainties of the future have played out. Consequently, Pannenberg looks at history eschatologically, from its end point, in order to acquire the necessary knowledge of God. "It is not so much the course of history," he reasons, "as it is the end of history that is at one with the essence of God. But insofar as the end presupposes the course of history, because it is the perfection of it, then also the course of history belongs to the revelation of God, for history receives its unity from its goal."[47] But how are we, mere historical creatures caught in our own time, to know the goal of history? Simple, says Pannenberg; it is shown proleptically in the resurrection of Jesus: "It is through the resurrection that the God of Israel has substantiated his deity in an ultimate way and is now manifest as the God of all men . . . Thus, the end of the world will be on a cosmic scale what has already happened in Jesus."[48]

From the point of view of the new historicists, Pannenberg is right to deny Christian idealisms and the notions of biblical inspiration, direct divine self-disclosure, and Christologies from above. Pannenberg means to stick with history and to keep the future open.[49] But for the new historicists, Pannenberg's effort to project a "universal history" through the proleptic event of Jesus's resurrection might be more naive than Hegel's efforts to unify history under the absolute idea; for Pannenberg not only presumes to comprehend the totality of the past, but the totality of the future as well. Pannenberg's willingness to believe in the unity and goal of history, whether or not that belief is based on the historical resurrection of Jesus, begins to appear just as nonhistorical as the efforts to unify history under an idea or a method. Hence, Pannenberg's religious historicism is decidedly not of the new historicist and American kind, which is pluralistic and uninformed by any sense of the totalities.

The question is, Can a method or a hermeneutic be both historicist and religious? This question is answered initially by two recent forms of biblical criticism, tradition history and sociological analysis. Together, these critical methods suggest a religious hermeneutic consistent with an American new historicism. Tradition history sees scripture as the outcome of a continuing process of the social reinterpretation of tradition. Sociological analysis makes a similar approach to scripture, but with an orientation informed by a concern for social science and for praxis.

Tradition history argues that what is religiously primary is not the religious scriptures, dogmas, practices, and rituals themselves, but the social histories of the people who formed those religious traditions. However, while social history is basic, it can be examined only by looking at the traditions. In specific times and places these traditions are formed to meet a people's needs in those times and places; however, these traditions were formed always in consultation with earlier traditions, but even these were formed to meet a people's needs in earlier times and places. This account conforms to the new American historicism in three ways: (1) that definitions cannot be taken from beyond history, either from dogmatic, scriptural, or eschatological abstractions about history or from some mystical or rational experience of something deeper than history; (2) that traditions are interpretations of social situations; and (3) that the interpretations refer merely to earlier traditions or interpretations.

Tradition history is an alternative to or an addition to the literary approach of biblical criticism that grew up under the guidance of Julius Wellhausen in the late nineteenth century. The literary approach centers on the scriptural text itself; and when it probes the history behind the text, it looks at literary evidence alone and does this only to explain the extant text. Tradition history, on the other hand, centers on the historical situation of the people who form the text; and it uses scriptural, doctrinal, and liturgical traditions, not as inherently important, but only as interpretations of historical situations. Tradition history reasons that social problems and needs cause a people to rethink their earlier tradition; and the rethinking leads to an oral expression and then to a new phase of the written text. For tradition history, a process of historical interpretation lies at the heart of the reality.[50]

In Europe tradition, criticism first was set forth definitively by Gerhard von Rad in his 1938 essay, "The Form-Critical Problem of the Hexateuch." Von Rad argued that the Hexateuch (the first six books of the Hebrew Bible) came about by means of ever-amplifying expressions of the covenant creed exemplified in Deuteronomy 26:5ff—that is, by re-expressions of the faith in the divine redemption of Israel, from the exodus from Egypt to the settlement in Canaan. The redemption story was told and edited from different locations in space, time, and history, using first the spoken creed, then the larger oral and literary units, then the principal sources of the Hexateuch, then the redactions leading to the Hexateuch, and, finally, the Hexateuch itself. Von Rad opposed this historicist and interpretation-centered account to what he calls the "high-handed methods of pneumatic theology."[51] In 1957, in his *Old Testament Theology*, von Rad restated his method, arguing that a historicist rendering of the development of the Hebrew Bible has made quite inadequate any effort to understand Hebrew religion in terms of general theological doctrines.[52] According to von Rad, each generation believed: (1) that it acted largely in continuity with the Israel of the past and its redemption story; (2) that it acted also partly in discontinuity—in order to reshape that Israelite past and that redemption story to answer the problems distinct to its own place in history. Hence, says von Rad, "a law of theological dialectic seems to have presided, a dimly or clearly felt need to hold the transmitted in suspension, and to correct it by means of accounts expressed in a strangely contradictory fashion."[53]

Apparently, von Rad saw himself rejecting not only a purely literary approach to biblical criticism, but also the prevailing German idealistic theology that grounded itself on the rational intuition of a reality beyond history. He claimed that the Hebrews took their religious identity only from historical events (including those events said to reveal Yahweh) and from historical interpretations of those events. Martin Noth joined von Rad in his 1940 "The Laws in the Pentatuch: Their Assumptions and Meaning," where he demonstrated that throughout most of their history, the Hebrews formed their laws, not as embodiments of any universal principles, but as ways of reordering their lives to meet specific new social and historical situations.[54] He extended this historicist account in his 1948 *A History of Pentateuchal Traditions.*

In 1977, *Tradition and Theology in the Old Testament*, an anthology edited by Douglas Knight, attempted to solidify and amplify tradition history for the next generation. Knight, writing what is perhaps the central essay, argues that, as the community of Hebrews reinterprets its past tradition in order to meet its new needs, this "tradition process creates new meaning."[55] Knight contrasts the tradition history method with efforts of Karl Barth to define all revelation in Christocentric terms and with the effort of Wolfhart Pannenberg and Rolf Rentorff to equate revelation with the sum of all historical events. Knight suggests that the tradition process always outruns what is currently seen as definitive revelation; future traditions always create new knowledge of God, indicating that the God of the future is always currently mysterious; hence, the equation of revelation with past tradition forgets the "ultimate mysteriousness" of God.[56] Robert B. Laurin notes elsewhere in this anthology that the early Christian Church's use of the Hebrew scriptures can itself be explained by the tradition history method; for the early Church creatively reinterpreted the Hebrew tradition to address the new events and needs experienced in the Church's own life.[57] And Hartmut Gese contends that the entire historical process of tradition development itself "reflects Israel's experience of God in history."[58] Among other prominent tradition history scholars not included in this anthology are James Sanders and Paul Hanson.[59] New Testament proponents of tradition history include Martin Hengel, E. A. Judge, Abraham Malherbe, and Robert Grant.[60]

The tradition history method is consistent with the new American historicism. It works without recourse to something beyond history that would unify, structure, or provide a goal for history. It implies that religion and scripture were created by the interpretations of traditions that, in turn, were created by the interpretations of still earlier traditions. As the interpretations answered the new needs presented by the new historical situations of the biblical peoples, the biblical religions evolved. None of this is to deny that the divine is active, even if the divine is known simply as the impetus to the tradition's growth. It is to deny, however, that the Hebrews, the Christians, or their God could be what they were apart from historical change. Take away historical change, and the biblical religions lose their distinctive character. Through most of its earliest life, there is little evidence that the actual biblical communities had recourse to a world "deeper" than the world of history. For the Hebrews particularly, when history went well, they went well; when history went poorly, they went poorly. There was no recourse beyond history. Consequently, it is within history, within a plurality of traditon-events and interpretations, that God was to be found.

Sociological criticism, the second movement in biblical criticism echoing the American new historicism, is well-represented in the collection entitled *The Bible and Liberation: Political and Social Hermeneutics,* first published in 1976 and published in a revised and expanded edition in 1983. In both editions, Norman Gottwald, the editor, argues that the volume is guided by two primary aims: "(1) To bring to light the actual social struggles of our biblical ancestors and to locate the human and religious resources they drew upon in the midst of those struggles. (2) To tap the biblical social struggles and religious understandings as important resources for directing us in the social struggles we are presently engaged in."[61] The contributors to the anthology advance a sociological analysis of specific biblical social histories, discuss original biblical meanings only in relation to those histories, and attempt to apply biblical meanings to twentieth-century life by applying those biblical meanings to contemporary social histories. The analysis is heavily oriented toward economic and political analysis, and it is heavily flavored by South American liberation motifs and Marxist paradigms of social analysis. One contributor cites José Miranda, that to "know God" in the Bible is to "know justice," and describes this conception as the idea "that God's presence is justice happening in the world."[62] Consistent with this representative passage, the volume avoids a reference to anything beyond history even in its definition of God.

In that same volume, Robin Scroggs lists sociological analyses of the New Testament. He selectively summarizes the theoretical frameworks working in those analyses in the following way: "(1) Troeltsch-like studies of unconscious social protest in the work of R. Scroggs and G. Snyder; (2) cognitive dissonance theory as applied by J. Gager; (3) role analysis as practiced by G. Theissen; (4) sociology of knowledge in the instance of W. Meeks; and (5) Marxist historical materialism in the writings of M. Machovec, F. Belo, and M. Cévenot."[63] To Scroggs's list, one could add many other books, including John G. Gager's *Kingdom and Community: An Anthropological Approach to Civilization* (1975) and Wayne Meeks's *The First Urban Christians: The Social World of the Apostle Paul* (1983).

The single most outstanding piece of sociological analysis has been Norman Gottwald's *The Tribes of Yahweh: A Sociology of the Religion of Liberated Israel, 1250-1050 B. C. E.* In that book, Gottwald takes his cue "from the methodogical insight that religion is the function of social relations rooted in the cultural-material conditions of life. This entails *a rejection of forms of theology that separate theology from religion and that abstract religious beliefs from the socially situated locus of religious believers.*"[64] For Gottwald, technical biblical scholarship works also as practical theology in the form of liberation theology; truly to understand the Hebrew Bible today is to apply it to our contemporary social situation—which now, as in the life of ancient Israel, primarily has to do with the struggle for the liberation of oppressed people. The liberation theology motif means a focus on the social history, with a new emphasis on the economic dimension of that social history. In the *The Tribes of Yahweh,* Gottwald says, "This theological structure of premonarchic Israel can be 'demythologized' according to its socioeconomic and communal-cultural referents, in contrast to the usual program of demythologizing into states of existential or mystical consciousness."[65]

Although the tradition history and the sociological approaches to biblical criticism have distinct emphases, at no point are they inconsistent with the hermeneutic implicit in the new American historicism. For, in all approaches, biblical religions are understood as created by a continual reinterpretation of past traditions from the standpoint of one's own newly problematic social context. And all approaches avoid extrahistorical referents for the word *God* and extrahistorical explanations of religion. They rely entirely on the plurality of historical events in order to account for past and present religious meanings.

While in this preliminary way these two groups of biblical scholars have begun to spell out a biblical hermeneutic unwittingly consistent with the new American historicism, they have not drawn the larger theological or philosophical implications of their work—implications that might suggest the contours of a theological historicism.

Surprisingly, this task has been initiated by people who work within the deconstructionist mode of philosophy and literary criticsm. I think particularly of Jacques Derrida, Susan Handelman, and José Faur.

Derrida has discussed the connection between his form of the new historicism, deconstructionism, and the historicism of the Hebrews in his essay on "Edmond Jabès and the Question of the Book." In his interpretation of Jabès, Derrida contends that the Hebrews redefined for themselves the ideas of knowledge and of God. Derrida, himself a Sephardic Jew (or, at least, once a Sephardic Jew) from Morocco, calls Judaism "the birth and the passion of writing," "the radical origin of meaning as literality." Here, *writing* and *literality* are metaphors referring to the construction of reality through the interpretation of the past. The writer knows that this construction one day will turn on the interpreter and interpret him or her; not only does the writer's writing construct reality, but, subsequently, this writing will write the writer. By contrast, *speaking* is the direct, uninterpreted communication of God's meaning, something that Derrida contends is more Hellenistic than Hebrew. In effect, the idea of "history," says Derrida, is born in this Jewish gesture of writing, for "there could be no history without the gravity and labor of literality."[66]

When the Hebrews left the primeval "garden" of their security with God and entered the "desert" of their wanderings, they left the place where the voice of God was heard and repeated in speech, and they became writers. That is, when they became wanderers, they were forced to see their own ever-changing interpretations as a source of their knowledge of God—hence, the gravity and labor of literality. The Pharisees, Derrida says, saw particularly well that "God no longer speaks to us; he has interrupted himself: we must take words upon ourselves. We must be separated from life and communities, and must entrust ourselves to traces, must become men of vision because we have ceased hearing the voice from within the immediate proximity of the garden."[67] Derrida quotes Jabès, "*The garden is speech, the desert writing. In each grain of sand a sign surprises.*"[68] The silence of God both causes the loss of what we would call a theonomous, Cartesian perspicuity, and gives people freedom—the freedom to rename the meaning of the present, to rename even God. Derrida quotes Jabés: *All letters form absence.*/ *Thus God is the child of his name.*'⁶⁹ While we might recognize that out of this process God is generated, we also know that in this process God is active. Jabés again, *"If, wrote Reb Servi, you occasionally think that God does not see you, it is because he has made himself so humble that you confuse him with the fly buzzing in the pane of your window. But that is the proof of his almightiness: for he is, simultaneously, Everything and Nothing."*⁷⁰ This God, which is itself "an interrogation of God," is not, says Derrida, the classical philosophers' God "who neither interrupted nor interrogated himself, . . . whose infinity did not tolerate the question, precisely had no vital need for writing."⁷¹

In his essay on Jabés, Derrida extends the implications of his Hebraic analysis to a notion of the Hebrew law. The law stands as the "Tables" within an original text, the Torah. The Jew does not place the original text outside historical contingency, as do today's structuralists. The Jew cannot decipher the law and thereby crack the code of a contingent and open history to give us the eternal truth at last. This is impossible for the Jew of the desert, who knows that any eternal meanings of the law are always already broken, signifying the rupture with the God of the origins. Nevertheless, because the law has not been lost, the Jew of the desert still interprets the law. The Jewish rabbi is unlike the poet, who must interpret without the benefit of an original text. The breaking of the original Tables, the negativity of God, gives the Jew a kind of autonomy and freedom; but this freedom and autonomy still depend on and translate the law, still depend on the chain of laws, on the negated tables and the silent God. Ironically then, a real style of the law still lives in a process, the process of continuous reinterpretation; this sytle is not ontological and extrahistorical, but it does extend a tradition.

In *The Slayers of Moses,* Susan Handelman analyzes the notion of the rabbi, using much the same deconstructionist motif, consulting Paul Ricoeur and Hans-Georg Gadamer, as well as Derrida. She lifts up the Hebrew concentration on the word, on hearing the spoken word—rather than on spirit, on seeing the nature of being. She sets a fundamental tension between Hebrew and Hellene, Jerusalem and Athens, Jewish Torah and Greek wisdom, sacred and secular, Jew and Christian. The Hebrew emphasized letter, not spirit. For Aristotle, the letter, the metaphor, lacks the reality of spirit, it produces nothing, adds nothing, even cancels itself by being empty of any proper and spiritual vision of being; "figures of speech are thus merely ornaments and not generators of meaning."⁷² For the ancient Semite, the metaphor is constitutive of reality. When the Hebrews introduced their scripture with the announcement that the heavens and earth were created in a divine act, and added that that act

The pen is mightier than the sword? NO SPEAK!

was an act of speech ("And God said, 'Let there be . . . .'"), the foundations of Greek ontology were threatened, says Handelman. Citing Hans Jonas, she notes that this "pitted contingency against necessity, particularity against universality, will against intellect."[73] In short, says Handelman, "the Rabbinic way of thinking is precisely that kind of linguistic-metaphorical hermeneutic which thinkers such as Gadamer, Ricoeur, Derrida, and others call for in their work."[74]

In his 1986 *Golden Doves with Silver Dots,* José Faur thickens the plot, arguing that "contemporary critical theory represents a radical shift in Western thought, resulting in new perspectives and methodology. This shift now allows for a better understanding of rabbinic semiotics and textuality."[75]

Derrida, Handelman, and Faur, then, have begun the task of developing an historicist and theological interpretation of Hebrew scripture. Their notions can serve as a preliminary way of extending the theological implications of tradition history and sociological analysis. And with tradition history and sociological criticisms, they, too, illustrate that a historicism can be religious.

Beyond this, I reiterate: all three movements of Hebrew Bible criticism operate out of a historicism equivalent to the historicism of the deconstructionists and neopragmatists. All these movements are historicist in the following ways: (1) interpretation occurs within history, refers to history, and shuns extrahistorical standpoints and referents; (2) the present signifier and the past signified, and those alone, both contribute to and place limits on the present interpretation and its viability; (3) because the present signifier contributes to the emergent reality, transcendental and materialistic objectivisms are denied; (4) because the past signified contributes, subjectivistic and relativistic nihilisms are denied; (5) because the viability of the interpretation is criticized by reference to the way it works in the histories that flow from the signifier and the signified, a kind of pragmatism is affirmed; (6) because in each instance the signifier to some extent determines the emergent reality, the responsibility of the signifier is emphasized; and (7) because a theology growing out of any of these historicisms could know only what lies within history, such a theology's God must be known only in history. Consequently, Hebrew historicism, deconstructionist historicism, and neopragmatic historicism share far more than a mild antipathy to extrahistorical metaphysics; they overlap in worldview, expistemology, tests of truth, implicit morality, and implicit theology. Consequently, the concept of history in Hebrew thought bears great and unnoticed implication for the concept of history in today's neopragmatic and deconstructionist new historicism.

THE RELIGIOUS NEW HISTORICISM IN NEED OF AMPLIFICATION

For all their value in unwittingly demonstrating the religious viability of American new historicism, Derrida, Handelman, and Faur betray their Continental origins. Their example calls for a more Hebrew—and, I might add, a more American—extrapolation of the theological implications of the new historicism. For all three seem still heavily affected by the spirit-matter dualism of Continental idealism. They concentrate on the linguisticality, the literality, of reality, reducing Hebrew religion to a religion of rhetoric and placing it on one side of a spirit-linguistic/material-nonlinguist dualism. They imply that Hebrew religion is an affair of the spirit—a surprising implication for this religion which so clearly affirmed a mind-body monism. Faur attributes to the Hebrews a "semiological view of the universe" amd calls the Hebrews a people of the Book. In his explanation of the Hebrew mind, Faur approvingly quotes Roland Barthes to the effect that "Man does not exist prior to language, either as a species or as an individual."[76] All three neglect the Hebrew preoccupation with God's involvement in nature, which, von Rad says, is the basis for all God's expression in social history, in words, and in laws.[77]

The problem with this dualism is that it does not permit a religious interpretation of the political and economic action so important to the tradition and sociological critics. Politics and economics involve physical behaviors and materials which cannot be expressed in words. The tradition historians and the sociological analysts need a theological outlook that would confirm not only the consitutive function of the metaphor, but the constitutive function of all acts and all experiences—an outlook provided by the original American religious pragmatism and radical empiricism.

Finally, just as the tradition critics and the sociological methodologists argued that Hebrew and Christian people's meanings cannot be understood except as they are seen in that people's own social context, it follows that these critics, themselves, should look to their own social context for an adequate theology.

The American frame of thought to which they could turn was best represented in the first four decades of this century by the sociohistorical method of the Chicago School, which was first formulated as a biblical method. It is an understatement to say that the sociohistorical method anticipated tradition history and sociological analysis. The fact is that the Chicago scholars had opened all the large windows, and had surveyed from those vantage points the biblical peoples, traditions, and texts for decades before the tradition historians and the sociological analysts had seen from afar this many-roomed mansion of historicist biblical criticism. In the last analysis, the point is not a perfect methodological consistency, but functional adequacy. The Chicago sociohistorical method not only provides a less dualistic analysis of the Hebrews than that offered by Derrida, Handelman, and Faur, but an analysis more relevant to American culture than that offered by the European scholars to whom the biblical critics typically turn. Generally, if American biblical scholars were to look into their own history for their historical method, they might find a theory more pertinent to the temper of Americans than that offered by von Rad's European, covenant-oriented, tradition history analysis. Further, they might find a social theory more germane and persuasive to the more capitalist, voluntarist, and demotic history of Americans than that found in many of the sociologists' Marxist analyses, more naturally rooted in Europe.

Despite these problems, it should be said that the recent biblical historicists have offered a powerful illustration of the religious viability of the new historicism. But to enlarge this account and to render the religious expression in a way more germane to American culture, a movement further back, into the Chicago School of religious thought, is required.

CHAPTER 3

The Chicago School

The University of Chicago's Chicago School of theology was fully "new historicist" sixty years before the current new historicism attained its mature voice. It saw clearly that reality is built from the chain of interpretations: people newly interpreting their social circumstance, in that light reinterpreting their traditions, thereby creating religious answers which became new traditions, after which new social circumstances arose, with the cycle repeating itself over and over again. Furthermore, the new historicism of the Chicago School utilized the American tradition of philosophy and theology to become a historicism that was American. Further still, the Chicago historicism was a religious historicism, beginning with a new historicist biblical criticism, moving into the area of the history of Christian thought and Christian ethics. During the first four decades of this century, the Chicago School demonstrated that a new historicism could be both American and religious.

Today's new historicists, particularly those with an interest in the American and religious uses of the new historicism, forget the Chicago School at their own peril. The Chicago School's historicism included a theologically sophisticated expression of a third option, a value-laden historicism, beyond objectivism and relativism. Any American religious historicism must develop eventually such a third option, but that is yet to be accomplished under the social and intellectual circumstances peculiar to the late twentieth century. Admittedly, the Chicago theologians worked in a less pluralistic era and they were less methodologically self-critical than today's historicists; nevertheless, the similarities between the Chicago theologians and the current religious historicists could make the Chicago example instructive. That example may speak to the tendency among today's historicists still to be implicitly dualistic, still to be influenced by a neo-Kantian tendency to identify what for all intents and purposes is real with the way people think and perceive, so that it is easy to see all of history as simply a chain of linguistic tropes (words, signs, "worlds," human interpretations), to ignore the world of nature, and to collapse natural history into human literary history.

45

The Chicago School theologians were influenced by the evolutionary and pragmatic naturalism of William James and John Dewey. These distinctly American philosophers had treated historical relations as themselves the deepest reality, and refused to base their thought on anything outside natural and social history. They went on to blur the things related in history, so that they treated as abstract and artificial the conventional distinctions between mind and body, spirit and matter, value and fact, person and world, God and world. For the Chicago School theologian influenced by this new worldview, it followed that religious truths necessarily referred entirely and exclusively to the valuational interaction of events in natural and social history.

The historicism of these theologians was thorough and distinct; with the possible exception of the latest writings of Ernst Troeltsch,[1] there was nothing in Europe like this American historicist theology. The many books of these historicist theologians were widely influential. The Chicago School of theology proliferated its students and influences to other universities, to divinity schools, and to many Protestant pulpits. Their prose was lucid, concrete, and affective; they had no category of the eternal and universal, so that the Germanic language designed to refer to the eternal and universal was for them literally useless.

Most prominent among the Chicago theologians were George Burman Foster, Gerald Birney Smith, Shailer Mathews, and Shirley Jackson Case; perhaps the Chicago School's most important alumunus was the Yale theologian Douglas Clyde Macintosh. At the University of Chicago, the Chicago School of theology was the counterpart to "Chicago Schools" of philosophy, sociology, education, economics, political science, and psychology. These schools of thought were influenced by John Dewey, who taught at Chicago from 1894 to 1904, and by his friend and intellectual confrere, George Herbert Mead who taught at Chicago from 1894 to 1931. The orientation of these schools was pragmatic, empirical, pluralistic, and in a peculiar way, American.[2]

The historicism of the Chicago School of theology is found in its sociohistorical method, which made history the primary religious authority. Here scripture, tradition, and reason were important not as independent authorities, but as clues to historical meanings. For the sociohistorical method, history is not built randomly, deterministically, or providentially. History is about societies, about the way they reinterpret their past to meet their present needs, and about the way that reinterpretation becomes itself the past for future societies. History is not the changing window through which we glimpse the unchanging world of extrahistorical reality; it is the changing window through which we view nothing but a changing world. The divine exists both in the changes of the world to which the window opens and in the changes of the window itself. The Chicago School theologians knew of no way of talking about the divine except through ever-changing historical interpretations of previous historical interpretations. For the sociohistorical method talk about God and Christ is talk that arises from old historical contexts and opens new historical contexts.

This movement toward an American theological historicism was attacked and overwhelmed. Protestant historicism suffered from a combination of forces: Pope Pius X's 1907 encyclical against modernism, stifling a Catholic modernism which was beginning to ally with Protestant liberalism;[3] World War I and the Great Depression, which fostered a more cautious and conservative religious outlook; more particularly, the 1927 arrival at the Divinity School of the University of Chicago of Henry Nelson Wieman, whose Whiteheadian metaphysics attracted many of the liberal theological students who otherwise might have pursued historicism. The most important attack came from American neo-orthodox theologians, influenced by German crisis theologians such as Karl Barth and Emil Brunner. In retrospect, it is the Niebuhr brothers, H. Richard and Reinhold, who stand out; but their work was representative of a cohort of like-minded American theologians.[4] They complained that the liberals, including the Chicago School theologians, were optimistic in that they failed to recognize that the fundamental human condition is disobedience to and guilt before a transcendent God. (To my knowledge, the neo-orthodox critics did not distinguish between the optimism referring to liberal idealism's and Transcendentalism's absolute God working in a monistic world and the optimism referring to the Chicago School pragmatist's limited God working in a pluralistic world;[5] liberals were liberals, and they were all optimistic.) These critics concluded that the human attempt to know reality in the deepest way through interpretations of history was doomed because history is so distorted by sin that it obscures rather than reveals what is most real. Instead of history, we must rely on scripture, neo-orthodoxy asserted, and find in scripture that divine justice and grace which brings to history its true and meaningful order.

It is widely recognized that beginning around 1960, neo-orthodoxy began to lose much of its plausibility; but it has not been widely recognized that this change suggests that the critiques advanced by neo-orthodoxy should be reexamined. More than for any other reason, neo-orthodoxy lost plausibility because it relied on an extrahistorical order. P. Joseph Cahill, although he is writing in 1984 and commenting on then-current theologies, describes the kind of change which led to the demise of neo-orthodoxy. He pictures theology as still controlled by the subterranean influences of the "Pythagorean theory of harmonic ratios and the chain of being," and, in effect, by the ideal of a harmonious universe. According to Cahill, this ideal "has never been peacefully integrated into the two great movements of modern times: that is, the development of the empirical sciences . . . and the thematization of historical consciousness." The consequence, says Cahill, is that the inherited and harmony-bound theological styles are "at the point of exhaustion."[6] That neo-orthodoxy is among those theologies subject to such subterranean influences and to the ideal of harmony can be illustrated by Reinhold Niebuhr's notion of love—which is set forth as a theory of harmonic relations between the person and God, between person and person, and within the person, and which is based on the essential nature of the human being, which is based in turn on the will of a God beyond history.[7] Nevertheless, even if today neo-orthodoxy and its successors are at the point of exhaustion, their critiques of liberal theologies have not been critically reexamined.

Ironically, the kind of prediction made by Cahill can be found just as neo-orthodoxy was introducing itself. In his 1936 *Great Chain of Being,* Arthur Lovejoy argued that the theory of evolution, together with a concommitant empiricism and historicism, had virtually vanquished the idea of the chain of being.[8] Who, he asked, reasonably could conceive of the world as emanating from the greater perfection of God to the lesser perfection of the contingent world? Clearly, Lovejoy said, history's major movement is now seen to be from the lesser to the greater. Earlier still, in 1917, young Henry Nelson Wieman in his Harvard Ph.D. dissertation argued that the ideal of harmony is counter-productive to creative historical action. Harmonious coordination, he argued, is achieved by eliminating disparate notes, whereas real natural and social evolu-tion occur through the addition of disparate notes. Wieman went on to acknowledge that the disparate note usually introduces conflict; nevertheless, he concluded that "it is not coordination but conflict which makes life worth living."[9] All this said, however, Cahill still is probably right in noting that only much later was the point of exhaustion reached for the theologies of harmony, if even then.

Now, near the end of the twentieth century, the cultural climate may be more receptive to the Chicago School than at any time since the 1920s. The new historicism in America, as well as those new pragmatic, pluralistic, and social scientific interests that lie behind the new historicism, affect the way people appraise their ultimate values and their implicit or explicit religious meanings. Of course, it is possible that all theologies—not only neo-orthodoxy, not only theologies of harmony—are exhausted. But if American religious thought is to survive the loss of the ideal of an extrahistorical harmony, it might do that by reaching an accord with historicism. The atmosphere more receptive to the Chicago School is signaled not only by the neopragmatic and deconstruc-tionist philosophies, but also by the philosophies of science of Thomas Kuhn and Paul Feyerabend[10] and the literary criticism of the Yale deconstructionists

J. Hillis Miller, Geoffrey Hartman, and Paul de Man.[11] Together, these thinkers add a new episode in the conversion of the great chain of being from what Lovejoy called "one of the most grandiose enterprises of the human intellect" into "the history of a failure."[12] Together, except at their subjectivistic, formalistic, and Eurocentric extremes, these thinkers not only would agree with the historicism of the Chicago School theologians, but they would suggest that a reconsideration of the sociohistorical method of the Chicago School theologians is warranted.

THE RELIGIOUS HISTORICISM OF THE CHICAGO SCHOOL

Neither Shailer Mathews nor Shirley Jackson Case was a born historicist. Case, particularly, saw himself not as the happy warrior for change, but as the reluctant victim of change. When he was a young man in the 1890s, higher criticism took from him the sense of the impregnability of the Bible. Soon Case was to recognize that not only the words but the thoughts of Jesus and Paul were a function of their historical context, and that all Christian knowledge was vulnerable to historical analysis. Not even Ritschl's extrahistorical essence of Christianity could stop the erosion, for that "essence" was itself the function of a passing historical context. Case confesses, "From concentration upon reduction and simplicity we turned to the study of variety and complexity. And soon we found ourselves groping about in a vast labyrinth."[13] By his own admission, Case had been a man for whom it was

> an irreparable disaster to be forced to abandon belief in the normative quality and eternal validity or at least a modicum of traditional dogma. The Heraclitean postulate that all is flux could surely not be true in the realm of Christian verities; somewhere the mind must come to rest in its search for dogmatic certainty. One might be forced to evacuate one or another antiquated stronghold, but surely there was somewhere in the rear an absolutely safe position yet to be occupied.[14]

Nevertheless, Case eventually was to set forth a historicism uncompromising in its attack on just such absolutely safe positions.

Although Shailer Mathews's childhood religious education was conventional,[15] sometime between 1884 and 1887 as a student in Newton Theological Seminary he asked a professor of theology whether Paul's rabbinical education could have affected his interpretation of Jesus. "To quiet me," Mathews recounts, "I was told I had better write a paper about it."[16] During the academic year 1890–91, Mathews studied history and political economy at the University of Berlin. There he "learned historical method in a field where there were no temptations to apologetics."[17] When, in 1894, he came to the University of Chicago to teach New Testament history, he saw himself as one who would write and teach "Christian Sociology," emphasizing the social origins and the social function of Jesus's teaching in particular. Around 1904, Mathews became chair of systematic theology and extended this sociological approach to the analysis of dogma. "So far as I know," Mathews was to say, "there were no precedents for the attempt except a volume by Hyde, *Social Theology*. But its method was very different from mine, which was simple."[18] (Unwittingly, more than seventy years later Norman Gottwald made a similar claim: his own *The Tribes of Yahweh,* he said, had presented "the *preconditions* for a new theological method which would employ the biblical records as ideological products and instruments of the social formation of Isreal."[19]) Mathews proceeded to set doctrinal development in the context of the larger social history and concluded that Christianity "was a religion rather than merely a system of doctrines."[20]

Case and Mathews together, more than anyone else, were responsible for the flowering of the "sociohistorical method" of the Chicago School of theology. The relevant publication of these men extends from Mathews's 1897 *The Social Teaching of Jesus* to Case's 1946 *The Origins of Christian Supernaturalism.* Mathews arrived at Chicago in 1894 and retired in 1933; Case arrived in 1908 and retired in 1938. Each worked within the Chicago atmosphere, pervaded as it was by Dewey and Mead, for a few years before developing his version of the sociohistorical method; and each continued to advocate the method in publications after leaving the university.

In Case's 1943 *The Christian Philosophy of History,* which is the best summary of the sociohistorical method of the Chicago School,[21] it is evident that Case is shooting at the rear guard of neo-orthodox theology. With a kind of dismay, Case recounts the way "at the opening of the twentieth century, historical thinking seemed to have become a permanent characteristic of the intellectual life."[22] Historical thinking had pervaded all aspects of thought, from the "physical realm," where geology and biological evolution saw nature historically, to the realms of culture, society, and religion. With this thinking, "the whole of civilization represented a progressive movement of expansion surely advancing, either directly or in zigzag fashion, toward higher levels of achievement."[23] Of course, it had been just such terminology of *progressive, expansion, advancing, higher,* and *achievement,* which had intially antagonized the neo-orthodox theologians. But for Case, such criticisms missed the point. Not only did neo-orthodoxy abandon the great achievement of constructive historical thinking and turn to complaining about the contradictions within historical life; not only had it "produced what may be called the 'cult of crisis,' propounded to offset what its devotees had scornfully termed the 'cult of progress';"[24] but the core problem was that neo-orthodoxy had measured history in terms of fixed and nonhistorical standards from the past, such as Augustine's standard of the *City of God*.[25] When earlier these standards had been overthrown, the orthodox theologians had drifted "into eddies of despair."[26] Now the neo-orthodox theologians were turning that despair into an attack on those liberals who were ready to live with history and to find in it grounds for social action.

Case's empirical orientation required the abandonment of all fixed and nonhistorical standards for history, whether they were neo-orthodoxy's standards from the past or philosophy's metaphycial standards. An empirical approach saw all standards as transient and historical. "Evaluational opinions must be left as free to develop as is the historical process itself. Judgments of what is 'good' and 'better' and 'best' are as fluid as is the stream of time."[27] Neo-orthodox criticism notwithstanding, Case maintained that there can be no absolute progress because there can be no absolute norm of progress. If we have no absolute standards, we affirm what is natural to our own situation, and this is correlative to our own novel and distinctive achievements, which, as new, are thought to surpass the achievements of former generations. We affirm, said Case, what suits our taste, and taste inevitably arises from "the value each successive generation attaches to its accomplishments over those of its predecessors."[28] Given this, "no one can fail to perceive numerous evidences of progress. Who would choose to return if he could to the conditions of life that enveloped mankind in primitive times?"[29]

Case may have best defined the religious historicism the neo-orthodox theologians rejected when he said, "One of the most elemental lessons to be learned from history is the fact that religion is integral to the process of life itself. In this sense, history may be said to make religion."[30] Each generation lives out of an inherited tradition, but also it lives under the values it currently finds most worthwhile. In the terms of its contemporary values, it "re-creates" the religious tradition it has received. No generation makes its religion from nothing; but neither does any generation simply replicate its religious heritage; every generation reinterprets and alters the religion given to it by the past. Gradually, then, a society's religion grows and assumes the distinctive characteristics which to future generations may seem to be immemorial. When Case says, "The making of religious history is a heavy responsibility to place upon mankind,"[31] his audacity can be understood. If religion is a function of history, and history is a function of societies, then, of course, the creation of religion is a social responsibility.

It is just this fact, Case believed, that the neo-orthodox theologians missed. In order to argue against such social and progressivistic interpretations of Christianity, the neo-Reformation theologians of Europe and America revived the traditional distinction between secular and the sacred histories. With what is finally an ontological dualism, they declared secular histories and their "religions" to be merely vain undertakings. In sacred and supernatural history, by contrast, there "is no evolution, no gradual unfolding of wisdom, no testing to distinguish between good and evil, no uncertainty or tentativeness about alleged truth. All is complete, final, and absolute in theory."[32] It is appropriate, therefore, for the neo-orthodox Christian to confess the failure of secular history in the sight of God, to abandon hope of ever basically improving secular history, and to use secular history primarily as the arena in which one stands as one asserts one's faith in the God of sacred history. Karl Barth rejected the social gospel and the movement for religious education, and called for what Case characterizes as a concentration on "a theoretical sphere of alleged revelation lying outside the realm of specifically human history."[33] In the last analysis, then, Case protests what he thinks of as the neo-orthodox reintellectualiza-tion of Christianity: their disappointment about the course of history led them to repristinate a two-level world (one historical and the other extrahistorical), and to argue that the real end of life is to affirm one's ideals rather than to work actively for the alteration of immediate history. It can be said accurately that Case in 1943 upheld the earlier generation's "social gospel," championed by Walter Rauschenbusch, in face of the fideism of Karl Barth, just as a genera-tion later Rauschenbusch's grandson, Richard Rorty, would uphold the social activism of John Dewey and William James in face of Martin Heidegger's fideism about Thought which, Rorty said, "turns us away from the relations between beings and beings."[34]

More specifically, Case saw religion as the continual communal reconstruc-tion of the past in order to meet new social needs. To understand the religion of the past, the historian must understand that reconstruction as it occurred in the past. To understand the religion of the present, the theologian must understand that reconstruction as it is occurring in the present.

If religion is the continual communal reinterpretation of the religious tradition to meet contemporary social needs, this makes historical reinterpreta-tion, itself, the religious authority. Scriptures, religious institutions, and theological dogmas must be understood and respected as interpretations by specific past generations to meet their social problems. But, Case emphasized, it was that social interaction and interpretation which produced the scriptures, and it was not the other way around; the historical reconstruction is the source, or parent, of the literary religion. To treat the literary religion—scriptures, institutions, or dogmas—as inherently authoritative is to make the child into the parent. Case is aware that the priority of literary religion is the prevailing practice; his argument is that it is simply backwards.[35]

Using these distinctions, Case created a sociohistorical version of the quest for the historical Jesus. In *Jesus: A new Biography*,[36] Case argues that the Jesus of history arises in the interaction between Jesus and his social history, whereas the Christ of faith arises in the interaction between a later generation and the Jesus of history. Of course, this is complicated by the fact that the gospels picture the Christ of faith for the gospel writers rather than the Jesus of history himself. Consequently, the biblical scholar's task is to go behind the gospels to find the Jesus of history so that the scholar's own generation can form more accurately its own Christ of faith. (In presuming that the scholar is capable of "discovering" such a Jesus of history, Case would appear to today's new historicist as naive.)

Religion lives, then, only in the present social interpretation. History as it was lived in the past is not religiously authoritative, but it does set the boundaries and give the contents for present interpretation. In *The Evolution of Early Christianity* (1914), *The Social Origins of Christianity* (1923), *The Social Triumph of the Ancient Church* (1933), and in *The Origins of Christian Supernaturalism* (1946) there are always two lessons: Christianity lives in the interaction between a current social environment and a received tradition, and in that interaction the people treat the received tradition not as authoritative, but as their object of interpretation. In fact, if one truly understands that an earlier religious expression was a specific interaction between that people's past and its own present, then one will understand that the tradition issuing from that interaction ought not itself be authoritative in the present. The genesis itself of that earlier interpretation means that faithfulness to its spirit requires that one not accept its content as authoritative. Consequently, Case concludes *The Social Origins of Christianity* by saying: "If he [the present-day Christian] has successfully visualized the devotion and the energy which characterized the ancients in the service rendered to their contemporaries, he can scarely fail to become a more zealous and effective servant of his own generation."[37] The same lesson pervades Case's *The Origins of Christian Supernaturalism*, written in 1946 to combat, once more, the tide of supernaturalism that was innundating the field of historical scholarship. He argues that supernaturalism was true for the early Church because it worked in that Church's social environment. Without its supernaturalist argument, the Church would not have been able to make a successful appeal to the supernaturalistic people of the time; and without that appeal, the Church would probably have been ineffective in the Roman Empire. But Case argues with equal vigor that that same supernaturalism is not true in the twentieth century because, finally, it cannot and will not work in the Age of Science. In short, newer forms of thinking have become "more efficient in supporting the ideals and aims of Christian living in a modern world."[38] Consequently, what was once true has ceased to be true;

and the new naturalism which once was not "efficient," and therefore not true, has become "efficient," and therefore true.

For Case, the concept of God, like everything else in religion, will change as the social-historical contexts of the interpreting community change. In the eyes of some Christians, the Hebrew people's task of sociohistorical interpretation was given to a divine Christ, who brought to humanity the extrahistorical and eternal truth. Then there were two Gods; the God of logos Christology and Greek abstraction was added to the historical God of the Hebrews.[39] Case argues that in the twentieth century the communities based on biblical traditions should return to a single and thoroughly historical approach. Case hinted at a naturalistic rendition of this God when he said, "The urge of the human race toward cultural advance and the pursuit of moral and spiritual ideals suggest to the thoughtful observer that there is some force in nature inspiring these efforts."[40] Or, he said, "The surest guaranty of progress lies in the very fact that [people] are inspired, as never before, by a restless impulse toward still higher attainments."[41]

But here, Case seems to flirt with a new absolute. He wants to base his speculations on a people's historical beliefs and on how those beliefs are developed, and he examines people's beliefs and how they are inspired. The "restless impulse toward still higher attainments" is the definition that is generated by a people who seek a "Deity who is integral to the normal historical process, knowledge of whom is derived from the observable phenomena of the world of human experience."[42] But does Case demonstrate, in fact, that this theory of God is derived from the observable phenomena of the world of human experience in his time? When it came to his own generation, did he feel that historical research and historicist theologizing were unnecessary? Is Case here indulging in his own form of ahistorical theologizing?[43]

Shailer Mathews best stated his version of the sociohistorical method in his *The Atonement and the Social Process*. The great temptation, Mathews thought, was to fail to treat the history of Christianity the way other history is treated and to fail to see the history of Christianity as a phase of general history. Historians of doctrines may be the true villains: "Instead of treating Christianity as a continuous group movement of people possessed of a common loyalty to Jesus, they seem to regard it more as a system existing apart from people. The effect of such a preconception is to center attention on doctrine and to make the great question for the theologian the truthfulness of any doctrine."[44] Rather than attending first to the doctrine and its truth, the theologian should regard first the people who formulated the doctrine. "Strictly speaking," said Mathews, "there is no history of doctrine; there is only the history of the people who made doctrine."[45] Change in doctrine is a function of change in the people;

doctrine is revised not when its theory is found to be conceptually flawed, but when a people's social order has changed.

Sounding very much like Thomas Kuhn's reputedly innovative 1962 *The Structure of Scientific Revolutions,* Mathews contends in 1930 that beliefs are threatened when a conscious tension arises between inherited beliefs and those new situations to which the inherited beliefs should, but no longer do, apply. Then the community must choose to abandon its inherited belief, to merely reiterate it, or to find a new belief which can comprehend both the new and the old situations. The process is driven by dominant social and political groups which make that pattern orthodox simply through accepting it; equally, "heresy is always the belief of a defeated party."[46] Mathews's explanation of the development of doctrine was built on the motif of revolution, just as Kuhn's is. In 1901, at the request of the Chautauqua Institution, Mathews had written *The French Revolution—A Sketch.* Later, Mathews was to say that in writing that book "I pioneered into the field of the presentation of history from the point of view of social psychology." "Unconsciously," he said, "I had laid a foundation for what seems to be the true method in theology."[47] In *Jesus on Social Institutions,* Mathews stated that "the Messianic hope is a phase of the psychology of revolution. To understand it one should be a student of revolutions."[48] Mathews's point is that beliefs are not first of all theories to be evaluated on cognitive grounds; rather, they are instruments used by revolutionary groups to address new social and historical problems.

Like Case, Mathews argues that an orthodox belief not currently true might once have been true. In a particular time it might have been not only victorious, but functionally the most socially advantageous, the best problem-solving conclusion. So to say that certain founders of orthodoxy were nearer the truth than certain heretics is to say that their conclusions were more advantageous for an early Christian community than were the conclusions of the heretics.[49]

In *The Atonement and the Social Process,* Mathews proceeds to describe the way various theories of the atonement attempted to resolve a social or political problem faced by the Christian community at various points in its history. To simplify vastly Mathews's story, previous to the modern era the death of Jesus received seven basic interpretations, each understandable as a response to the social situation and the social psychology of the people propounding the interpretation. First, the Messianic theory of the death of Jesus addressed the problem of the Hebrew Christians as they struggled to make sense of the fact that the Messiah had not arrived according to expectations. Second, the sacrificial theory of the death of Jesus addressed the problem of Gentile Christians who needed an alternative to ritual sacrifice in cult religions and in Judaism. Third, Paul's acquittal theory of the death of Jesus addressed the problem of a people accustomed to juridical systems and dominated by the fear that they would be found guilty when the great day of judgment dawned. Fourth, the Johannine sonship theory addressed the problem of people living in the eastern Roman Empire who were preoccupied more with their connections with the Godhead than with problems of sin. Fifth, the Augustinian theory of atonement dealt with the problem of people in the western part of the Roman Empire who were distraught from the breakdown of the empire and sought a City of God led by a Christ who would restore order. Sixth, the Anselmian theory of atonement in its rationalistic and nonscriptural form attempted to answer the imagined queries of Arabs, Jews, and ancient Greeks, all of whom were the intellectual superiors of the medieval Christian and none of whom accepted the Christian's scriptures or tradition. Seventh, the substitutionary, Reformation theory of atonement expressed the social needs of those people outside the old Roman Empire who chose to assert their independence from the Roman curia by erecting the notion of a monarchial God with punitive justice.

When a particular theory of the death of Jesus prevails, the people take the theory literally. It is for the theologian, said Mathews, to see that the theory is primarily an analogy for addressing a new social problem, and then to assess the functional value of that analogy in the social practice of a people.[50] While acknowledging that theology typically has taken its analogies from politics, making it a form of "transcendentalized politics," Mathews contends that in the current age, a more adequate analogue is needed. Mathews came to prefer science as an analogue.[51] Leaning heavily on evolutionary and sociological theory, Mathews argued that we should look to "our experience of the relation of an organism to its active environment and of individuals to groups."[52]

A year later, in 1931, Mathews's *The Growth of the Idea of God* traced the ways in which the idea of God, from the pre-Hebrew God to the contemporary God, has changed to meet social needs. This book did for God what *The Atonement and the Social Process* had done for Jesus, showing that the concept of God was altered to meet changing social needs.

Mathews' historicism caused him to reject all efforts to establish an essence of Christianity. He moved toward a pluralism, arguing that the term *Christianity* has always been relative to the social conditions of the Christian peoples, and the social conditions are always changing. "In fact," says Mathews, "the only definition that can possibly be given to Christianity is that it is the religion professed by people who call themselves Christians."[53]

Finally, it must be noted that even Mathews had difficulty living within the brave new world of sociohistory he had done so much to build. For example, in *The Atonement and the Social Process* just a page after nominalistically defining Christianity as the religion professed by people who call themselves Christian, he asks "Was Jesus correct? Can one think of any reason or beneficient purpose in the cosmic process, and is love rather than coercion a basis upon which to build human society and organize one's own individual life?"[54] We might ask, however, whether this question does not seek just that timeless, universal essence Mathews had just ruled out. Or, in his 1928 *Jesus on Social Institutions*, Mathews implies that we can separate the specific teachings of Jesus, which are relative to Jesus's own times, from "the principles which such specific teachings expressed."[55] Or still earlier, in his 1924 *The Faith of Modernism*, Mathews argues that while the doctrines of the Christians are specific to an era, "the basal Christian attitudes and convictions" of the Christians are "the permanent element in our religion."[56] But it must be asked, If what is real for a people arises from their social context, and if social contexts continually change, how is it any more possible to hold for permanent principles, attitudes, and convictions than it is to hold for permanent doctrines? Are they not all creatures of the social context, without any general or enduring meaning? Is Mathews really speaking historically, rather than rationalistically, when he talks of universal and enduring principles, attitudes, and convictions? But if so, how? Are his generalizations of a type different from those he rejects?

Ironically, a few of Mathews's specific efforts to describe what is general in the Christian attitude have been relativized in ways beyond his control. In *The Faith of Modernism*, Mathews claims that the test of Christianity throughout all time is its "active loyalty to Christ and his message that God is fatherly and that men, therefore, ought to be and can be brotherly."[57] Within half a century it became apparent that the words *fatherly* and *brotherly* (let alone *man*) are not general metaphors. Rather, they, with other notions, have conveyed a specifically masculine picture of our society and its religious realities, which for many men as well as women not only fail to resolve religious needs, but add new problems and needs to the society ostensibly using them to resolve needs. Further, throughout most of his career Mathews pictured God as "the personality-producing activities of the universe." Today Mathews's characterization can appear anthropocentric and psychologistic. It is hard to resist seeing such a God's preoccupation with humans and with their pyschological constitution as just the sort of absolutization of one's own modern, Western concerns that Mathews so vigorously denounced in the writings of others. Finally, it often appears that Mathews treats his own scientific analogy as unencumbered by the political baggage Mathews finds in all other analogies. But it is increasingly clear in the late twentieth century that the scientific analogy, far from leaving behind religion's history of transitory, political analogies, may be our own supreme political analogy, supreme partly because

it so effectively cloaks its political tendencies behind its claimed innocense as
"pure science." To take a single example, the sudden and universal loss of the
human gene is today quite possible because so many scientists made the political
decision to develop nuclear arms. As Paul Feyerabend has stressed, scientific
reasoning not only works like, but to a large extent is, a political maneuver[58]—in
ways which, no doubt, would have surprised Mathews.

While Case and Mathews are mentioned most prominently as the
sociohistorical methodologists *par excellence,* in fact their careers were
overlapped and in important ways preceded by the careers of Gerald Birney
Smith and George Burman Foster, both of whom were Chicago School
sociohistorical religious thinkers.

Smith set forth the elements of the sociohistorical method in 1910 in the
American Journal of Theology in his section of a jointly written article entitled "The Task and Method of Systematic Theology." Smith begins his argument by noting a weakness in just that pietistic and Continental liberalism
that might have seemed most appropriate to early twentieth century America.

> A disciple of Schleiermacher declared that the theologian had only to look within
> himself for the material with which he was to deal. But further reflection showed
> that the experience cannot be taken simply as a storehouse from which permanent
> conclusions may be drawn. Experience has a history; it is conditioned by historical
> circumstances; it varies with changing environment.[59]

To have the courage to abandon the authorities of dogma, scripture, or church
external to experience does not entitle one to still the chaos by finding a new
absolute within experience, whether that be Schleiermacher's "absolute
dependence" or Ritschl's sense of values derived from Jesus. For there is still
the empirical fact that internal experience, like everything else, has a history;
it varies from time to time and from place to place. There are, in short, qualities
of religious experience other than those found in the psyches of nineteenth-
century German Christians.

Does the loss of the capacity to generalize on the basis of any particular
kind of experience mean, then, the end of theology? Smith begins his answer
by arguing that the situation for religion is not as new as it might seem.
Theology has never been characterized by any "static body of doctrine"; no
historical period ever has been content to accept the "unchangeable truths"
of an earlier period.[60] Even a doctrine that was understood to be timeless because
its object was timeless—such as the doctrine of the trinity—has never been
static, has always been newly interpreted. Smith, in short, argues that a little
empirical examination shows that change is not the threat it might seem to
be. In fact, it is nothing new; we have survived it over and over again already.

Smith proceeds to note that doctrines have changed because people's problems have changed, and new religious doctrines have been accepted because they seemed to offer a solution to these new problems. Smith's continual reference to the social origins of doctrines indicates his own historical empiricism, just as his continual reference to practical answers suggests his own pragmatism. As a matter of fact, Smith argues, Christian thought has always worked not only empirically, but pragmatically. Using the twin planks of empiricism and pragmatism, Smith lists the "four main tasks to be accomplished in the scientific formulation of the religious beliefs which ought to be held by men today": "(1) the historical understanding of the growth and significance of the religious ideals which constitute our social inheritance; (2) the analysis of present religious needs; (3) the interpretation of these needs in such a way as to suggest religious convictions which shall be at the same time practically efficient and rationally defensible; and (4) the apologetic defense of the theological convictions reached."[61] The first task is the empirical examination of the religious history. The second and third tasks combine the methods, first the empirical examination of the present needs, then the proposal of pragmatic resolutions of those needs through religious convictions. The fourth task is the demonstration of the pragmatic success of the proposed convictions. It was not long before Smith was calling the second and third tasks *constructive dogmatics,* a phrase designed to emphasize that theology must formulate new beliefs appropriate to the new contexts in which people live.[62]

In 1914, Smith distinguished the "Christ of faith" from the "Jesus of history," and argued that the Christ of faith was not an imitation of anything timeless within or beyond history, but was itself a historical creation. Furthermore, the Jesus of history, not only is not an object of imitation, but is virtually unknown, for this actual Jesus is not evident on the surface of even the New Testament, which already is filled with various Christs of faith, various meanings of Jesus for the peoples who wrote the New Testament. Each subsequent era found itself with different religious needs, and, hence, with different Christs of faith. To use Smith's words: "If the emphasis in our Christology is to be determined by asking what Christ actually accomplishes in our experience of salvation, any significant change in the nature of religious experience will directly register itself in the content of christological doctrine. The Christ of faith will be defined in relation to the actual experience of the Christian."[63]

Smith based his historicist theory on evidence of people's pragmatic practice in church history; beliefs, he discovered, had won "their right to exist by their power to satisfy men's needs."[64] This prevailing pragmatic practice points to the ultimately democratic character of the actual history of Christianity. In his 1917 "Christianity and the Spirit of Democracy," Smith suggested that Christianity's extrahistorical elements came not from its earliest ideas, but from those autocratic and imperialistic political systems with which Christianity has cohabited for most of its existence. Even the authoritative use of the Bible as a religious criterion is a function of such authoritarian systems. Smith argued, "the extent to which the dead hand of the past is strangling the religious life of today should be more generally recognized."[65] Nevertheless, Smith does not affirm that in principle a generation should simply and speculatively invent its own truths, nor that there is no God to be discovered; but he does affirm that any generation can play its democratic part in the evolution of religious truths rather than subserve itself to the will of previous generations or to the authority of purportedly extrahistorical truths. Admittedly, says Smith, this "throws on the living generation a far larger responsibility for the discovery of ideals and aims than has previously been supposed."[66]

Smith's fullest exercise of the historicist method occurs in his 1913 *Social Idealism and the Changing Theology*. The book analyzes traditional moral norms in terms, first, of what in history originally occasioned them and, second, of their functional worth in early twentieth century society. Smith recognizes the original social utility of Jesus's eschatological ethic and of medieval Christendom's ecclesiastical ethic, but says they fail in twentieth-century politics and economics. With regard to its functional worth he criticizes the Christian ethic of his own time, particularly with regard to its disdain for the marketplace, a disdain created by the combined acceptance of an eschatological worldview and ignorance of modern economics. The consequence, he says, is that the field has been left to shallow secular economic theories.

The overriding conclusion of the book is that a consciousness of method is of enormous importance in the analysis of religion. It does not pay for the student to identify religion with a particular content of religion, because content changes with historical change. What is stable in the study of religions are the empirical and pragmatic procedures for the study of religion. Consequently, the only stable factor in the study of religion is a "a reliable *method* of ascertaining the meaning of religion."[67] However, Smith does not advocate a preoccupation with method, certainly not to the neglect of the religious contents specific to one's own time.

Finally, the reader might wonder why methods should be less vulnerable to the effects of historical change than contents are. If Smith objects to the absolutization of experience (let alone dogma, scripture, or church), how can he absolutize method?

George Burman Foster often is not treated as a member of the sociohistorical Chicago School.[68] However, Charles Harvey Arnold, probably the most devoted historian of the Chicago School and a particular champion of Foster, has called Foster's 1906 *The Finality of the Christian Religion* "the prototypical work" of the emerging Chicago School of theology.[69] In that book, Foster does talk like a sociohistoricist, at least to the extent of arguing that religion is guided neither by an authoritative reality nor by a necessary law; it is shaped by the unpredictable dynamics of historical change. He argues that actual religion is unlike both "authority-religion" and the old "naturalism" of the sciences because actual religion is wed to meanings within a particular world, while they are committed to cognitive abstractions (whether supernaturalistic or mechanistic) about all worlds. As a historical reality, religion asks about the worth in the historical particular. History, itself, "is a worth-science rather than a cause-science."[70] It is concerned with "the utilization of facts for purposes of knowledge," whereas science is explicitly dedicated to a more Platonic quest for "the true essence of things back of phenomena, colorless and changeless, without the earthy smell of sense-qualities upon its garments— the triumph of thought over perception."[71] History does not attempt to subsume everything under the category of eternal laws, to give everything an exhaustive causal explanation. History looks at what is individual and allows for "a remainder that is incomprehensible—something inexpressible, indefinable, ineffable." This remainder involves both human freedom and something inexpressible to which that freedom refers.

However, as Foster very well knew, students of religion are never content to leave the matter there. In addition to a meaning of the historical particular, they want an interpretation of the sweep of history. They want to determine the essence of a given religion, to move on to a higher historical science which can postulate the connections among the particular facts. In effect, students of religion aspire to something approximating the "nomothetic" sort of inquiry typical of the natural sciences. While Foster rejects the deductive tactics of what he calls "post-Kantian idealism" as a legitimate route to such an essence, he has sympathy with an inductive approach.

However, after praising induction in principle, Foster admits, "in all the foregoing discussion there is a painful defect which it is difficult to obviate . . . . A strictly objective and impartial determination of the essence is impossible."[72] It is impossible because only a person can interpret larger historical manifolds, and a person's "psychic forces" depend on that person's social history. The movement from the personal, to the sociohistorical, to the consequent loss of the possibility of determining a general essence, is implicit in the following paragraph, which concludes the chapter on method in *The Finality of the Christian Religion:*

> Finally, determination of essence is *construction* of essence, since the task is personally conditioned. That is, it is not simply a datum to be received, but

a reality to be created ever anew. Hence the significance of the influence of personal subjective presuppositions. But if the conception of Christianity is conditioned by the personal attitude toward it, this personal attitude is conditioned in turn by the age of the world in which one lives, the type of civilization of which one is a member, the stage of culture to which one belongs, and the local and temporal currents or drifts from which one, try hard as one may, cannot hold himself aloof. All in all, therefore, the task is not simply scientific, but moral, and thus belongs to man's larger vocation of forming an ethical personality through pain and struggle, perplexity and sorrow. Once personal, man must be free—free lord of the essence of the Christian religion.[73]

Foster not only radicalizes the dependence of interpretation on the interpreter, saying that the essence is a construction, a creation, of the interpreter, rather than the induction of what is truly general. He says also that the interpreter, while partially free, is also, to a large extent, a construction of the society in which he or she lives—meaning that the personality which is lord of the essence is not an individual personality but a social personality. For this reason, all claims to general understanding and all claims for the finality of Christ based on such general understandings fail. They are caught in their particular age; nomothetic explanations of finality claim to transcend the shifting social conditions surrounding the deducer, but that claim is unwarranted. Behind all claims for finality is a reliance on a doctrine of inspiration, establishing that one's own reading of the general meaning of scripture is correct. But again, as Creighton Peden has said, when Foster "demonstrated that the inspiration theory rests ultimately upon the *testimonium spiritus sancti internum,* his attack was essentially historical . . . ."[74]

Foster's historicism is universalized in his 1909 *The Function of Religion in Man's Struggle for Existence.* Here he historicizes even the sciences, opposing *The Finality of the Christian Religion,* where he had conceded that the sciences aim for "a knowledge of the legal necessities which rule all process in timeless unchangeability."[75] Citing Poincaré and George Herbert Mead, Foster suggests that temporal and spatial qualities, even the number system and Euclidean space, are to a large extent human constructions![76] Foster extends this to the five senses: "If our eyes and ears borrow from nature the perceptions from which we then make the thoughts which pass muster as truth for us, still fantasy is jointly active in the very first impressions of the senses, in the contact of the senses with the world. Even our very sensations are no mere gifts to us, but creations by us."[77] Certainly, this condition applies to religion as well, for, says Foster, "it cannot be denied that our god-faith had its origin in human fantasy."[78]

Foster, however, refuses to give a negative or merely subjectivist interpretation to this historicism; and as with the postmodernists at the other end of his century, he moves clearly beyond the forced option of scientific objectivism

and relativistic nihilism. He argues that, even though the specific image we
give God is a creation of our imagination, the religious faith makes a claim
on the world:

> Certainly ours is an ideal-achieving capacity. But the fruits of the ideal are grown
> and borne by a tree whose roots strike deep into the soil of the real. We who
> achieve ideals are a part of existence as a whole. Therefore we may assume that
> existence as a whole has an ideal-achieving capacity. The world is such as to produce
> ideals, or, at all events, such that the ideal may be produced . . . . The word
> *God* is a symbol to designate the universe in its ideal-achieving capacity.[79]

Admittedly, religion is a series of social constructions; but this does not mean
that religion is merely subjectivistic with no external and historical object.
Foster's point is orthodox in that it argues that people reconstruct their religion
not on a subjectivist fantasy, but with a reference to God, to a reconstructive
trend in all natural and social history.

Foster, then, was interested not only in denying the essentialism of science
and religion, but also in denying the opposite problem—that science and
religion might be historicized in a way that they would make them meaning-
lessly subjectivistic. In his 1907 article "Pragmatism and Knowledge," Foster
saw a newly fashionable scientific nominalism as an effort to reduce, without
remainder, human knowledge to human imagination. Sounding much like
a Hilary Putnam protesting the extremes of the relativists, Foster rejects those
scientists for whom "formula and law alike are devices for the manipulation
of phenomena and the achievement of practical results—in a word, for orientation of the self in the world of phenomena, and not for the intellectual apprehension of reality."[80] Such scientists claim, he says, that they would just as
little think of calling their laws "true" as they would think of calling them
"blue." They claim to be describing mere rules for action. But, responds Foster,
either you are bad at predicting, which means your particular rule for action
is worthless, or you are good at predicting, which means that your particular
rule is worth a great deal; in both cases, the worth of the particular rule seems
to be a reflection on its truth as a commentary on the world. Foster argues that
one must make a distinction between "raw facts" and "scientific facts," and
seek with constructed scientific facts to interpret the raw facts accurately enough
for rules for action to work. Equally, religion may be a construct of human
imagination, but no one can use that construct beneficially if it so misconceives
the objective world that the construct fails to work. Or, to play with Foster's
terms: there is a raw history and a believer's history, and the believer's history
must be sufficiently true to the raw history to allow the believer's history to
work beneficially for the believer.

Remembering that Foster had been excoriated by those who called him a humanistic atheist,[81] it is ironic that he was a true conservative in his respect for a "Whole Reality" by comparison to which human constructions paled:

> After all, the total humanization of reality is an audacious and unwarrantable proposition . . . . This modern anthropocentric Humanism and Copernicanism are mutually exclusive. It may well be that the statement of the Whole Reality in terms of the human is not a tribute to Its wealth and strength, but an insinuation of Its poverty and weakness. It may well be that there are more things in heaven and earth than we dream of in our new philosophy.[82]

We might push Foster, as we have pushed Case, Mathews, and Smith, to explain how an antiessentialist can generalize about the "Whole Reality" and the divine "ideal-achieving capacity of the world."

Instead, it may be appropriate to consider this problem as it seems to have infected Smith, Mathews, and Case, as well as Foster. For they all have failed to explain the implicit absolutes in their work or to defend themselves against the charge of an inconsistency between their overt historicism and their covert ahistorical absolutism. By the standards of the late twentieth century, each of these thinkers seems surprisingly unselfconscious about this predicament. While this is true, I think that they might be defended as historicists who anticipated a third option, just as had James and Dewey, whose approach they followed (but whom these historicists, irony added to irony, almost never cited). Consequently, they could argue that their "absolutes" were based not on extrahistorical foundations, but were temporary generalizations that were pragmatically successful in their specific sociohistorical context. If this is true, they could not be indicted by a false and inappropriate dichotomy: that either something is sheerly relative, historicist, and ungeneralizable in any way whatsoever or it is sheerly absolute and ahistorical. Instead, they were working with absolutes within their historical horizon, and that is a third way of speaking. Theirs were the temporary, local, pragamatically successful (or so they hoped) generalizations.

THE CONSEQUENCES OF THE CHICAGO SCHOOL

A double irony smiles on the demise of the Chicago School and its liberalism. The crisis theologians of Germany, particularly Karl Barth and Emil Brunner, as well as the neo-orthodoxy theologians of America, particularly Reinhold Niebuhr, claimed to be pessimistic realists, and declared that liberalism was optimistic about human nature and naive about history. On occasion the Chicago liberals, or "modernists," (the Chicago School answered to both terms), did act their part. Like optimists, they did claim to know evolutionary progress; and they complained that neo-orthodox theologians, like pessimists, did neglect the real and positive potentials of human history. But in the short run, history itself proved both characterizations partially wrong. For neo-orthodoxy's pessimistic characterization of incorrigible human pride was accepted with such alacrity that liberalism was all but routed from the academic study of religion; and the apparently virtuous humility implicit in this acceptance was not something pessimistic neo-orthodoxy could have anticipated. Conversely, liberalism's optimistic message about people's intelligence was spurned and neo-orthodoxy was embraced with an apparent ignorance that optimistic liberalism could never have anticipated.

These ironies may be, however, only superficial. For the deeper belief of the neo-orthodox, finally, was not pessimistic but optimistic; and the deeper belief of the liberals, finally, was not optimistic but pessimistic. Neo-orthodox theologians, just as the Reformation theologians before them, were actually optimists in the sense that they believed that the Lord of the universe was so preoccupied with welfare of the few worthy occupants of one planet that this Lord would do virtually anything to rescue them. Conversely, the empirical liberals of the Chicago School, just as many ancient Hebrews before them, were pessimists in the sense that they believed that humans had no access to anything that would rescue them from the perils of history. They found no extrahistorical securities; one must live within an inescapable, inexorable, and insatiable history—which sooner or later eats everything alive.

Nevertheless, all this said, the Chicago School did not die completely with Case in 1947. While the sociohistorical method may be found more vividly today in a nontheological new historicism, it lives vicariously in three areas of American religious scholarship: theology, church history, and biblical studies.

First, the sociohistorical method of the Chicago School affected the American theological movement called *process theology*—perhaps the most important school of thought in academic theology today. The Chicago School parentage of process theology is neglected by those process theologians who have tended to see themselves as the uncompromised, legitimate philosophical children of Alfred North Whitehead's *Process and Reality* and/or Charles Hartshorne's rationalism. Nevertheless, John Cobb, Jr., Bernard Meland, and Larry Axel have all recently pointed out the lineage extending from the Chicago sociohistorical method to certain aspects of process theology.

John Cobb, while recognizing that process theology is commonly thought to be virtually a Whiteheadian theology, nevertheless argues that process theology can be defined by reference to the central theological tradition at the University of Chicago Divinity School from the mid-1910s until the 1960s. In his 1980 article entitled "Process Theology and the Doctrine of God" and in his 1982 *Process Theology as Political Theology,* he describes the themes tying the sociohistorical method of the Chicago School of theology to process theology. In *Process Theology as Political Theology,* he shows the points of continuity and difference between Mathews in particular and the Chicago founders of process theology: Henry Nelson Wieman, Charles Hartshorne, Bernard Meland, Bernard Loomer, and Daniel Day Williams. Cobb treats the sociohistorical method as an effect of the "Social Gospel" movement in Protestant theology in the first few decades of the century, meaning that the sociohistorical "method had its unity, not in a theology, but in the conviction that the Christian churches had the responsibility to address the injustices of the class society being produced by industrialization and that the Bible, properly understood, required concern for these issues."[83] Cobb shows the affinities between Mathews's sociohistorical method and the process theologians: an opposition to supernaturalism and to binding authority, a loyalty to current tools of scholarship and to outcomes of the best empirical thought, and a preoccupation with forces operating in the natural or the secular world. But also he notes that the process theologians departed from the sociohistorical method by stressing metaphysical issues and neglecting the social and historical study of religions. In the last analysis, Wieman is a metaphysician who aspired to define empirically the universal nature of God as the creative event; Hartshorne is a confessed metaphysician who aspired to establish on the grounds of *a priori* reason the necessity for and the nature of God. Both implied that history cannot create what is fundamental, for they both thought that basic theological and philosophical ideas arise from universal, eternal, and therefore ahistorical characteristics of reality. (I might add that Edward Scribner Ames, another Chicago liberal generally within the process orientation, stands with Wieman and Hartshorne, for Ames also sought universal and timeless generalizations about the psychological genesis of religious experience.[84]) Cobb ruefully notes: "It would have been quite possible to assimilate the sociohistorical method also within a Whiteheadian context, and if this had been done, process theology would have been richer and more adequate."[85] Nevertheless, the process theologians do share much with Mathews and his Chicago School colleagues.

Bernard Meland, in his 1984 "Reflections on the Early Chicago School of Modernism," raises the question of the influences of the Chicago School on process theology by distinguishing idiosyncratic from nonidiosyncratic aspects of the Chicago School. Meland is critical of Mathews and Case to the extent that their work is tied idiosyncratically to "a social evolutionism that has since had to be revised." But, says Meland, "what does persist as a haunting thesis concerning Christian faith and its history as these figures presented it is the cultural orientation of religion itself, and the realization that, for all the specialized cultic developments within the Church's history, its real history lay in the wider sweep of the cultural mind and experience . . . ."

Consistent with this is G. B. Smith's definition of *modernism:* "the attempt to interpret religious belief in such a way as to bring modern ideas into the service of religion"—thus making modernism a generic rather than a specific term, for every period seeks to bring its own "modern" ideas into the service of religion.[86] More ambitiously, Meland sees the sociohistorical method as a precursor to current theologies of culture and to current theologies of secularization, and as a challenge to the cultic canons of scripture and dogma. In this nonidiosyncratic Chicago wake can be found the empirically oriented process theologians, most particularly Meland himself, as they attempt to establish what Whitehead called the "adequacy" of an idea to the best thought of one's own day.

Larry Axel, in his 1978 "Process and Religion: The History of a Tradition at Chicago," has made a more direct case for the continuing importance of the sociohistorical Chicago School in current process theology. He has argued that the sociohistorical school and process theology share a basic view of reality: that it is nonstatic, atomic, relational, and processive. Following Dewey, Mathews developed an evolutionary and organismic picture of reality. Accordingly, he saw reality as the whole processive concatenation of events in which creatures and communities grow through time and in interaction with their environment. Axel, quoting Kenneth Smith and Leonard Sweet, puts it this way:

> In recognizing the passing of absolute notions of space and time and the mechanistic conceptions based upon them, in viewing matter as primarily activity rather than substance, in utilizing evolutionary, processive, and relational understandings of God and religion, he [Mathews] may be said to have 'anticipated the cardinal presupposition of process philosophy.' Indeed, Mathews believed 'that there is nothing more fundamental and elemental than processes; nothing transcends or undergirds processes. Everything that exists is either a process, an aspect of a process, or a relation between processes.'[87]

In a muted way, the Chicago School lives on at the University of Chicago in the Jamesean orientation of Don Browning (especially his 1980 *Pluralism and Personality: William James and Some Contemporary Cultures of Psychology)* and in the Deweyan and Hartshornian orientation of Franklin Gamwell (his 1984 *Beyond Preference: Liberal Theories of Independent Associations).* The new historicism of the Chicago School is even more vividly embodied in the recent theological writings of David Tracy. It appears that he has relinquished his effort to name "common human experience" (in his 1975 *Blessed*

Rage for Order: The New Pluralism in Theology) or to name categories that
"all reasonable people" can accept (in his 1981 *The Analogical Imagination:
Christian Theology and the Culture of Pluralism*). His 1987 *Plurality and
Ambiguity: Hermeneutics, Religion, and Hope* more completely adopts the
recognition that people know what they know from the standpoint that their
histories have given them and that histories are in fact plural so that no specific
understandings will be universal. He has moved beyond the "modern belief:
the belief that somehow we can think our way through once more"; and he
has more completely adopted the postmodern belief that "all experience and
all understanding is hermeneutical."[88] But, as with the "third option" Chicago
School theologians, Tracy does not allow his historicism to drive him into a
subjectivistic or relativistic despair. He is sharply critical of those deconstructionists who reduce language to illusion—"the illusion that history and society
can be kept at bay while we all enjoy the surf of signifiers"[89]—and of the Rortian
tendency simply "to change the subject" when religious questions arise. Tracy
sees historicism as a place where one still can distinguish between history and
fiction, where one still can "know what actually happened," and that permits
one still to hope "that revelations from God have occurred and that there are
ways to authentic liberation."[90] Nevertheless, despite Tracy's, Browning's, and
Gamwell's notable appreciation of their theological and philosophical ancestors
and their clear recognition of the importance of historical understanding, none
of the three connects his work (anticipated though it is by the Chicago School)
to the "Chicago aura" that still hangs in the rooms in which even now they
teach and write that same work.

Second, the Chicago School's sociohistorical method lives vicariously also
in church history, and perhaps more effectively there than in process theology.
In 1968, Jerald C. Brauer argued that there had been three major perspectives
in the writing of American church history: (1) the period typified by Robert
Baird, from the 1840s to the 1920s; (2) the period typified by the environmental
approach of Peter Mode and William Warren Sweet, from the 1920s to the
1950s; and (3) the period exemplified by Sydney Mead and typified by a
combination of the environmental approach and the history of ideas, from the
1950s until at least the late 1960s, the time of Brauer's analysis.[91] When he
discusses the second period, Brauer closely associates the "Chicago school of
environmental historians" with the sociohistorical method of the Chicago
School, for both treated the social context as the key to interpretation. As "the
first serious attempt in America to make church history a responsible scientific discipline at home in the university,"[92] the environmental school not only
regarded social context as the key, but more generally described Christianity
as a thoroughly historical phenomenon, produced in and shaped by its historical

context, rather than as a phenomenon God engendered outside of history and spawned in history. Consequently, historical analysis can access Christian meanings. In addition to Mode and Sweet, the environmental method was exercised by University of Chicago historians such as John T. McNeill, Matthew Spinka, Harold R. Willoughby, and W. E. Garrison. Brauer mentions reasons for the eventual diminished prestige of the environmental method: the excessively simple way in which it was utilized (identifying what was distinctive in American religion by one or two or three characteristics), the lack of a theological dimension, and the onslaught of the antihistorical neo-orthodox theology, which not only distinguished Christianity from religion, but largely dissociated the word of God from the events of history. Nevertheless, the sociohistorical method lived on in the third period in the writings of Winthrop S. Hudson, H. Shelton Smith, Robert T. Handy, and Lefferts A. Loetscher—the last three especially in their *American Christianity: An Historical Interpretation with Representative Documents.* But here Brauer focuses on Sydney Mead and his *The Lively Experiment,* for "it was Mead's synthesis of the sociohistorical concerns with the fresh approach of the history of ideas that gave birth to the new perspective in American church history."[93]

Among current church historians, Martin E. Marty, despite all his earlier reservations about the tendencies of the earlier sociohistorical church historians,[94] and despite all his recent disparagement of the late-nineteenth-century liberals,[95] is himself among those who most faithfully utilizes sociohistorical analysis. In his 1976 *A Nation of Behavers,* Marty argues that contemporary religious history cannot be understood properly through the regional and theological methods used to study the Colonial Period, nor through the denominational and institutional methods used to study the nineteenth century, nor through the political methods (the demonstration of how religion affects the secular world) used to study religion in the twentieth century. Marty argues that these approaches are not now functional in demonstrating the way people use religion to meet their problems—that is, the older approaches do not demonstrate people's religious pragmatics. Marty proposes a fourth approach: that church history must begin to explain religious phenomena as the efforts by religious groups to meet their social problems. This is accomplished not by looking at the intellectual, institutional, or political aspects of religion, but at the practical behavior of groups. In that his method is "a species of social history," Marty says, "it would concentrate on habit and conduct and practice, on religious social behavior."[96] Marty argues that this "people's history" has a long career, going back almost a century to J. B. McMaster's *History of the People of the United States.*

Quoting Peter Berger and Thoman Luckmann, Marty calls the four approaches to the study of religion "maps"; then, metahistoriclly, Marty contends that "mapping is part of what today is called 'a social construction of reality'."[97] Marty reminds the reader that the epigraph for his book is Wallace Stevens's line, "We live in the description of a place and not in the place itself." All histories, then, are literally created from within history by our interpretations of, our constructions on, history. Why in his brief comments on the lineage of his functional and constructive method he does not cite his Chicago School predecessors is not immediately apparent. Nevertheless, I think it is accurate to conclude that his method is a descendent from the sociohistoricism of the Chicago School.

Seven years later, in his 1983 "Two Integrities: An address to the Crisis in Mormon Historiography," Marty clearly rejects a correspondence theory of truth realism. For the historian, Marty says, "objectivity seems to be a dream denied." " What results, all thoughtful historians agree, is not a reproduction of reality, which cannot be grasped even by people on the scene during events, but 'a social construction of reality'. The historian invents."[99] Playing on Paul Ricoeur's notion of primitive naivete and second naivete, Marty distinguishes between the literalistic test of faith (Was Joseph Smith literally a prophet or literally a fraud?) and the test of faith which believes "not in spite of but through interpretation" (Does or does not Joseph Smith's story enable a people to acquire a usable past?). Through interpretation, Smith becomes someone who allows a people to see history on the basis of a useful set of presuppositions and understandings, and thereby to do what otherwise they could not do. Marty is so intent on distinguishing this essentially historicist view of the second naivete from the literalist view of the primitive naivete that he will contend that "faith is dependent upon testimony, not sight, not 'proof,'" and that people can disagree despite the fact that they agree on the "material traces of actual past events."[99] Nevertheless, Marty refuses to leave it all at the level of imagination; he ends by requiring that one show the way textual traces ground one's interpretations, and that one empirically, even pragmatically, demonstrate that these interpretations have rendered life practically "satisfying."[100] It is apparent that Marty continues to play the sociohistorical option into an era of hermeneutical writings (Ricoeur, Heidegger, and Gadamer).

Finally, the sociohistorical method of the Chicago School is implicit in recent developments in biblical criticism. In Chapter 2, I noted that the unacknowledged American precedent for the tradition history critics, the sociological critics, and the deconstructionist critics of the Bible is the sociohistorical method of the Chicago School. These biblical critics, however, failed to explain the historical dependence of their own historicism on any American empiricism, let alone the sociohistorical method of Chicago.

The same sort of irony (the historical forgetfulness of the historicists) is pointed out most effectively in the "The Watershed of the American Biblical Tradition: The Chicago School, First Phase, 1892–1920" written by Robert Funk in 1976, previous to the flowering of the tradition history and sociological methods in American biblical studies. Funk begins by identifying William Rainey Harper, an Old Testament scholar from Yale who endorsed the best German literary and philological scholarship of the day, and who, as the first president of the University of Chicago, retained an intense interest in Chicago's Divinity School. Harper was animated by the trust that all-out literary scholarship would vindicate the "evangelical truth." In the course of building the divinity faculty, he hired Ernest Dewitt Burton, whom he thought would be his ally in the literary approach. However, Burton, in an 1898 epoch-making article in *The American Journal of Theology*, advanced an alternative to Harper's own approach. Burton contrasted his own "biblical criticism," which uses all varieties of historical evidence to determine a truth about the relation between God and humanity, to Harper's literary interpretation, which avoids questions of historical truth because they would distract from the task of describing the literary meaning itself. Biblical criticism seeks answers to questions of truth by critically assessing the literary meanings in the context of the factual history surrounding the text. In pursuing this aim, Burton used narrative history, a history of the sequence of interconnected events in which the text was written and to which it refers. Funk describes Burton's task and influence this way:

> Burton wants to give priority to the narrative history, and to emphasize the human element in the biblical interpretation of that narative, owing to his predilections for scientific method. But in assigning these priorities, he in fact reverses the position of Harper and his orthodox predecessors by looking first at the history underlying the biblical documents and only then at the biblical interpretation of that history. In this he anticipates the social history of Christianity so characteristic of Mathews and Case.[101]

Burton's biblical criticism takes a thoroughly historicist position. For Burton, "Scripture has lost its primary function. It is to play an ancillary role at best."[102] Not only, then, is religion to be understood by way of history, but as the history changes, so does the religion. Funk quotes Burton saying that it is our duty "to enact our part in the continuous evolution of that religion and its continuous readjustment of itself in doctrine and life to the needs of successive ages."[103] Although Mathews's 1897 *The Social Teaching of Jesus* precedes Burton's 1898 "The Function of Interpretation in Relation to

Theology," Burton effectively initiated the more technical and methodological work on the sociohistorical method.

Funk argues, however, that while Burton and the sociohistorical method may have prevailed temporarily at Chicago, Harper's literary criticism method succeeded nationally. Again, ironies light this analysis in several places. First, Harper—the first president and (with John D. Rockefeller) the virtual founder of the university, who cared more about biblical studies than any academic field, who cared especially about his literary approach, and who personally hired Burton as an ally—this same Harper lived to see Burton pipe Harper's own divinity faculty in the opposite direction. Second, Harper, who as an administrator would be naturally diminished as a scholar, nevertheless, came to stand at or near the head of the American literary school that nationally came to prevail over the local sociohistorical school. Third, the sociohistorical method failed nationally despite the fact that in showing scripture's relation to history it had faced the major question of biblical theology, the authority of scripture. By contrast, the literary school, animated by an unspoken evangelical trust in the authority of scripture, never bothered effectively to raise the question of how to estabish scripture's authority, in history or beyond history. By consequence, as it lived in seminaries and in religion departments of denominational colleges, the literary method was a "kept" scholarship; it was supported despite the fact that it had not paid its way by answering this central question of Biblical studies.[104] For the literary scholars it was enough to assume that the scriptures have authority, and then, using nineteenth-century German textual scholarship, to turn and fight it out with the fundamentalists. Given the current prevalence of the literary approach, this makes the Society of Biblical Literature, Funk says in this, his presidential address to that society, "a fraternity of scientifically trained biblical scholars with the soul of a church." Fourth, the sociohistorical method, while it was "a better index to common American consciousness" and "may reflect the broader drift of cultural history," nevertheless "has not basically affected the course of biblical scholarship in America"—in fact, it "has disappeared from the record as though it never took place."[105] It was overwhelmed by the literary approach Harper and his allies acquired from the Germans. America had developed a historical method for examining a historical literature; it was a method germane to American experience; yet America abandoned that method in favor of a German method which replaced the primacy of history with the primacy of religious assurance.

Funk anticipates that—what with the new importance of university departments of religion—the era of kept biblical scholarship may be passing. And, in fact, much does seem to be happening in tradition history, sociological, and deconstructionist biblical scholarship since 1976 to fulfill Funk's predictions.

Nevertheless, the sociohistorical method, which spoke so representatively of an American style of thought, still is neglected—a fact that not only demonstrates the anomaly of historicists neglecting their own history but deprives these same historicists of an interpretation best-suited to their American context.

As we have noted, this is not the only unexplained case of silence toward the precedent set by the Chicago School; it is a silence common among process theologians and many appropriate church historians as well. The cost to an American theology is untold, for how can it be said what would have been yielded by a greater attentiveness to the style of American historicism? At the least, the fuller development of a third methodological option might have occurred—an option proposing an empirical and valuational historicism. And the conclusions reached with such a method might have been socially useful.

However and nevertheless, the sociohistorical method of the Chicago School remains, by and large, the lost voice of a lost tribe.

CHAPTER 4

The Hidden Empiricism

In odd moments, today's American new historicists appear to be animated by values; and in some unaccounted way, these historicists appear to know these values. Yet usually they say almost nothing about these values nor about the social goals they envision, let alone about how they know them. In fact, to talk about the way values are known, to introduce epistemology at all, appears to them anachronistic or at least something they themselves prefer not to do. So, like people with blocked dreams, what the new historicists seldom speak of seems to be nothing at all. When their critics say that their unwillingness to explain how they know their values makes them subjectivists, relativists, even nihilists, the current historicists are merely puzzled. Why would people want to draw such conclusions? They feel that they simply act rationally, merely seek the kind of satisfactory outcome any university intellectual wants. Yes, they subscribe to a sort of pragmatism, but that is not a program guided by values; it is simply a method. Why should they be asked to add to that pragmatism some explicit claims about knowledge—particularly, some knowledge of values?

[handwritten margin note: on what are they basing their philosophy ↓ not American!]

Nevertheless and anomalously: these new historicists do act from values; they seldom speak about values; and when they speak about values, they seldom say how they have come to know their values.

Decades earlier, the original and classical American historicists could conceive of no pragmatism without an antecedent empiricism. It was from this empirical knowledge that they gained their values, and this they admitted. However, today's new historicists seems not much concerned about the original historicists; and when they do turn to them, it is for their pragmatic method, not for their empiricism, and certainly not for insights about the way this empiricism yields values.

To explore these anomalies of the current American historicists, I advance a case study, a portion of the work of a single religious thinker—Joseph Haroutunian, a mid-twentieth-century American theologian, Calvin scholar, and unselfconscious pragmatist and historicist. Working backward, I discuss first an informal talk he gave in 1964, near the end of his career, and, then, his first book. *Piety vs. Moralism*, published in 1932. I move from his nonempirical pragmatism of the 1960s to his warning in the 1930s against the shallowness of just such a pragmatism. Only then do I discuss the larger anomaly of the current American new historicists.

A CASE STUDY: JOSEPH HAROUTUNIAN

In fall 1964, on a faculty retreat soon after his 1962 appointment to the faculty of The Divinity School of The University of Chicago, Haroutunian unburdened himself to his new colleagues by offering "Theology and American Experience," a statement which he called not a finished statement, but one delivered for the purpose of encouraging discussion. By all accounts it did. The paper was not laced with scholarly qualifications, equivocations, hedgings, and modesties. It was raw and provocative.

Haroutunian began by arguing that American theologians typically have appropriated European theology, and consequently have provided for the American people a theology which has little to do with the distinctively American character of experience. "Thus theology and American experience have been perennially at odds, and the Church in America has had to live to a large extent without the benefit of logic."[1] The paper calls for research into what might be an American theology:

> In fact, it is doubtful that there is a prospect for American theology at all without a new knowledge of the history of theology in this country. America may not have produced an Augustine or a Schleiermacher, but its hope of producing theologians who shall do more than live off the European mind has little chance of being realized unless the history of theology in America is studied, not as a tributary of European theology, but, for all its derivative character, as an expression of American experience.[2]

In order to develop the prospect for an American theology, Haroutunian initially isolates a single aspect of the physical and social condition of the European emigrants: the building of a new life in a challenging environment. He refers to the American who was distinctively marked by experiences "in the woods and on the prairies, in settling down on new lands and in building up new towns, in fighting nature and in making things."[3] Without saying so, Haroutunian adopted, several decades after its demise, not only the general sociohistorical method of the Chicago School, but the specific method of what Jerald Brauer would call "the Chicago school of environmental historians."[4]

According to Haroutunian, three American motifs rose to prominence in this physical and social situation. First, Americans have worked for specific ends, without the typically European concern for first principles, theory, speculative foundations, or contemplation. Second Americans have unabashedly worked to diminish the Adamic curse, and they have attained a well-being which in other places and times was "beyond the reach of the many." Third, and most important, Americans have striven for individuality: they did this—not as Europeans typically did, through dependence on the authoritative institutions of church, state, and society—but through the cooperation of common people. In arduous physical circumstances, the American has "a new sense of his fellow-humanity through his steady dependence upon those around him without whose cooperation he would have failed in his pursuit of happiness."[5] This concept of individuality through cooperation has yielded three distinctly American notions: (1) goodness is not obedience to institutions, but fair play in cooperative enterprises; (2) freedom is found primarily not in the rebellion from the restraints of an institutionalized social order, but in collaboration in a common social venture; (3) reason is not primarily the capacity to envisage an order (which, after all, the institution represents), but the capacity to attain a desired consequence.

Focusing on American reason, Haroutunian argued that it has grown out of the American physical habitat. Because that habitat was distinct, so was the reason.

> Neither the life nor the prosperity of the American was caused by a social and cosmic order. What confronted him in his habitat was not an established order, but the society of his fellowmen who were with him busy making a home in a new land. What impressed him about nature was not so much its order and beneficence as the work it took to make it serve his life and prosperity. His hardships and struggles were indeed due to natural law. But natural law was the occasion not of good and order but of evils and the necessity of overcoming them . . . . Truth was not so much the given as the accomplished; reality was not so much out there as at the end of hard work; wisdom was acquired more by intelligence than by contemplation; things were made to cohere rather than found coherent; and the Good gave way to good things which although mutable were solid as well as available.[6]

In America, then, human reasoning was not the eye for envisioning the True or the Real or the Cosmic Whole, but the instrument guiding work on the environment, making life more satisfying.

When he turned to European reason, Haroutunian again looked at the influence of habitat. Why, asked Haroutunian, should the European treat the true as something given, and again, Why should the European pay homage to the given?

The given as such does not wear a badge of excellence. One may have to yield to its power, but one does not have to bend the knee before it. Where, in the European tradition, does truth get all this prestige in its sheer giveness if not in the Establishment, social or supposedly cosmic, which attributes to itself the sovereignty and inviolability of the ultimate? The European devotion to empirical and rational truth as the Given corresponds to the European experience in which the given Order, social and presumably cosmic, is the effective incarnation of God.[7]

The establishment (monarchial authority, class status), then, is the social cause of the European trust in contemplated orders.

In the course of his 1964 talk Haroutunian's pragmatism became increasingly explicit. He had begun by saying that ideals are selected for their capacity to function in the distinct social habitat. This led, in turn, to a concern for method. The American, always preoccupied with the need to act in the face of obstacles, never content merely to copy orders, is concerned with method because there is no alternative. There is no given Reality to provide constancy in this fluid and task-centered American world; the only constant is a procedure for attacking an always inconstant environment. The American arrived "at his truth or reality not by objectification but by operation. Since not intuition but method has been the way to reality, the given Object, whether as Nature or as God, has had no logical and proper place in the American mind as formed by American experience."[8] As his discussion developed, it became increasingly clear that that method was a pragmatic method. (And here, incidentally, Haroutunian addresses a long-standing conundrum in American religious historicism: Why should an orientation so devoted to concrete achievement be so preoccupied with the abstract discussion of method? When Haroutunian's answer becomes clear—that only procedure is left standing in a world where the ontological eternals have fallen—it echoes Gerald Birney Smith's conclusion decades earlier.) Nevertheless, despite this attraction to method, the American typically did not stop with method, but used it to attain practical outcomes: thus, the American "has kept method and results together, and sought truth by operation rather than by vision."[9]

Having stated the need for a pragmatic theological method, Haroutunian cast about for an appropriate American theology. Twentieth-century American orthodoxy and neo-orthodoxy, he said, are imports from Europe; they deal in the supernatural and the neo-supernatural. They are "a negation in general of American experience."[10] While American religious liberalism qualified as "an American theology," too often it was preoccupied with European procedures and displayed no consistent adherence to American experience. And it failed to deliver the solid criticism a good theology should offer because it incorporated pragmatism only superficially.

Romanticism about nature ✓ in art music poetry

Consequently, America still needs a theology that explicitly acknowledges several features of American experience. First, Americans see nature, not as the embodiment of something personal and moral, not as the embodiment of any ultimate reality or cause, but as something morally neutral on which one must use method, intelligence, and labor; consequently, they properly reject any natural theology. Second, Americans have no vision of the infinite and need a religion capable of addressing the particulars of life. Third, while Americans will not look to the Great Being of natural theology, they will look to the God of the Bible, the God who speaks and acts in human history. While the words and works of this God are different from the words and works of people, this God will be known in acts of human communion. In fact, "it may well be the business of theology in this land to explicate the logic of communion in American experience."[11] But the test for such a new theological logic will be pragmatic: "neither the clarity nor the truth of an idea can be arrived at apart from its consequences."[12]

we don't respect the environment

Now Haroutunian's 1964 "Theology and the American Spirit" applied to theology what, in effect, was a historicist method, for like today's American new historicists it looked to history itself to test its conclusions. However, Haroutunian's own 1932 *Piety versus Moralism* argues for the retention of an element virtually absent in Haroutunian's 1964 statement, but crucial, I believe, to the distinctively American religious thought. The 1932 book, which established Haroutunian as a young and powerful interpreter of American experience, describes the decline and fall of the New England Theology. It records how the late-eighteenth-century Calvinists and the liberal Unitarians and Arminians failed to include Jonathan Edwards's piety in their moralistic theology. Although they did relate their thought to the new scientific, commercial, and humanitarian spirit of the times, they left out the pious heart of Edwards's American reinterpretation of Calvinism. The result was a case of "the faith of the fathers ruined by the faith of their children."[13]

Edwards' piety as experience, values, emotions?

When Edwards's piety was omitted, his empiricism was omitted. Edwards, Haroutunian maintains, "put the theology of Calvinism upon the basis of an empirical piety, and defended its doctrines philosophically and rationally."[14] From his childhood Edwards, in a distinct way,[15] experienced the natural world aesthetically, and through this experience he felt the spirit of God. That experience of the divine "Being in general" in the things of the natural world is an extraordinary experience, not to be confused with a person's ordinary experiences. Nevertheless, Edwards is willing to treat this extraordinary experience as a form of perception and to call it a "sensible effect" or a "sensation," and on this basis Haroutunian can talk of Edwards's "empirical piety."

According to the 1932 Haroutunian, Edwards's disciples and later champions soon "reverted to governmental and legalistic conceptions of Calvinism, and under the influence of new political and humanitarian principles, modified Edwards' theology, subtly, variously, and greatly."[16] They reduced his empirical piety to a morality without aesthetic or spiritual weight (William Hart); or to a humanitarian doctrine of universal goodness, "friendly affection," and formal legalism (Samuel Hopkins); or to the acknowledgment of God as a "moral Governor" or "glorious Monarch" (Joseph Bellamy); or to happiness through obedience (John Barnard).[17] The liberal Unitarian and Arminian thinkers repeated from their own anti-Calvinist standpoint essentially the same moves. They regarded piety and religious affections, whether from Edwards or from the Great Awakening, as dangerous and irrational, and replaced them with an unemotional humanitarianism. Haroutunian cites William Ellery Channing as the prime instance of this reaction. In short, Edwards's successors replaced piety with moralism, the source of religion with one of its derivatives. For Haroutunian, it made no sense: Edwards's morality had meaning only because it was based on the pious perception of the spirit of God in the things of this world; Edwards's successors abandoned the piety and simply ascribed meaning to something which by itself had no meaning.

Haroutunian predicts that again piety will emerge: that "the optimism and the humanism of the nineteenth century have already lost their rational quality"; "that a revival of the 'tragic sense of life,' together with the wisdom and sobriety which grow out of it, should be forthcoming"; that, as Haroutunian says in 1932, "if the humanitarianism of Channing is modern, a post-modern mind is already in the making."[18]

The question is, does Haroutunian, himself, thirty-two years later, contribute to that American postmodernism, or merely to another version of modernism? It is noteworthy that the Haroutunian of 1964 introduces no empirical piety, no empirical sense of the spirit of God in the external world; when empiricism is mentioned, it is positivism that is treated and then dismissed, understandably, as a merely European form of the "given." Never does he refer to "piety" or to the affectional and nonpositivistic empiricism which Edwards had set forth. Granted, Haroutunian does refer to the need for knowledge of a God who acts and speaks. But never is this Biblical theism "naturalized" in the way Edwards had naturalized it, showing how that God could underlie nature's activities. In fact, in 1964 a natural theology is declared impossible for Americans.

This is not to deny the remarkable insightfulness of Haroutunian's 1964 depiction of American experience and religious sensibility. Haroutunian's statement is classic, and has been unaccountably ignored, languishing in the pages of an alumni quarterly. Furthermore, that statement is consistent in several important ways with *Piety versus Moralism*—a book which claims that European and medieval Calvinism must be thoroughly reconceived if it is to be meaningful for contemporary America, much as it is reconceived in the 1964 statement.

But our question remains, Has not Haroutunian's 1964 pragmatism omitted that affectional empiricism which, he said in 1932, lies at the center of a distinctively American theology? And, if so, how is Haroutunian's late theology more coherent than the moralism to which he objected in 1932.

A FLOATING PRAGMATISM

Like the Haroutunian of 1964, today's new historicists work out of an American spiritual history, but omit the key to that spiritual history. The American spiritual history—possibly extended to the Edwardsean theology and its pietistic successors but certainly extended to the classical American pragmatism—was based on an empirical piety which included social interaction only as a derivative; the current new historicists have retained the derivative interactionism and have discarded the kernel of empirical piety. When today's new historicists test how a hypothesis interacts with future events, they elevate pragmatism as their expression of interactionism. And with this pragmatism they are able to make even moral judgments about what, for example, is good for communities. But this is a moralism without a pietism, a social interaction without the earlier pragmatist's reason for interaction. By comparison to the pragmatism of their predecessors, this pragmatism merely floats.

This omission is awkward for today's new historicists, for when they do talk of where ideas originate (including their ideas of pragmatism), they attribute them not to heaven nor to iron laws of nature but to earlier people. However, just those earlier American people who had so many of their ideas, including their idea of pragmatism, clearly began with an empirical piety— an affective form of empirical perception, a radical empiricism. Only subsequently did these ancestors introduce a pragmatic test; and then only because radically empirical perception is too vague to pass strict tests of meaning and truth.[19] Nevertheless, not only do today's new historicists not tie their pragmatism to the pragmatism of their ancestors, not only do they omit the radical empiricism on which their ancestor's pragmatism stood, they cite no real historical source for moral values. Today's historicists, as historicists, claim they acquire thoughts, not spontaneously, but from a reinterpreted past. Yet they tend to treat the values that inform their pragmatism as unsupported by the past, as virtually freestanding, self-authenticating.

Because something of the original genetic endowment has been forgotten, the historicist creature now walks with a limp. Today's new historicists, consistent with Edwards and James and Dewey, have evaluated their judgments by asking whether they have contributed to present and local history. They have rejected both the authority of past dogma and the authority of extrahistorical realities; they have emphasized ideas that had consequences most satisfactory in immediate history. However, in their legitimate preoccupation with the test of immediate history, they omitted something perhaps too obvious for easy recognition. Epistemologically speaking, how does one know that an idea has consequences that are satisfactory? What does "satisfactory" mean? What, in Rorty's terms, does it mean "to cope with environments?"[20] What does any neopragmatist mean by a conversation that is somehow more than enjoyable, that has some socially beneficial yield? Surely, when Rorty wants to cope with an environment, he does not mean simply to do anything with the environment; he means to make it somehow more satisfactory. But again, What would "satisfactory" mean?

What, in short, is the criterion for these pragmatic or functional tests? Today's historicists seem to have become so obsessively resistant to any authority at all—let alone the authority of past dogma or the authority of extrahistorical referents—that they lost a clear sense of why, on what grounds, something might be declared valuable in their own history or in any history. Forcing a dichotomy, regarding two possibilities as exhaustive of all possibilities, they have said: If you reject the bad criterion of authority, then you reject all criteria—even the nonauthoritarian and historical criterion of radical empiricism, the criterion introduced by James and Dewey, let alone the pietistic criterion by Edwards.

The problem with this maneuver is not that it misses out on the comfort of a criterion that is nicely bedded in authority or extrahistorical realities, for that omission is explicit and consistent with the original new historicists. The problem is practical, merely implicit, and inconsistent with the original new historicists. The current new historicists, lacking an evaluative criterion, are not able to say why one theory with one historical outcome is to be preferred to others. And without such an explanation, they cannot discriminate intelligently or help others discriminate intelligently among theories. There is no account, for example, of why one prefers a Marxist, bourgeois, Christian, Hebrew, or liberationist theory to a fascist theory, as long as each can be made meaningful by demonstrating some effect. There may be the Gramscian Marxist historicism of Frank Lentricchia, there may be the bourgeois historicism of the university philosophers, there may be the liberal historicism of the Chicago School theologians, there may be the theistic historicism of ancient Israel, there may be the liberationist historicism of Norman Gottwald. But, if more than one of these is possible in a given historical situation, how is one to choose among them? Certainly, any historicist might point to his or her own criterion and call it better simply because it comes out of his or her own tradition—because, thereby, it feels more genteel. But traditions convey many criteria. How is one to say which is preferable? So in a given situation how is the fascist criterion better or worse than the Marxist criterion? How would the Marxist criterion be better or worse than the bourgeois criterion? How would the Christian criterion be better or worse than the non-Christian criterion? For that matter how would the insane historicist with an insane criterion be distinguished from the sane historicist with a sane criterion—let alone, an evil historicist from a good historicist? Does it all come down to merely subjective preference, after all? But none of today's new historicists admits to such subjectivism.

Far less confusing and far more complete would be an account that discussed the way history yields criteria, an account that introduces, in short, some sort of historicist epistemology. If criteria for the desirable outcome are operative in fact, it would be better to know where they come from and to examine them, rather than simply to affirm them. While an awareness of how criteria grow from a historical tradition does not validate them, it does allow one to be more critical of them, more capable of openly nurturing them, or more capable of protecting oneself from accepting them simply because, for example, they are locally fashionable . The epistemology of the original new historicists permitted at least a vague awareness of the cognitive and non-cognitive historical sources of opinions and values. Admittedly, it pointed to experiences that were provincial, nonobjective, confessional, relative, communally specific. But these experiences were accounted for and subject to open examination; they were consistent with the stated historicist claim that what we know is an interpretation of our history.

Apart from some such account for why a particular form of historicist coping is "satisfactory," are people likely to follow the lead of the new historicists? Are they actually moved by a historicist interpretation whose goals are unaccounted for or are admitted to be merely arbitrary? Would not these people prefer to go on calling the new historicists merely relativistic or nihilistic—as they have already? And if people are unpersuaded, what practical difference will such a historicism make? Do today's neopragmatic new historicists become nonpragmatic?

This question can be applied to any of the new historicist philosophers, but Rorty, again, provides the most vivid case. He omits explicit consideration of such a criterion for determining whether an outcome is satisfactory. He will praise a pragmatic historicism, but offer no grounds for preferring one historical goal for pragmatic action over another.

Rorty's selective adoption of pragmatism shows even in his treatment of James and Dewey. First, Rorty systematically deprives James and Dewey of everything except their pragmatism. He praises James's pragmatism, but acts as though James had never advocated the radically empirical appraisal of goals, including religious goals[21]—which James himself chose to couple with his pragmatism. Rorty praises Dewey's pragmatism but treats his effort in *Experience and Nature* to find an empirical basis for his goals for action as merely Dewey's inexplicable inconsistency.[22] Rorty praises James and Dewey as "the great pragmatists" to whom his *Consequences of Pragmatism* looks,[23] yet he faults those who say, just as James and Dewey once said, "that language does not go all the way down—that there is a kind of awareness of facts which is not expressible in language and which no argument can render dubious."[24] Rorty never seriously asks why both James and Dewey, who were not uncritical and who did avoid extrahistorical foundations, still pushed beyond language and grounded their pragmatism on just such an empirical awareness. Did they simply lack purity and the rigor? Or did they know something that Rorty, like Haroutunian, seems to have forgotten? And was it this knowledge which made their writings widely persuasive to two generations of Americans?

Furthermore, and despite Rorty's attacks on an inexpressible awareness of facts, is there not just such an inexpressible awareness sleeping beneath the surface even of Rorty's writings? Why does Rorty write as he writes if in fact he is as narrowly pragmatic in his historicism as he expects others to be? John E. Smith recently said, "Since no thought, philosophical or otherwise, proceeds without assumptions, it is imperative that a candid disclosure of these assumptions be made at the outset." There are no "privileged starting points," Smith says; we always begin, "in the middle of things with a set of inherited beliefs made up of funded experience."[25] Every act of writing inevitably inherits or creates its own orbit of meaning and value; otherwise, there would be no coherence to the body of writing. When Rorty denounces the norms operative in the philosophies of others, does he not express norms of his own—norms that drive his denunciations? Further, if he has such norms, how does he know them?

Does not Rorty's own orbit encompass metaphysical regions—albeit historical rather than extrahistorical regions? Of course, Rorty never commits himself to a systematic expression of universal principles, but he does commit himself to a definite worldview. Rorty's rejection of logocentrism claims a nonlogocentric world just as surely as the logocentrists claim a logocentric world. Simply for his pragmatic method to make any sense at all, the world must work one way and not another. To claim that we are capable of freely, deliberately, and purposively coping with environments to get a better outcome or of freely, deliberately, and purposively conversing with people holding opinions incommensurable with our own is to deny that the world is completely determined, completely random, or completely indifferent to human intention. At the same time it is to affirm: that the world, while not completely determined, is ordered enough for acts to yield predicatable consequences; that the world, while not completely random, is disordered enough to allow room for choice; that the world, while not completely indifferent to human intention, is indifferent enough to override unrealistic intentions. As William James said, the pragmatist's world is a world characterized by possibility. It is a world that includes some things that are neither necessary, nor impossible, nor actual. Possibility means that "there are no preventative conditions present, but that some of the conditions of production of the possible thing actually are there."[26] Rorty also accepts the world status of possibility when he characterizes pragmatism as the notion that "there are no constraints on inquiry save conversational ones—no wholesale constraints derived from the nature of objects, or of the mind, or of language, but only those retail constraints provided by the remarks of our fellow-inquirers." Rorty calls this "accepting the contingent character of starting-points."[27] Again, when Rorty proposes that "language goes all the way down" or speaks of "the ubiquity of language," he advances a *Weltanschauung*. Except for its amputation of the nonlinguistic, it differs little from James's own, rather starkly stated worldview: "For pluralistic pragmatism, truth grows up inside all the finite experiences. They lean on each other, but the whole of them, if such a whole there be, leans on nothing. All 'homes' are in finite experience; finite experience as such is homeless."[28] In short, Rorty's rejection of idealism, positivism, and of classical theology is not a chaste refusal to play at all. He does not walk into the thin, clean, innocent air of metaphysically unencumbered talk. He simply enters another encumbered room, this time decorated for pragmatists. And the question, again and with greater emphasis, still is this: How does Rorty or any other neopragmatist know that their world is as they assume it is? What unacknowledged epistemology operates here? How does it yield the values Rorty treasures?

In declaring that "philosophy" (with a lowercased "p") should supersede "Philosophy" (with an uppercased "P"), Rorty argues that the new pragmatic "philosophy" should leave behind the entire "interlocked Platonic notions" of "Philosophy, Truth, Goodness, and Rationality."[29] Rorty himself, however, does not abandon all value commitments, but is inclined to lift up his own alternative and clearly normative understanding of truth, goodness, and rationality. After reminding philosophers that pragmatic philosophy can enlarge human freedom, he exclaims, "There is indeed no better cause."[30] Rorty ends his 1979 Eastern Division American Philosophical Association presidential address by praising James and Dewey for offering "a hint of how our lives might be changed."[31] Is Rorty's encouragement not a functional equivalent to the nonpragmatist's claim for some value in the world? Does Rorty not provide at least a personal criterion for assessing the possible truth and meaning of all statements? Is his antipositivist or anti-idealistic commitment less valuational than a pro-positivist or a pro-idealistic commitment? He does work from within history and not, as Plato did, from beyond history. Nevertheless, he advances criteria for evaluating history; and this enables him to evaluate thought, much as Plato did. And, once more, How does Rorty know about these values and criteria?

How, if not as a general moral criterion, does Rorty's concern for community work? As noted in Chapter 2, Rorty objects to Continental metaphysical preoccupations finally on moral grounds: that they turn us "away from the relations between beings and beings," away from "our loyalty to other human beings clinging together against the dark."[32] He objects to the search for "objectivity" for the same reason: it neglects solidarity with local and present communities, a project which warrants our deepest commitment.[33] Apparently, the break with extrahistorical metaphysics is animated in part by moral norms. But criterion for criterion, is Rorty's criterion of the good in communal relations less a moral criterion than some extrahistorical criterion of the good in objective truth? Of course, Rorty's criterion refers to something within history—and not beyond history. But is his criterion for that reason less of a criterion than is the other? If it is a criterion, how does Rorty come to know that it is true in his world?

Interestingly, as noted earlier,[34] other new historicists cited—Putnam, Goodman, Lentricchia, and Bernstein—also refer finally to the creation of community as the moral criterion justifying their historicist project. Lentricchia, for example, strenuously advocates a Gramscian Marxist social ideal; his historicism is based on an obviously felt but nevertheless unexplained belief in the value of community. But how do they come to know these moral criteria?

A similar ambiguity regarding values is evident among the Chicago School theologians. In their pursuit of pragmatism, they, too, neglected consideration of epistemology; and yet they, too, were animated by values. On the surface, they seem to have been purely pragmatic and nonempirical. They were clearly opposed to the introduction of nonhistorical sources, so they assessed the validity of their interpretation of Christianity not by reference to a mystified scripture, creeds, or institutional authorities, but by reference to how successfully their interpretation squared with the social experience of their own times. But this reference to their own times implied their acceptance of the values of their times. Accordingly, the Chicago School theologians were criticized with some justice as being creatures of their own era, for it is apparent that they were driven by hidden commitments to values suspiciously typical of their own times. The Chicago School theologians acknowledged that for them adequacy consisted in the conversion of Christian language to meanings appropriate to the twentieth century. Shailer Mathews, for example, defined theological modernism as *"the use of the methods of modern science to find, state and use the permanent and central values of inherited orthodoxy in meeting the needs of a modern world."*[35] Or, in the area of economic issues, Mathews would excoriate American capitalism and conclude a discussion of Jesus's moral stance by saying: "All this, it must be admitted, brings Jesus close to the general position of socialism."[36] It is hard to resist the conclusion that the Chicago theologians were animated by commitments to value, and that among these values were not only the values of the biblical world, but of "scientific method" and left wing economic and political theory. Their historicism, in short, was heavily influenced, if not dominated, by value criteria that were never clearly examined.

Bernard Meland, as a later member of the Chicago School, came to recognize that pragmatic historicism must be driven inevitably by an experiential criterion of value. Meland makes this point over and over in his writings, and illustrates it even in his analysis of Haroutunian's 1964 article. In a brief critique published with that article, Meland argues that when Haroutunian cited the Bible, he implicitly acknowledged that he was "unable to take Pragmatism straight." As Calvin said, "we put on the spectacles of Scripture when looking at history." Haroutunian's Calvinist biblicism offered a means for seeing in "the experiences of history depths of meaning relating to ultimate demands which might otherwise escape us in our immediate perception of events."[37] Meland concluded that, unwittingly, Haroutunian was uncomfortable with a pragmatism which would not be guided by a historically experienced criterion of value.

Equally, for Cornel West the prophetic, Afro-American Christian experience serves as an explicit empirical source for what works in his theological essays as an evaluative criterion. Although West does not make much of empiricism, he at least does not hide his empirical norms.

But it was George Burman Foster, at the very beginnning of the Chicago School, who wrote most aptly of the problems encountered when a pragmatic historicism fails to acknowledge that it is guided by criteria taken from experience. In his 1907 article entitled "Pragmatism and Knowledge," Foster worries about the "new philosophers," by which he refers to unnamed pragmatists. Finally, they focus so exclusively on the pragmatic consequence that they deny the cognitive source—that is, they deny that the hypothesis in question is based on knowledge of the world. Foster begins by saying that current scientific thinkers have concluded that religion has no basis in knowledge because its assertions are unverifiable and therefore invalid. Religious assertions express merely the baseless feelings of the religious. But then, when the religious vent their indignation at this, the scientists respond, "Why do you find fault with me any longer for my attitude to your knowledge . . . since I assume the same attitude to my knowledge." In other words, these scientists treat science itself as "only a rule of action, a device for getting results for life—this is Pragmatism."[38] But here Foster himself responds, "*either,* science is not competent to forecast—but in that case it is worthless as a rule of action; *or,* it is competent to forecast, in a more or less imperfect manner—but in that case it is not worthless as a means of *knowledge.*"[39] Foster concludes that science does not freely create the "facts" with which it works; rather, it knows facts and is conditioned, limited, and guided by those facts. Equally, the relations between the facts—pointed to by scientific laws—are known to be "*true,* and not simply devices of the pragmatist to serve as supernumeraries in the seriocomic play of human life." Then, through an illustration, Foster shows the implication for religion: "And, as to the world of religion, let any functional psychologist try to act upon the idea of God, no matter how it arose, and at the same time disbelieve in his existence; he will find that no action will follow, if *ontological* reference be denied to the facts."[40] In short, to be meaningful, pragmatic philosophy, natural science, and religion must acknowledge not only that it is the world that is interpreted, but that this interpretation guides inquiry. Foster was unequivocal in his claim that religion is based on some experience of God as the ideal-achieving capacity of the universe.

In instance after instance, it appears that pragmatic historicism must be augmented by historical knowledge whereby values can be acquired. On rare occasions, the Chicago School historicists—particularly in the person of Foster—contended that empiricism was capable of perceiving the valuational depths of the world, and of doing this without violating the claims of pragmatism.

AN EPISTEMOLOGY THAT IS NOT "THE EPISTEMOLOGY"

But have we come this far only to return to a quest for extrahistorical foundations? Should historicism return to the old modernist attempt to answer skepticism by showing how we know? Is not the insistence that a pragmatic historicism be augmented with a kind of empiricism merely one more call for what Rorty designates "epistemology," meaning that effort, begun with John

Locke, to recover security through an examination of how we know? And has not that particular epistemology of empiricism been effectively eliminated not only by Hume long ago but by Thomas Kuhn and Paul Feyerabend today? So is not the need for a kind of empiricism really just that craving we should learn to kill?

This question, itself, works out of a false dichotomy, neglecting the possibility of a third kind of epistemology, one that is historicist and nonfoundational. This can be illustrated by reference to Rorty. While Rorty and today's new historicists sometimes denounce epistemology in unqualified ways, their real protest against epistemology is directed against "foundational epistemology," toward, in Rorty's words, that "desire to find 'foundations' to which one might cling, frameworks beyond which one must not stray, objects which impose themselves, representations which cannot be gainsaid."[41] "Epistemology" for Rorty finally is the search for something commensurable, "a set of rules which will tell us how rational agreement can be reached."[42] "Epistemology" becomes, then, a code word for denouncing modern philosophy's effort to find foundations by finding how we know, when finding how we know means using representational theories. However, as Jeffrey Stout argues, "Rorty's opposition to epistemology as the quest for rules of commensuration does not entail antipathy toward 'epistemology' in the perfectly innocuous sense of [to quote Ian Hacking] 'reflection on the possibility, nature, and content of numerous kinds of knowledge'."[43] The implication of Stout's comment is correct; there is a third and unexamined term between foundationalist epistemology and no epistemology at all. But this does not alter the fact that Rorty and the neopragmatists tend to be so mesmerized by their negative characterization of the foundationalist epistemology of modern philosophy that they erect a false dichotomy ("epistemology" or no epistemology at all), thereby ignoring all other theories of knowledge.

Ironically, in his 1981 *Flight from Authority*, Jeffrey Stout advances his own dichotomization, making a move similar to Rorty's. Stout's "meditation on the motivations behind, and the merits of, historicist orientation in philosophy" may be, in fact, the most complete such meditation about current philosophy; and yet it, too, rejects "epistemology," including the epistemology of empiricism.[44] Stout tends to oppose his historicism to all epistemology. Stout claims that the inadequacy of empiricism, like the inadequacy of idealism, can be demonstrated by an historicist anlysis, and that empiricism simply can and should be replaced by the "new historicism" which he advocates.[45] Stout's version of historicism involves both Willard Quine's notion of holism and the Ludwig Wittgenstein's notion of meaning-as-use. Holism demonstrates that the "ideas" of an idealist or of an empiricist or the "meanings" of a language analyst are far narrower than the web of factors in which those ideas and meanings actually are involved. A more complete recovery of a word comes from examining its varying uses in history. Words and their changes are functions of history and its changes, and inquiry into such words eliminates the need for epistemology.

On the face of it, Stout defends his historicism and his rejection of epistemology consistently by setting it in the history of modern philosophy, beginning with Descartes's personal battle with skepticism. The *opinio* that Descartes received from tradition had once been made "probable" by the citation of the regnant authorities, usually theological; but when those authorities became divided in the mid-sixteenth century, *opinio's* probability was undercut. Hence, the aggravation of Descartes's doubt, and his strong desire to so fortify *scientia* that now it, rather than *opinio,* could provide the impregnable barrier against skepticism. Descartes developed the *cogito* of the autonomous individual, and made it into the foundation of *scientia.* But his project eventually backfired; *cogito* would not carry the weight he placed on it primarily because of its subjective status. Efforts to resolve this new skepticism about the subjectively isolated *cogito* came to be, more than anything else, the dominating task of three hundred years of modern philosophy. The philosophers "began to take preoccupation with the implicitly skeptical subjectivity of the veil of ideas as their own professional obligation and distinguishing mark," even into the twentieth century when professionalized philosophy was seen as "a foundational discipline with epistemology as its most basic part."[46] There was, to use the phrase Stout uses for his title, a "flight from authority," a rejection of the leaders whose judgments had once authorized *opinio,* and an effort to ground thought, particularly moral thought, in autonomy—autonomous thought by autonomous individuals. Stout attacks this Cartesian and post-Cartesian attempt at autonomy, whether it ends in sheer skepticism about all forms of justification or in the foundationalist epistemology of modern philosophy; he argues that both skepticism and modern philosophy ignore the historical locus of everything we do and say. Hence, Stout can dismiss "empiricism" as simply the British and, then, the American side of this misguided epistemological foundationalism, and pursue instead a nonempirical and nonepistemological historicism.

But, interestingly, hidden and unacknowledged within Stout's pages is his own "third term," his unorthodox epistemological empiricism. The argument of Stout's book appears to deconstruct itself by according experience more trustworthiness than the book's denial of empiricism would seem to permit. This point is so obvious that it can go unnoticed. After all, historicism obviously is founded on a kind of experience of social contexts. Contrasting his new historicism to the idealistic historicism of the nineteenth century, even Stout will claim that the new historicism "has more to do with empirical approaches to language and sociological conceptions of knowledge than with an idealistic philosophy of spirit."[47] Or, in another context, Stout contends, "If we ever achieve a general theory of justification that is worth having, it will probably be a sociological theory of the kind that emerges from extensive historical and anthropological research."[48] Obviously, these are calls for a kind of empiricism, a kind not driven by the quest for certainty, a kind not pre-occupied with the "realism" which uses the correspondence test of truth, a kind not trying to ape the ostensible style of the natural sciences, but a kind of empiricism anyway. It will see David Hume's category of "custom" not as a despairing acknowledgement of the failure of the true empirical quest, but as the introduction of perfectly good empirical evidence of a more informal sort. It will see the new probability as Locke and Hume sometimes saw it, as the introduction of "the tradition of 'sound human judgment,' not that of foundationalist epistemology."[49] It will be a kind of empiricism and a form of epistemology, even if Stout has no interest in using those words to describe it.

The point is not as trivial as it might appear. Stout, Rorty, and other new historicists or neopragmatists are inclined to force dichotomies. They see the history of modern philosophy as "epistemological" in the foundationalist sense, and as "empirical" in a realist sense (when, that is, the epistemology is not idealist); and to that tradition, they oppose their historicism and pragmatism. Consequently, they disregard "epistemological" and "empirical" in describing their own enterprise. Treating the terms as univocal, they simply give them over to the tradition and opt for chastity. They profess to live without a theory of knowledge and without an empiricism. They never seriously inquire about the possibility that there might be a third option, something between the accep-tance of modernist epistemology and its empiricism and the complete denial of epistemology and empiricism. They avoid this inquiry even though they, themselves, operate implicitly out of an empiricist epistemology. Consequently, they never seriously inquire about the possibility of a postmodern epistemology and empiricism. They ignore the claims that unorthodox, nonfoundational, and distinctively American empiricists might have made, and how they might have escaped the sins of the orthodox epistemology and empiricism.[50]

Their forced dichotomy may make their pragmatism and historicism less persuasive and less likely to prompt historical action, for it precludes serious discussion of the way beliefs, including beliefs about values and criteria, arise from experience. Most people still want some explicit discussion of what beliefs are based on—whether it is officially called epistemology or not. They know that knowledge is had, and originates somewhere, and that it makes a difference from where. (Stout's own book-length testimony confirms this; for he assumes that we simply cannot understand current philosophy, morality, and religion if we refuse to discuss carefully the history from which they arose.) In fact, when today's new historicists reject all forms of epistemology and empiricism, they invite the charge that they are unpersuasive because they are subjectivistic and/or relativistic. This is true even of Stout's *Flight from Authority,* dispite Stout's valiant and, I think, largely persuasive effort to show how objectivism and sub-jectivism, or absolutism and relativism, are obsolete alternatives, mere conumdrums from the dualistic world of modern philosophy.[51]

In short, although Stout offers an encyclopedic discussion of recent philosophy, his general neglect of empiricism allows him to specifically neglect American radical empiricism. Here the problem is compounded, for this involves Stout not only in the neglect of an epistemological explanation but in the violation of his own methodology. By Stout's own account, one of the two basic standards of historicism is that "historical insight must be essential to self-understanding."[52] Using that standard as a critical criterion, Stout applies it mercilessly, faulting the "tradition of Descartes and Kant" for its failure to "account for its own history," faulting religious ethicists David Little, Sumner B. Twiss, Ronald Green, and John Rawls because they do not understand the historical traditions in which they stand: Little and Twiss for not appreciating their logical empiricist heritage; Green for not evaluating the neo-Kantianism entailed by his use of Rawls; and Rawls for not appreciating his own neo-Kantian heritage. Stout's entire book is guided by "the purpose of exemplifying historicism."[53] Consistent with this purpose, Stout reveals his own dependence on a pragmatism which began in mid-century, a pragmatism which, with Feigl, Carnap, and Reichenbach, "re-entered American philosophy on little cat feet, first with this one tentative paw but then suddenly on all fours—a calming fog of blurred distinctions," but finally grew to something more thorough in Quine's 1951 "Two Dogmas of Empiricism."[54] Stout wants a holistic historicism "consistent with the best in American pragmatism."[55] But—and here the problem arises—what does Stout mean by "the best in American pragmatism?" Does it really begin with Feigl, Carnap, Reichenbach, and Quine? Rorty thought it began in James and Dewey. If it were James and Dewey, or at least involved James and Dewey, why does Stout not make this clear? If Stout were to exercise consistently the historicist criterion, should he not trace his own historicism back to James and Dewey? Again, for Stout: "Situated freedom is a creature of space and time. To locate ourselves in *our* situation, and thereby to make informed moral action possible, is largely to construct the narratives in which the interaction of character and circumstance can be brought to light."[56] Why, if this is what historicism means, did Stout treat his situation as a situation of European thought (not American thought) until around the 1940s and 1950s, when he switches to America by taking up the narratives of Feigl, Hempel, Quine, and Rawls? If Stout had traced sonsistently *our* situation in space and time, would he not have traced his pragmatism back to the classic American pragmatists? And might he then have questioned his rather thorough rejection of "epistemology" and "empiricism," a rejection James and Dewey avoided because they took the trouble to redefine those terms in a new way, peculiar to their own American historical situation?

And if Stout had traced his own historicism to the work of James and Dewey, might his own moral criterion have been easier to understand? Stout's closing plea falls perfectly in line with the moral pleas offered by all of today's new historicists: "The real hope for rational discourse lies in the will to create communities and institutions in which the virtues of good people and good conversation can flourish. Philosophy is no substitute for that, but its value can be measured by the contribution it makes."[57] Coming at the end of the book, this hope leaves the reader breathless. How, for example, is it possible to talk about "virtues," "good people," "good communities," or of any criteria at all, after all forms of epistemology and empiricism have been rejected? Apart from some kind of knowledge, how does Stout know the meaning of virtues and good communities, or that to work for these virtues and communities is a desired pragmatic objective? A clearer connection with the epistemology of the American radical empiricists might have given the brain the oxygen it needs for answering such questions.[58] For Dewey and James did have an empiricism which enabled them forthrightly to offer their reasons for their normative judgments.

James and Dewey need not have been disqualified as ancestors of the new historicists. The empiricism of James and Dewey, just like the historicism of Rorty and Stout, is not foundational, it does not seek commensurables, it is not born of the quest for certainty; and it rejects just that dualism which would cage the subject's knowledge within the subject. In fact, James's entire philosophical project is born not of the crisis regarding *opinio,* where authority disagreed with authority, nor is it born out of the solipsistic predicament of the subjective ego. James does not fit Stout's paradigm of the "flight from authority." He was propelled, not by flight, but by something close to its opposite: a yearning to overcome his loss of authority, his sense of personal helplessness caused by positivism. James was so intimidated by positivism's "automaton" picture of the human self that he was rendered virtually immobile for portions of 1869 and 1870.[59] Like Rorty and Stout, James struggled for a morality that might be founded on something more than a flight from authority. But unlike Rorty and Stout, James—as well as his successor, Dewey—

was able to trace his hopes and pragmatic objectives through a kind of empricism to a kind of knowledge of values.

Let me state the matter one last time, again using Stout's *Flight from Authority* as a case study. I am suggesting that the continuing need for an epistemology can be stated as a question about the use of historical understanding for understanding generally. According to Stout, historical understanding is not something foundational, not something standing at the end of what would otherwise be an infinite regress, offering "beliefs that require no additional reasons for their justification" or that are "immediately justified."[60] But neither is historical understanding dispensable ("It is hard to imagine *dispensing* with historical understanding without dispensing with understanding altogether."[61]). The question is, What is the relation of historical understanding to understanding generally, if it is indispensable but nonfoundational? More specifically, if historical understanding is indispensable, does it provide a kind of awareness that understanding must have? And if so, is the recognition of the need for this awareness implicitly a call for admitting a kind of epistemology, particularly, a kind of empirical epistemology? If so, what kind of empirical epistemology, and how would it differ from the positivist epistemology historicism has had to reject? Here Stout's powerful book is strangely silent.

Stout appears—but only appears—to answer this question by a distinct and third approach to theological understanding. Obviously, theology is finished if it must continue to react to modernity as Alisdair MacIntyre says it has in the past: that is, either by accommodating so thoroughly to modernity as to lose its distinctiveness or by becoming so remote from modernity as to become incomprehensible.[62] Rudolf Bultmann and Paul Tillich may have become so concerned with satisfying an existentialist modernity that they lost their capacity to speak for a religion grounded in tradition; Karl Barth may have become so committed to tradition that he lost credibility in the modern world. To a Popperian this means, How can theism become meaningful enough to be refutable and still remain an authentic theism? Or, How can theism retain its relativity to its own tradition without becoming irrationalistically relativistic? To most twentieth-century philosophers this means, How can theism be evaluated in terms of universal criteria of validity or meaningfulness and still not be so trimmed to these criteria that it stops talking about God? In the last analysis, Stout says, this is a modernist dilemma, still dominated by the quest for absolute certainty in the face of skeptical questions, still caught in a dualism which seeks freedom from the materialistic chaos by the exercise of universal spiritual laws. The real question is, can historicism offer to theology a third kind of understanding, one between obstinacy and acquiescence, one between irrationality and empty universality?

Stout thinks so, and in this he sides with Thomas Kuhn's escape from the relative-universal dilemma through "mapping the variables of this relativity in social and historical space"; [63] with Larry Laudan's claim that rationality is found in "doing (or believing) things because we have good reasons for doing so";[64] with Donald Davidson's contention that we can understand another culture by seeing "a shared background of entrenched assumption."[65] Stout most explicitly states his own use of this third and historicist understanding in the following terms:

> The reasons to which I can appeal in justifying my decisions, and therefore the reasons relevant to anyone's assessment of my rationality in reaching these decisions, are determined by my situation—not only the epoch and culture into which I was born but also various other autobiographical facts that distinguish my reasoning from that of my fellows. The reasons available to you might well differ, given the facts of your situation. You might then reach conclusions which, while justifiable for someone in your situation, could not be so for me in mine. Grant for now that no rules of adjudication, neutral with respect to our differences, can be brought forward to resolve these differences.[66]

With such an outlook, then, one might adopt a theism which claims neither universalism nor a particularistic, irrational, relativitistic fideism. Citing Davidson, Stout seems to conclude that the irrationality of a multiplicity of mutually contradictory positions will not arise because each position shares enough with others to prevent a relativistic irrationalism.[67]

But this is only an apparent explanation of the distinctiveness of historicism's understanding and of the possible knowledge on which it is based. Neither Stout, nor any of today's new neohistoricists, nor most of the Chicago School theologians, is really very convincing in explaining what there is about *"our* situation" that is so enthralling, that inspires an alternative understanding that can quiet the call of universal truth. Stout admits confinement to his epoch, culture, and autobiographical facts, just as Rorty acknowledges a provincialism and ethnocentrism,[68] all characteristics which usually count against understanding. So, what exactly is the appeal of this historical knowledge that enables us to hold onto it? Is there something about local knowledge which makes it convincing? If our history is so basic and crucial that it can give us our theism, the basis for our morality, and the direction of our particular life, should we not at least describe it, to say how it is known, to say how it is valuable? If, in short, the thick history in which we live offers us that criterion on which we base all our value commitments, must we not be more demanding in how we know it? Can the matter really be passed off as just local history and left there? There are all sorts of local knowledges which we try to abandon. What, for example, is there about the local knowledge Stout seeks that makes it true and proper, and how is it known?

I am suggesting that these questions cannot be resolved except through a greater discipline and self-consciousness about how and what we know through our historical experience. Only through such care can we hope to perceive, and to perceive critically, the values we derive from our history. Apart from such epistemological, historicist inquiry the confidence that engenders moral action is hobbled, and the pragmatist will not have the effectiveness he or she above all seeks.

Stout, today's neohistoricists, and the Chicago School theologians seem to have become so preoccupied with fighting the philosophical and theological mistakes of the past that they have forgotten what specifically it is that gives the reasons for fighting at all. Yes, they have acknowledged that there are goals and values; they have to do with the virtues of good community and good conversation. But is any comment on goals and values sufficient, without an indication of how, in this strange new world, we can know them and of how this awareness requires us, in turn, to adjust and readjust our historicisms and pragmatisms?

James and Dewey believed that an historicism must be based on a special kind of experience, explained by a special kind of epistemology. They were always leery of focusing on what was clear, distinct, merely factual within our known world. They always knew that, to cite Conrad Hilberry's "Fisherman," we become so preoccupied with the hand and the eye that we forget the body . . . and how it is known:

Wet to the knees, the fisherman studies the twist
and fall of water then drops the fly in a pool
beyond a log. He takes the subtle trout.
Like finds like. His hand and eye are cousin
to the fish, that canny bit of river.

A feeling stirs in him like a thin mist
on the water. It rises with his breath
penetrant as shame, he thinks, or regret.
Nothing to do with the trout, it is a smell
almost remembered—the heaviness of an attic
or the musk of leaves. His heart is hidden in it.

Hand and eye know their trade, but the body is
the whole canyon, the river falling ignorant
over rocks and debris, over the fisherman's
boots, over the precise scales of the trout.
It is osier, marsh grass, the broken cliff,
vague browns and greys and greens rumbling
in their sleep. It will not rise to the lure.[69]

It is, in short, a knowledge of something which stirs like a thin mist on the water that provides, finally, the true reason for acting effectively, out of the past, for the future. This knowledge is not simply an invention of the self. It is felt with the whole body—with the entire self using a combination of perceptions—and it tells about the ethos, the ambience, the atmosphere, the whole situation. For Hilberry, this knowledge tells about a world which is not balanced on the precise scales of the trout and which will not rise to the precise lures of, for example, our professional philosophies or theologies. This knowledge perceives what William Carlos Williams in *Paterson* called "the roar of the present,"[70] or what Charles Olson called the "energy" of the situation.[71] It attends to the vague values which actually dominate our lives, rather than to our precise justifications. If Stout wants to be guided by holism, here it is, amply stated by the poets, amply explicated by the classical American pragmatists, a holism not merely of words connected to words, but of the entire psychophysical web of words and bodies, and of natural and social histories.[72]

This is not to argue that the current neopragmatists or neohistoricists are entirely ignorant of this radical empiricism (though they have not named it). Stout will emphasize the importance of *"describing* the fuzziness that is there," and of resisting the temptation to "think that a clearer picture would be a better one."[73] And every one of his new historicist predecessor will attack the tradition of "clear and distinct ideas" established by Descartes.

But, effectively, they have not only ignored but spurned the radical empiricism through which values might be perceived—an empiricism for which James, Dewey and a number of American theologians found it important to labor at length.

CHAPTER 5

The Radical Historicists

. . . . Once the Bomb was used and the enormity of its effects
realized, it had the impact of Copernicus, Darwin, Freud—of
any monumental historical theory that proved, fundamentally, how small people are, how accidental their prominence, how subject to external manipulation. When the
Bomb dropped, people not only saw a weapon that could
boil the planet and create a death-in-life; they saw yet one
more proof of their impotence. We live in a world of "virile
weapons and impotent men," wrote the French historian,
Raymond Aron, shortly before his death in 1983. We saw a
vision of the future in Hiroshima, but we also saw ourselves,
and (again) we did not like what we saw. . . . [1]

Basic securities were blasted away by unexpected
developments. The bomb loosened people's hold on their presumption that
through their cognitive abilities they could control their fate. It allowed people
also to recognize that history changes not only thought and language, but
attitude.

What the bomb did for us in the late twentieth century was done for
William James and John Dewey in the late nineteenth century by another event:
Charles Darwin's reinterpretation of nature. While the late nineteenth century
mind was affected by a variety of social phenomena—the Civil War, Reconstruction, the struggle for an American identity in the community of Atlantic
nations, the increasing influences of industrialism and science, a complacency
born of new prosperity—it was only Darwin who struck James and Dewey like
the bomb struck us. Furthermore, just as the bomb demonstrated to us not
only human weakness but human immorality, so Darwin pictured a nature
guided not only by accident but by violence. Both the bomb and Darwin
suggested a closer empirical look, and that revealed not only impotence but evil.

99

Further, just as the bomb was the perfect twentieth-century preparation for an utterly historicist hearing of the world, so Darwin was the perfect nineteeth century preparation for an utterly historicist hearing of the world. We see the bomb interpreting us, and we are trying to decide how to interpret it. Darwin saw the interpretive imagination at work in nature: creatures through variations saying how they interpret their past; creatures through selection saying which variations will be accepted and which rejected.

In "The Influence of Darwinism on Philosophy,"[2] Dewey notes the remarkable departure of Darwin from prevailing worldviews, whether Greek or Christian. After Darwin, species were no longer imprints from eternal stamps; rather, they were literally created in the temporal dynamics of natural history. The implications for philosophy were profound. In James's "Great Men and Their Environment," which sets forth James's theory of social history, Darwin is juxtaposed to Herbert Spencer. Darwin's emphasis on the unlimited creativity of random, spontaneous variations refutes, James said, Spencer's mechanistic interpretation of evolution. Darwin did for our thinking about history, says James, what Galileo did for physics.[3]

The thinking of Dewey and James became empirical, but in a new way. They abandoned any sort of dualism that would restrict empirical examination to the material impressions of the senses. For example, Dewey and James concluded that Darwin could not be restricted to some physical world with no influence on distinctly human value; rather, they applied Darwin culturally as well as materially. For Dewey and James, the cultural and the material were parts of one history, and this history created itself as it crawled.

Early in their intellectual lives each had had allegiances to worlds beyond the world of history, worlds that allowed them to confine empiricism to the material world known by the five senses. James as a medical student was intimated by the then-prevailing mechanistic interpretation of human identity, which found reality in material laws impervious to historical contingencies and known through the observation of the five senses; he later disparagingly called this the automaton view of human nature. Dewey as a young philosopher was a Hegelian; he later villified the intuitionism of that approach. Although mechanism's laws of science or Hegel's laws of reason advocate a kind of evolutionism, they appealed, nevertheless, to a law of nature or to an Absolute which itself remained as it was, unaffected by random historical variation. Once James and Dewey abandoned such extrahistorical foundations, they had to look to natural and social history alone as the seat of both body and spirit. History's spontaneous variation and natural selection created all the life there was. But for James and Dewey an empiricism of the five senses could not carry this load; empiricism was enlarged to include experience of thoughts, decisions, and feelings of living things.

For James and Dewey history—even natural history—carried values as well as physcial causes. Nature was not a blind physical mechanism; nature was the bearer of good and evil, as well as matter. When Darwin described the human as a product of variation and selection, and not a creature determined by divine, scientific, natural, or rational forces from beyond the worldly process, a certain sobriety seemed in order. Finally, life came to be seen as a dramatic struggle, in which those species that still stood in life's battle—the overwhelming majority of which already had fallen—stood not by personal virtue, not by the grace of God, not by reason, but by a historical and morally ambiguous cunning which allowed them to keep their blood from spilling in a bloodthirsty environment.

James's recognition of evil in this evolutionary context is striking. "Doesn't the fact of 'no' stand at the very core of life?" James asked.

> I find myself willing to take the universe to be really dangerous and adventurous, without therefore backing out and crying 'no play.' I am willing to think that the prodigal-son attitude, open to us as it is in many vicissitudes, is not the right and final attitude towards the whole of life. I am willing that there should be real losses and real losers, and no total preservation of all that is. I can believe in the ideal as an ultimate, not as an origin, and as an extract, not the whole. When the cup is poured off, the dregs are left behind for ever, but the possibility of what is poured off is sweet enough to accept.[4]

Earlier James had asserted, "If this life be not a real fight, in which something is eternally gained for the universe by success, it is no better than a game of private theatricals from which one may withdraw at will. But it *feels* like a real fight— as if there were something really wild in the universe which we, with all our idealities and faithfulnesses, are needed to redeem; and first of all to redeem our own hearts from atheisms and fears."[5] In his last essay, James quoted Benjamin Paul Blood: "Not unfortunately the universe is wild—game flavored as a hawk's wing."[6]

The question is, What kind of empiricism is this, that both refuses to be confined to the material world of the five senses and that perceives values, like the evil in nature, as well as facts? James called it a radical empiricism; Dewey called it immediate empiricism. The new historicism exercised by James and Dewey worked out of this empiricism, and became a historicism capable of discussing values as well as words.

Def. radical empiricism

I am contending that radical empiricism is central to the work of James and Dewey because their thought was occasioned by the recognition that everything depends on accident and creative choice in history, and that there is nothing extrahistorical to save the day. It was this perilous condition that drove James and Dewey to seek a more complete empiricism, for now so much more had to be derived from history.

In this analysis of history, as much clarity as possible was needed. Pragmatism, as we will see, was their method of clarifying the "buzzing, blooming confusion" of the empirical reports on this fact-value world. Although Charles Sanders Peirce, by James's own testimony, invented pragmatism. Peirce does not figure in a major way in this account because Peirce's pragmatism was a method not for marrying history's irredeemable confusion but for escaping that confusion, for deciding what was real generally, extrahistorically, beyond and above historical contingency. Peirce was not a new historicist, but, by his own account, a "scholastic realist of a somewhat extreme stripe."[7] Pragmatism was to aid in finding the meaning of universal "intellectual concepts." Further, it had nothing to do with the "qualities of feeling"[8] that James and Dewey derived from the radically empirical account of the world.

Here I discuss the radical empiricism of the classical American philosophies of James and Dewey. I will show how this gave them a "radical historicism," one open to values in ways that the new historicism is not open today. Finally, I show the theological adoption of this radical historicism by two, little-recognized, latter-day Chicago School theologians, Bernard Meland and Bernard Loomer.

The point is, that this fuller epistemology and the fuller historicism it reveals allowed the classical American philosophers and the theologians who depend on them to show where they find their values and norms, and thus potentially to be more persuasive, more pragmatically successful with their readers than are today's new historicists. The objective, after all, is to develop a historicism that will be pragmatically effective in its own history. The classical American precedent could contribute to this objective today if it were to be appropriated more fully by today's new historicists—for whom, after all, it is a historical antecedent.

FROM RADICAL EMPRICISM TO RADICAL HISTORICISM

James's initial admiration for eighteenth-century British empiricism, the empiricism we today would call a positivism, was real. He accepted the positivistic empiricists' demystification of idealism; while these positivists may be too "tied to their senses," they are properly and "positively shocked by the easy excursions into the unseen that other people make at the bare call of sentiment."[9]

Nevertheless, James objected to positivistic empiricism as early as the third paragraph of his first philosophical essay, the 1876 "Remarks on Spencer's Definition of Mind as Correspondence":

What right has one, in a formula embracing professedly the "entire process of mental evolution," to mention only phenomena of cognition, and to omit all sentiments, all aesthetic impulses, all religious emotions and personal affections? The ascertainment of outward fact constitutes only one species of mental activity. The genus contains, in addition to purely cognitive judgments, or judgments of the actual—judgments that things do, as a matter of fact, exist so or so—an immense number of emotional judgments: judgments of the ideal, judgments that things *should* exist thus and not so.[10]

[margin annotation: What about emotions?]

James went on to note that Spencer had argued that evolution was a theory about survival, and that survival was nothing more than a material question of adjusting the inner self to the facts of the outward environment. But experience itself, James retorted, indicates that such a scheme is impoverished. Physical survival is only one of many interests, and often a subordinate interest; humans, in fact, find survival a supportable interest only in the presence of other interests. Principal among these other interests is the desire for greater richness of experience; and that desire is ignited only by emotionally entertained ideals. Spencer, committed as he was to the notion that mind is purely derivative from the material environment, could not permit the introduction of a telos toward greater richness because that smacked too much of a spontaneous mental contribution. Also, Spencer forgot that "not a cognition occurs but feeling is there to comment on it, to stamp it as a greater or less worth."[11] James may not have decided to treat such value judgments as empirical—as experiences of the world, rather than as merely private feelings—until 1884, when in *Mind* he argued that evaluative experience is based on the relations between facts rather than the experience of facts themselves. This led James to call for a new, a more thorough, a radical empiricism.

James opened further room for his radical empiricism when he broke free from dualism in his 1904 "A World of Pure Experience."[12] If the positivistic empiricism involves the five-sense experience of a material world, a truly adequate radical empiricism involves neither material objects nor spiritual subjects but the "pure experience" of interaction between a self and its world. We feel simply the "instant field of the present," the world in its multiplicity, nothing more and nothing less; and the sense of inner or outer, spiritual or material are merely reflections of how we deal with the present.

James's "radical empiricism" was his claim: (1) that experience alone is reliable testimony about the world, (2) that what is experienced are relations between things as well as things themselves, and (3) that beyond experience and the relations and things experienced, there is no transempiricical whole. It is our experience of relations that conveys the qualities (including the values) we feel. Both rationalistic idealists and positivistic empiricists had said that it was the self who supplied the relations; James argued that the relations were external to the self. It is to these relations that our experiences of qualities and values refer. "We ought," James said, "to say a feeling of *and,* a feeling of *if,* a feeling of *but,* and a feeling of *by,* quite as readily as we say a feeling of *blue* or a feeling of *cold*."[13] We feel how the world comes to us with a directedness or with resistances; we know the world as coming with a tendency. As long as we live in a world of pure experience, for the time being we can conclude that the world with all its felt qualities and values "is *just what we feel it to be.*"[14]

This affectional experience works in special ways in religion, which to James was not the particular reaction but "any total reaction upon life." To get at total reactions, said James in *The Varieties of Religious Experience,* "you must go behind the foreground of existence and reach down to that curious sense of the whole residual cosmos as an everlasting presence, intimate or alien, terrible or amusing, lovable or odious, which in some degree everyone posseses. This sense of the world's presence, appealing as it does to our peculiar individual temperament, makes us either strenuous or careless, devout or blasphemous, gloomy or exultant about life at large."[15]

James acknowledges that radical empiricism testifies to external relations that "nine-tenths of the time are not actually but only virtually there."[16] Thus, if every radically empirical testimony is not to be suspect, radical empiricism needs a method for distinguishing that nine-tenths from the one-tenth that is meaningful and true; this method is pragmatism. James ends his 1878 article on Spencer by embracing pragmatism, not for its inherent importance, but as a method for evaluating pure experience. Pragmatism is introduced as a way of sorting out and selecting which among our unreliable, empirically based theories "in the long run works best."[17] In 1884, James allowed that without evidence of practical effects, one had a right to be suspicious of the radically empirical testimony. "If your feelings bear no fruits in my world, I call it utterly detached from my world; I call it a solipsism, and call its world a dreamworld."[18] In 1904, James argues that when a dispute arises about which experiences are true, the pragmatic method "consists in auguring what practical consequences would be different if one side rather than the other were true."[19] It is a way of distinguishing those experiences which are merely subjective from those which are not.[20] Radical empiricism stood to pragmatism, in short, as Darwin's variation stood to his selection: the former is the germ, the latter merely differentiates the viable from the nonviable germ.

Finally, James's radical empiricism leads to a radical historicism that makes the social environment the first context and the last evaluator of meaning and truth, including the meaning and truth of qualities and values. History, not the individual, is the final context of change. Radical empiricism requires that the individual is the source of growth, for the individual is not entirely passive to the realities of the past, but also active—that is, creative—in reading those realities in the light of what the individual brings to the world. In that early and prophetic essay on Spencer, James argues that, because what we bring affects what we perceive and because what we perceive is true if it works, then:

> The knower is an actor, and co-efficient of the truth on one side, whilst on the other he registers the truth which he helps to create. Mental interests, hypotheses, postulates, so far as they are bases for human action—action which to a great extent transforms the world—help to *make* the truth which they declare. In other words, there belongs to mind, from its birth upward, a sponaneity, a vote. It is in the game, and not a mere looker-on; and its judgments of the *should-be*, its ideals, cannot be peeled off from the body of the *cogitandum* as if they were excrescences, or meant, at most, survival.[21]

The self, in short, generates the variations which fuel history. However, James moved on toward a historicism: while the self is the source of variation, it depends on history and on nothing beyond history, the past history it perceptually feels and the future history that pragmatically selects its variations. History is both gatekeeper and judge, both stage of new variations and slaughterhouse of old ones. This historicism is "radical" because it recognizes that history is important not only as the stage and judge of facts, but of relations, qualities, and values as well.

It is this radical historicism that today's new historicists do not recognize. Their nonradical historicism sees history as a stage and judge for the linguistic and the cognitive, but not for the values that hide beneath but still operate within the new historicism. James's recognition of this valuational dimension of history and the epistemology atuned to this recognition, gives to James's work a completeness and, thus, a persuasiveness lacking today.

Equally under the influence of Darwin, John Dewey also called for a kind of radical empiricism as the basis for his historicism. Admittedly, Dewey's orientation in many ways diverges from James's. For James, Darwin initially challenges how we understand the individual and psychology. For Dewey, Darwin intially challenges the way we understand society and the way it develops. Dewey begins in the social arena while James moves there only to answer the solipsistic predicaments of a purely psychological philosophy. Dewey develops a naturalistic cosmology, James only hints at such an outcome. These differences do not materially affect, however, the fact that each thinker eventually advocated similar empiricist epistemologies and radical historicisms.

In his undergraduate years at the University of Vermont, Dewey received his Darwinian orientation from a T. H. Huxley text on physiology. Dewey confesses, "subconsciously, at least, I was led to desire a world and a life that would have the same properties as had the human organism in the picture of it derived from study of Huxley's treatment . . . . I date from this time the awakening of a distinctive philosophic interest."[22] From this he took "a sense of interdependence and interrelated unity" which served as "a kind of type or model of a view of things to which material in any field ought to conform." Admittedly, this did not keep Dewey from first publishing what he would call "highly schematic and formal" articles "couched in the language of intuitionalism," nor subsequently from falling under the spell of Hegel. In the last fifteen years of the nineteenth century, however, Dewey said that he "drifted away" from Hegel, and took with increasing seriousness the obligation of philosophy not to schemes of thought but to the practical and material orientations of thought.[23]

In autobiographical comments, Dewey says that the influence of James is the "one specifiable philosophical factor which entered into my thinking so as to give it a new direction and quality."[24] What hit Dewey was that James's *Principles of Psychology* grounded psychology in biology, in the body in its action, rather than in some static and structural picture. For Dewey, James's biological foundation, first, refuted British sensationalistic empiricism's presumption that knowledge is based exclusively on sense data; and second, "led straight to the perception of the importance of distinctive social categories."[25]

Dewey's acceptance of James's psychology led to his own variation on James's radical empiricism, which in 1905 he named "immediate empiricism." What we experience, he argued, is all we have; and this is only what it is "experienced as." Herewith Dewey opposed himself to the traditional distinction between what something really is and what it appears to be; his point is that such distinctions are based on the illusion that we can receive some authoritative and objective version of the world, and then distinguish that version from some less-than-authoritative and merely subjective version of the world. Furthermore, Dewey contended that "experience as" is much broader than cognition, or "knowledge as." To treat knowledge as somehow basic is to begin in abstraction, even if that knowledge is empirical. "Empiricism, as herein used," Dewey explained, "is as antipodal to sensationalistic empiricism, as it is to transcendentalism, and for the same reason. Both of these systems fall back on something which is defined in non-directly-experienced terms in order to justify that which is directly experienced."[26]

In his 1925 *Experience and Nature,* Dewey called immediate empiricism *"empirical naturalism* or *naturalistic empiricism;* and he begins to identify the ways "experience as" is broader than "knowledge as." Dewey accepted James's characterization of experience as double-barrelled—that is, as including both what and how, both thing and response. "Experience as," then, includes the "hows" and responses, including the affectional responses, that the positivists had excluded. Dewey's naturalistic empiricism treats this integrated experience as the starting point and authority for epistemology. Naturally, it opposes the matter-spirit dualisms which treat as real only one-half of the whole, whether that half be the material half represented by positivism or the spiritual half represented by idealism, even if such half-truths do satisfy an unrecognized moralistic preference for what is simple, certain, and permanent.[27] Most important, against both positivism and idealism Dewey claims that values are perceived, and they exist not in the private and historically disconnected emotions of the self or in an ideal world apart from the world of history. Although values may be perceived only in the margins of experience (beyond the cognitive, the clear, and the distinct), they do exist in history, which is both material and spiritual.

In his *Art as Experience* and *A Common Faith,* both published in 1934, Dewey identifies the specifically aesthetic and religious nature of these values and connects the aesthetic and religious functions with evolutionary theory. Both books focus on a single evolutionary problem: How is a creature to readjust itself to its environment when a previous union with the environment has been disrupted by either that creature's change or the environment's change?

Aesthetic experience, in the last analysis, is a response to such change. First, the creature feels emotionally the discord between itself and the environment. Then reflection is induced, and this phase is the heart of the sciences. The third and distinctly aesthetic phase occurs when the "desire for restoration of the union converts mere emotion into interest in objects as conditions of realization of harmony."[28] At their deepest these objects are not things, but experiences; and they are aesthetically real whether or not eventually they are set in the physical form of an artwork or a performance. The artist specializes in feeling and discerning the discord between creature and environment so that he or she can more sensitively bring "to living consciousness an experience that is unified and total." The artist's creative contribution, however, is not sheer subjective creation out of nothing. The artist is an empiricist imbibing values from the world: "The live animal does not have to project emotions into the objects experienced. Nature is kind and hateful, bland and morose, irritating and comforting long before she is mathematically qualified or even a congeries of 'secondary' qualities like colors and their shapes."[29] On the other hand, the artist is no passive observer, but creatively interprets the world he or she perceives. Dewey's aesthetic is not only empirical, but is historicist in the sense that art results from the artist's analysis of a social environment and in the sense that the artist's interpretation is partially creative of a social future. It is a radical historicism in the sense that it includes the values of history in addition to the facts of history.

Equally, Dewey's picture of the religious in *A Common Faith* is evolution-based, radically empirical, and radically historicist. Religious acts confront the problems of evolutionary disharmonies between the creature and the environment—disharmonies that require either the response of accommodation whereby the creature adjusts itself to the environment or the response of adaptation whereby the creature adjusts the environment. When these adjustments are not merely particular in their forcus, but general in that they reorient the environment and the creature in their entirety, then the adjustments are religious. The attitude which guides the adjustment is properly called faith, where faith is the imagination of the whole in ways which permit new adjustments. As with aesthetic experience, Dewey treats the religious act: as an experience rather than an artifact, such as a specific doctrine, institution, or ritual of what Dewey calls "religion"; as neither a function of the creature alone nor of the environment alone; but as the interaction between the creature and the environment. Because one's invironment is one's social and natural history, the religious harmonizing of the self with its world is historical.[30]

For Dewey, the religious interpretation of history is indispensible. (Of course, Dewey attacked "religion," as against "the religious"; but the attack against religion was directed against trivializing faith through indentifying it with mere intellectual assent, with mere ceremony, or with merely conventional attitudes—practices then and now common in organized religion. In this, Dewey's attack was analogous to that of such religious prophets as Kierkegaard.) For Dewey, the fate of humans depends on the existence of God; that is, humans depend on the existence of "some complex of conditions that have operated to effect an adjustment in life, an orientation, that brings with it a sense of security and peace."[31] In *Art as Experience,* Dewey threw off the mantle of the critic of religion, and was more articulate religiously than he was to be in his book on religion. In *Art as Experience,* he pictures religious feeling as directed toward "the extensive and underlying whole." "the background which is more than spatial because it enters into and qualifies everything in the focus," "the deeper reality of the world in which we live in our ordinary experiences." that without which "parts are external to one another and mechanically related."[32] It appears, then, that without God people would not see how the parts of their histories are related, and they would be afflicted with meaninglessness. For Dewey, God is the wholeness in history that fosters ever-new adjustments between creature and environment—a wholeness which the creature imaginatively intuits through religious faith. In a *A Common Faith*, Dewey extends the point by citing Santayana's contention that without the religious "all observation is observation of brute fact, all discipline is mere repression."[33]

It is in this aesthetic and religious margin of experience, where "experience as" exceeds "knowledge as," that immediate or naturalistic empiricism is indispensible. Repeatedly, Dewey notes that the great sin of the religions is their loss of the imaginative reach beyond the merely factual, seen most clearly in their positivistic doctrines of a supernatural God and supernatural ritual. Properly, religious faith refers to something which "cannot be apprehended in knowledge nor realized in reflection. Neither observation, thought, nor practical activity can attain that complete unification of the self which is called a whole."[34]

Aware that faith is so murky it prevents precise and direct empirical discrimination, Dewey introduces the pragmatic criterion in order to permit the evaluation of faith's judgments. Exaggerating the pragmatic, Dewey can say, "The actual religious quality in the experience described is the *effect* produced, the better adjustment in life and its conditions, not the manner and cause of its production."[35] But what this statement possesses in clarity, it lacks in comprehensiveness. For Dewey also acknowledges that religion's pragmatic effect would be impossible if it were not the consequence of something that originated in a religious experience of the world.

Today, Dewey's view of religious faith should be called historicist. The "wholeness" that is God is not a logos, nor a static structure—not, in short, an extrahistorical reality. By his use of the word *God,* Dewey refers, evidently, to a pervasive urge within social and natural histories toward ever-more comprehensive and enriched integrations between ever-evolving worlds and their ever-evolving creatures. This urge arrives in history not through the imposition of extrahistorical and static structures, but simply is resident in the historical process itself. This historical tendency works through the interaction of two factors which are historical themselves: (1) the creature's imaginative vision, and (2) the contingent and temporal possibilities of the world. "The new vision does not arise out of nothing, but emerges through seeing, in terms of possibilities, that is, of imagination, old things in new relations serving a new end which the new end aids in creating."[36] The locomotive did not exist before Stevenson, Dewey says; but its conditions did, and Stevenson's imagination and the conditions collaborated to create something new. The religious works similarly; it specializes in the whole; it works as an interaction between the imaginative creature and its world in its entirety; and it is fostered by God ("some complex of conditions which have operated to affect an adjustment in life"). The religious operates within history, uses historical resources, responds to an experienced "complex of conditions" in history, and works pragmatically to reestablish the equilibrium between the historical creature and its historical world.

It is in this historicist context that Dewey's recognition of evil may best be understood. Dewey is aware that his own position can be called "a sentimentally optimistic recourse."[37] He is not particularly impressed, however, when religious supernaturalists avoid optimism by expressing their "pessimistic belief in the corruption and impotency of natural means." For "this apparent pessimism has a way of suddenly changing into an exaggerated optimism."[38] Just those people who disparage the optimism of the naturalists are sublimely aware that the cosmic deity is obsessed with the desire to save their souls. Having safe-harbored themselves, they then are free to see history as so distorted that anyone hoping to improve it is a sentimental fool. Well, says Dewey, this "is too easy a way out of difficulties." We live unavoidably in history and history is unavoidably ambiguous. "There exists a *mixture* of good and evil," so that the most we can hope for is that "the disorder, cruelty, and oppression that exist would be reduced."[39] It is Dewey, in short, who is so unsentimental, so nonoptimistic, even so pessimistic, that he denies the sublime world of the religious supernaturalist, and determines to live and die in a history that is always ambiguous.

This sense of the unavoidable evil of history lends urgency to the quest for radically empirical grounds for some kind of unavoidable good, and for the hope and meaning such good might foster. Through his immediate empiricism Dewey claims knowledge of values operative in the occasions of history and of a valuational tendency operative within the whole of history. This completer knowledge, in turn, can enable people more effectively to pursue the good and to persuade others of its reality.

Here Dewey, unlike today's new historicists, attempts to explicte a radical historicism—one that would establish how values are known and to ground them in history. Again, our point is that this gives to Dewey's new historicism a completeness and a persuasiveness lacking in today's new historicists.

RADICAL HISTORICISM IN RECENT THEOLOGY

I have contended that greater explicitness about the values used by today's new historicists is needed. Until those values are uncovered, suspicions about the relativism, subjectivism, formalism, even nihilism of the current new historicists are warranted; and their apparent good advice is understandably unheeded. Until then, regardless how frequently the new historicists might claim that they have gone to a third position, beyond their critic's invidious dichotomy (if not objectivism, then nihilistic relativism), they will lack the credibility to make that third option persuasive. I have suggested that they can make that option pragmatically effective if: (1) they develop an epistemology that offers a warrant for it, and (2) they use this epistemology to open a radical historicism that includes a place for values in the historical world.

I have suggested that in the American scene that epistemology might be a radical empiricism, and that that empiricism is distinctively American.[40] Like an early sedimentation, this empiricism had been solidified and fixed as early as the eighteenth century, showing particularly in the writings of Jonathan Edwards. But it was soon covered from view, and until James wrote, few tapped it openly or were colored obviously by its element. Again, however, after a generation it was mostly covered.

Further, I have argued that the historicism opened by this radical empiricism could be called radical because it used all the experiences of history: the affectionally perceived and value-laden relations within history in addition to the sensuously perceived facts of history; the pre-refined, the pre-winnowed, the pre-abstracted impressions of history as well as the refined, winnowed and abstracted ideals of history.

On the whole and ironically, today's historicists seldom ask what they might learn from the radical empiricists who lie within their own American historical locus. This is more than an aesthetic irony. It is an irony with a distinct functional implication: when they neglect their predecessors, they obscure how they might locate their own values, thereby overlooking the key to their third and more adequate option in philosophy and theology, which might allow them to be more socially persuasive.

What is sought, then, is a constructive emendation to today's new historicism. In this constructive dialogue it is the specifically theological voice out of the past that is most convincing—particularly the voices of Bernard Meland and Bernard Loomer. They speak most directly of the need for a radical empiricism that exposes the religious values in history, largely missing in today's new historicism. To locate, historically, Meland's and Loomer's voices, I note first their comments on nuclear war (the event that may have struck them as profoundly as Darwin struck James and Dewey) and then their views on education (which was, after all, their life's work and a practical activity that reveals their general outlooks—for as John E. Smith has said, "the educational curriculum is a mirror of the universe").[41]

Both Meland and Loomer were educated and spent the majority of their careers at The University of Chicago, were highly influenced by the Chicago School, and moved beyond what they had learned from that school—primarily by recovering a radically empirical tradition which the Chicago School had neglected. For them, radical empiricism had general theological implications;

it suggested even a view of history. Furthermore and not incidentally, crucial to that view of history was the presence of evil.

According to Meland's and Loomer's radically empirical orientation, the philosophical and theological libido for abstraction carries a real danger, especially when it eliminates the concrete. In the Hellenistic West, abstract schemes sometimes replace the plurality of the historical world with a monolithic and essential world; and, with no apparent logical necessity but with an unnerving regularity, these schemes picture this essential world as an ideal world. The social importance of such essentialist schemes is that they ostensibly tell us how to receive that unambiguously ideal world into the actualities of history. Because such abstract schemes eliminate from actuality (beginning as they do, not with the richness of the actual world, but with the order of the ideal world), they overlook certain aspects of history, and in particular they overlook the presence of evil. Further, they imply that the responsibility for introducing the ideal into history lies not with historical creatures but with an extrahistorical reality of some kind.

It could be argued that Meland's and Loomer's empiricist epistemology and their discernment of evil in history intensified each other. Free from at least an explicit commitment to schemes pointing beyond history, they could look at the evidence for historical evil more directly. Their resulting consciousness of historical evil pushed them in turn to be even more empirical. Because they became relatively inured to the fact that evil permeated even the theological authorities—the scriptures, the institutions, the scholarship, the *a priori* reason—they relied even more on what an empiricism might add to their understanding.

Meland's and Loomer's radical empiricism can be expressed this way: if your empiricism is based not only on the facts perceived by the five senses, but on the relations between the facts perceived by the affections as well, then you will be aware of a broader range of phenomena. Meland preceded Loomer in urging the reader to remember that the phenomena are both attractive and repulsive, both creative and destructive, and to oppose the theological tendency to treat the attractive and creative phenomena as the more real. Loomer went on to argue that when specific creative phenomena are isolated and identified with the ultimate, the ultimate becomes a one-sided abstraction, which is to say that it is not empirically adequate to the world in which it is thought to be ultimate. He argued that an empirically radical experience of the deepest resources of history in its entirety is always mixed, always involves both attraction and repulsion, both the creative and the destructive.

When Meland and Loomer rejected were the last chapters of the more rationalized and domesticated religions, as those chapters drew the line, blinded one eye, and found something nice to say, whether about communities, about metaphysical foundations, or about God. Meland's and Loomer's effort was to keep both eyes working, and, as a result, to see both the good in history and the evil in history and to find this commentary on the ambiguity of history also a theological commentary.

Now keeping both eyes open is what made them radically historicist— that is, allowed them to see history itself as formed also by spiritual values that are ambiguous. And their effort, while exceptional in its time, was both unoriginal and American. For they followed the radical historicisms of William James, John Dewey, George Herbert Mead, Alfred North Whitehead, William Carlos Williams, Carl Becker, and many others in a peculiarly American form of practical, empirical, pluralistic, and historicist thinking.

These various outcroppings of radical historicism often resulted from erosions in social history, As for Meland and Loomer, they had witnessed World War II, were deeply affected by the cosmological meanings of the new physics, by the cultural pluralism introduced by closer relations with Asia, by the McCarthyism of the 1950s, and by the prevailing shallowness of higher education. The atomic bomb, in particular, became for them a metaphor. These events, in turn, seemed to have had two kinds of effects on the thinking of Meland and Loomer: (1) a loss of the modernist confidence that the world was rational and tractable, that it could be understood by and controlled through strict methodologies which would give certainty through cognition; and (2) a loss of the Christian-Hellenistic confidence that the evils of history could be separated from the ultimate goodness of history. These general effects are reflected in the views of education espoused by each of them.

Bernard Meland's comments on education are set against the historical backdrop of the years immediately following World War II. In his first two books after the war, Meland makes initial reference to the shape and feel of current historical events, as he does in almost every book written thereafter. *Seeds of Redemption* is based on lectures written for delivery during what turned out to be the weeks of the atomic bombing of Hiroshima and Nagasaki. The "Preface," surely written after the bombing, opens with these sentences.

> The energies of new growth are pushing beneath the soil of *a world become a desert* . . . . Something radically redemptive must occur within five years or less, changing in decisive ways, if not the hearts of men, at least their ways and organized efforts . . . . No one is really realistic who has not faced the possibility of the utter end of this human venture as history has known it.[42]

He proceeds to discuss the collaboration of physics and chemistry with governmental and industrial power, and the ineptitude of the spiritual culture in answering the perilous question of the times. He exclaims at one point: "Let our people face the fact! We have all failed."[43] In the 1947 lectures comprising *The Reawakening of the Christian Faith,* Meland makes reference to the "tragedy that stalks our path."[44]

In each book he traces the social problem in large part to the prevailing, narrow, science-based and technology-based understandings of human nature, and the ways in which they have led to practices, including educational practices, which distort the human spirit. Accordingly, *The Seeds of Redemption* recommends an epistemological solution: "the awakening in religion itself to an empirical understanding of the processes of grace and redemption that proceed from the creative work of God."[43] Similarly, in *The Reawakening of the Christian Faith,* Meland is struck with the epistemological sources of the problem: "Once one is seized by the disturbing idea that reason and observation give only truncated accounts of existence, one is no longer able to be complacently empirical, nor content to remain inhospitable to imaginative efforts to comprehend the human problem in its vaster context."[46] Meland moves quite naturally, then, from a social history dominated by the bomb to a view of education that is empirical but not "complacently empirical."

Meland's most extensive treatment of education is his 1953 *Higher Education and the Human Spirit.* The book argues that the abuse of education is caused by narrow views of human nature. Meland faults educational theorists for making this mistake; and he singles out John Dewey for his unduly behavioral interpretation of education and Robert Maynard Hutchins for his unduly intellectualistic interpretation of education. Meland believes that Dewey usually reduces pragmatism to what is practical in resolving physical predicaments, while by comparison William James properly had included in pragmatism what is practical in resolving nonphysical (that is, moral, aesthetic, and religious) predicaments as well. For James, the key to pragmatism is not exclusively what is active, but what is particular, whether it be theoretical, emotional, passive, or active.[47] Hutchins's analytic approach, on the other hand, had stressed principles and premises, and emphasized coherence rather than behavior as the core of the intellectual life. Education for Dewey tended to be guided by behavioral ends; for Hutchins, it was guided by intellectual ends. Meland cited as similarly truncated the moral view of human nature taken by Kant and the rationalistic view taken by Aristotle, and spelled out the overly narrow educational objectives which followed from those notions of human nature.[48]

For his part, Meland relies on James and Bergson and calls for a more inclusive view of human nature and for the philosophy of education which follows from that view. This third view, between behaviorialism and intellectualism, between moralism and rationalism, is open, Meland claims, to the depths of life, the subtleties of relations, and the imaginings of the human heart—all properly central not only to the human spirit but to the educational processes which will nurture that spirit. Meland advocates an "appreciative awareness" for which the authority is the "wisdom of the body," not the clear and distinct structures of behaviorism and intellectualism. While Meland looks to Alfred North Whitehead and, to a lesser extent, to the nonbehavioristic writings of John Dewey and Henry Nelson Wieman, he follows most explicitly James, who offered "the most impressive justification for sensitive awareness in thought which is to be found either in philosophical or psychological literature."[49] Meland calls for an awareness which "takes as its starting point the mystery of what is given in . . . the rich fullness of the concrete event with all of its possibilities and relations, imagined or perceived."[50] He stresses the sense of the physical relations which connect events, and the vague and adumbrative meanings which underlie the surfaces of mere consciousness.

The implications for education are obvious. Education, which is crystaline in its clarity and which treats adversely all that is smeared or otiose, finally prefers the part to the whole, the superficial to the profound. For Meland, education should begin with a Jamesean appreciation of physical complexities rather than with a Cartesian antagonism for imprecision. Only later, gradually and tentatively, should discriminations be added to these uncritical initial perceptions. New pedagogies and curricula should be built on this approach—for example, the arts should become a major resource in liberal learning.

The implications for theological study also are obvious. Religious faith and inquiry should begin with "our attachment to life as creatures," with this "most elemental condition of existence."[51] Meland identifies God not as universally implicated in all forms of life, the evil as well as the good, but exclusively in those "facts and meanings that define life as good." Meland goes on to say that "without the incentive to say that life is good, without the impulse to praise life, the religious response cannot emerge—save as a retreat from existence."[52] Nevertheless, with a historicist rigor rare among theologians Meland saw evil as so basic to the world that "the problem of good" (how can goodness enter a world so fundamentally evil?) appears at times just as real as the problem of evil (how can evil enter a world so fundamentally good?).[53] There is, Meland allowed, a slight margin of goodness in the world, and the explanation for this margin is a God who is "qualified by his goodness." "God's goodness may thus be viewed operationally as his participation in events which move toward qualitative attainment."[54]

While Meland does not arrive at the point of naming God ambiguous, his sense of the ambiguity of theology itself may be more complete than that of any American theologian. In his last book, *Fallible Forms and Symbols,* he criticizes the presumption of mid-twentieth-century theologians, particularly their lust to establish the correctness of their own theological forms and symbols. That presumption of "seeking to wrest the fire and efficacy of reality . . . is blasphemous, and carries within its own degree of dementia."[55] His theological colleagues and their work suffer from an appalling intellectual pride, and this is a direct consequence of their failure to recognize the myriad ways in which life outruns their cognitive appraisals—their inattentiveness, really, to what could have been learned from American radical empiricism.

For Meland, this leads to a radically empirical pedagogy, where God is found in the immediacies of experience, or nowhere. In *Fallible Forms and Symbols,* the term *God* refers to the "Creative Passage" within the stream of events; God is found in the thrust of creativity operative in the myths and structures of communal history. In addition to the conservative Christian emphasis on the presence of God within the cultic experience and the liberal Christian emphasis on the presence of God within personal experience, Meland argues for the presence of God within culture: the total complex of human gestures, languages, arts, and symbols. Meland is, more than anything else, a cultural theologian, but unlike Tillich and other Germanic thinkers, he sees culture not rationally in its ontological logos, not mystically in a numinous oneness, but historically in an observed congeries of plural phenomena. In this he saw himself as extending the Chicago School's sociohistorical method,[56] but his empiricist and historicist horror at scholarly pretension and his empirical appreciation of the subtle and the contingent surpassed anything found in his Chicago predecessors.

Above all, Meland's adoption of radical empiricism as a device for probing the valuational depths of history could serve as a corrective to today's new historicism. Today's new historicists. without an epistemology and without a way of expressing the values they affirm and apparently intuit in history, suffer from a void in their thought that Meland's use of James could serve to fill. Meland finds an American way, a way germane to his own culture, to discern the moral, aesthetic, and religious burden of history, and offers a more complete and, for some, a more persuasive historicism.

Equally, Bernard Loomer seems to have translated the social crises of his day into views on the nature of education. In retrospect, he seems to have probed more extensively and disturbingly the implications of an empiricist epistemology and a theological historicism. Finally, his notion of the ambiguity of God (an idea perhaps never systematically expressed in American religious thought) carries profound and practical implications for today's new historicism.

In 1947, during Loomer's tenure as Dean of the Divinity School of The University of Chicago, he proposed to his colleagues a response to the threat of nuclear war. His proposal was born of the special circumstances at the University of Chicago: the first sustained nuclear reaction was accomplished at the university with Chicago scientists in December 1942; in late summer 1947, the research scientists at Oak Ridge, Tennessee had just been placed under the direction of The University of Chicago; in the intervening years the university remained the nation's preeminent center for nuclear research. By fall 1947, Loomer says, it was apparent that "a new world was emerging before our very eyes. Most of us were increasingly cognizant that this new world of atomic power posed a serious threat to humanity's future, but we felt powerless to offset the seeming autonomous direction and decisive role of this new force in human life."[57] After extensive discussions, Loomer, as Dean, led the Divinity School faculty to propose that the University of Chicago community "could discharge its moral responsibility and continue its research in atomic energy only under conditions such as the three following which should be presented to the United States government: (1) that the United States government immediately call a constitutional convention for the purpose of establishing a world government; (2) that the Marshall Plan be extended to any nation which attends the convention; (3) that upon the adoption of the constitution the United States will surrender its knowledge of the atomic bomb to the world government."[58] In the last analysis, this was a Lysistrata proposal: if the government failed to agree to these conditions, the scientists at Chicago would terminate all research contributing to nuclear weapons development. The desperation of the times is connoted by the extremity of the proposal.

But the resolution was killed by the council of the academic deans of the university, a defeat which affected Loomer profoundly. According to Loomer, what finally was at issue was the "integrity within the University as a whole."[59] Integrity for an educational institution is lost when the relations between the several areas of the university, as well as the relations between the university and the society, become dis-integrated. Integrity for the researcher is lost when research is dis-integrated from its social consequences, from other areas of human inquiry, or from the researcher's sense of moral responsibility. The resounding defeat of the resolution represented the dis-integration particularly in relations between departments (the unwillingness of one department to consider another department's request that it terminate its nuclear research) and in the relations between the university and the government (the unwillingness of the university to consider its responsibility for the government's use of weapons the university had made possible). For Loomer, the defeat of the Divinity School's resolution meant the loss of a unique and historic opportunity. In his perceived world of education, it was a palpable evil.

A few years later, in his 1951 "Religion and the Mind of the University," Loomer argued that such dis-integration was endemic to the professorial mind wherever it is found. He contended that the "god of the university professor is specialized competence. His whole intellectual life is defined in terms of it and all the rest of his life is dependent upon it."[60] Competence is rated above integrity not only in the typically narrow commitment to a discipline, but in the even narrower commitment to one's own research within a discipline.

Much like the current new historicists thirty years later, Loomer argued that integrity calls for an interdisciplinary conversation and a pragmatic standard. "A constructive and adequate theology," he said, "must prove itself to be such in terms of its more fruitful intellectual implications and consequences for other academic disciplines."[61] Apart from such a proof, a discipline deserves to be forgotten. However, unlike the current historicists, Loomer contended that the theologian must work specifically at a noncognitive and radically empiricical level of knowing. The student of religion, for example, demonstrates the consequences of religion by making scholars in other disciplines "aware of the implicit religious assumptions in terms of which they have been operating," and by analyzing those assumptions for their adequacy.[62] These assumptions, like all religious assumptions, are not primarily intellectual. "Religion's greatest contribution," Loomer said, "may not be exclusively or even primarily intellectual."[63] The theologian's work in the academy may involve, for example, an analysis of the class-born presuppositions animating the work of an economic or political theorist or the deep ideological and historical commitments of two rival groups of physicists; and it may determine that these assumptions are so fundamental that they are religious.

In his 1965 "Reflections on Theological Education," Loomer extended his notion of integrity to assert that academic degrees should be awarded on the basis of "an achieved maturity." Here integrity refers to the integration among the student's various ideas and the integration between the student's ideas and his or her nonintellectual life. "In theological education the movement toward integrity becomes perhaps most intense at the point of the relation between our ideas and our emotional life."[64] When Loomer included aspects of emotional life as qualifiers for the awarding of a degree, it was as though he had calculated his words to offend his "disinterested" colleagues. Whether that is true, Loomer's theory of education was exceptional in being pragmatic (asking about the bearing of the student's ideas on society) and in being radically empirical (declaring that the student's emotional experience is germane to his or her cognitive experience).

The approach Loomer develops in his comments on education is most vividly expressed in his 1978 "The Size of God"—published, together with a biographical introduction and several critical responses, in *The Size of God: The Theology of Bernard Loomer in Context*.[65] He opens by professing not "the wisdom of the sojourner, who was made in the image of his creator and who travels lightly through his terrestrial pilgrimage because his destiny is a transcendent home," but "the wisdom of the evolved earth-creature, whose spirit had its origin in the flames of the stars and the dust of the planet, whose home is the earth, whose destiny, or that of his descendents, may be extinction or life among the stars, and whose fulfillment as an individual and as a species requires a deep attachment to the humanizing processes of this life."[66]

To convey this American religious naturalism, Loomer returned explicitly to the earlier history of radical empiricism, and used that as his key: "The present discussion, " Loomer said, "continues the empirical tradition within this general understanding of the nature of things. It was James who suggested in 1907 that 'some kind of an immanent or pantheistic working *in* things rather than above them is, if any, the kind recommended to our contemporary imagination.'"[67] Accordingly, Loomer moved beyond his typical talk about method and made an effort to characterize experienced fact. This effort led, in turn, to the awareness of unavoidable ambiguity in human life, six characteristics of which Loomer enumerates. First, each decision involves ambiguity because what it accepts always contains some evils and what it rejects always contains some goods. Second, because we are partially constituted by relations with the world, we cannot avoid internalizing the evils of that world along with the goods of that world. Loomer divides into third and fourth kinds of ambiguities the various and unavoidable ways in which just those energies which promote growth and good results are the same energies which promote internal degeneration and bad results. Fifth, we necessarily work at cross purposes with ourselves, for we can be sustained only if the full expression of some of our potentials are stifled. Sixth, because our virtues and vices have the same origin, they cannot be separated; if you want the virtues, you must retain the associated vices; there is no avoiding it.

Now when theologians hide these human ambiguities, Loomer said, they do it by selective emphasis—which is to say, by abstraction. It is just such abstraction about human nature and about human ideals that led to abstract theories about the unambiguous perfection of God. Theology, in fact, generally tends to be animated by a "passion for perfection," a desire to find a realm free of the admixture of evil. This passion more than anything is "a protest against the unmanageable vitalities of concrete life. It is yearning for the bloodless existence of clean-cut orderly abstractions. It is, in short, a yearning for death."[68] Loomer insists that ambiguity, not perfection, itself must be valued in theology, because ambiguity is unavoidable in life as it actually is.

Radical empiricism, then, led to the unorthodox account of God that characterizes the essay. No longer, Loomer implies, should one attempt to understand God through either rationalistic theory or through a one-sided concentration on the good. God, says Loomer, must be "identified" with the "totality of the concrete actual world," not with a part of or an abstraction from the totality.[69] The implication is clear: there is no way of avoiding the recognition that if the world is experienced as ambiguous, then God must be ambiguous. If evil is inherent in the concreteness of the world, then evil is inherent in the reality of God. We find in God both the attractive and the repulsive, the constructive and the destructive valencies in history. God is exemplified both in "an expansive urge toward greater good" and in "a passion for greater evil."[70] Loomer separates himself, then, from Charles Hartshorne, Henry Nelson Wieman, and Alfred North Whitehead, as well as from more orthodox Christian theologians, when they all propose the unambiguous goodness of God. However well-intentioned, they tend to worship not the God of the world, but the human ideal of perfection. For Loomer there is no "problem of evil"; God is no longer uniformly good (God's influence is as likely to be destructive as to be creative); consequently, the existence of evil is no puzzle.

What is left for religion after such an argument? Clearly, it is no longer the search for the perfect order, but for the fullest range of historical data, including the range of good and evil. It should aim, above all, to achieve for society the aesthetic appreciation of the pluralities of history, in all their unreconciled diversities and incompatibilities. Loomer introduced the word *stature* to describe the nature of a person or of a group achieving that appreciation; and stature came to supersede *integrity* as Loomer's key word. *Stature* is the drive to internalize the fullest range of experiences possible—just to that point where a fuller range would create so great an internal diversity that internal unity would be destroyed. Certainly, Loomer's earlier notion of integrity had been a mandate towards comprehensiveness; but it aimed to make life benignly and rationally cohere and it missed the wildness of the world, the unexpected and irresolvable ambiguities within the full range of experience. Stature focused on just those ambiguities, particularly the ambiguous combination of good and evil in all things. The greater the diversity of experienced contradictions, the greater the stature, for stature is a "a function of the inclusiveness of the communal web in which we feel at home."[71]

Loomer's own version of the aesthetic category of unity in diversity had become caustic, and it had caustic implications for religious life. To religiously serve stature is to promote as much diversity as an individual or a group can tolerate without losing its own identity, "to create those kinds of relationships from which more complex individuals and societies of greater stature may emerge."[72] Loomer's particular inference from this was that religion should foster the appreciation of the full range of God's ambiguity, the appreciation that God is "the organic restlessness of the whole body of creation."[73]

The implications for the new historicism would seem to follow directly, although Loomer did not state them. The most complete knowledge of history would be an empirical account of the ambiguities of history. When today's new historicism focuses on the emerging differences in words and ideas through the temporal chain of texts, it is certainly consistent with Loomer's program. But to the extent that the new historicism neglects values and the ambiguities among values in history, it neglects the fullest and, perhaps, the most crucial aspect of history. For Loomer, God would be the organizing center for a new historicist approach, for God is the most comprehensive expression of our history's continuous movement toward greater stature. The idea of God would function in the new historicism as an expression of history's drive for ever-larger unification through time of the full range of diversities, including valuational diversities. Theology, as the effort to describe our history's vector towards increasing ambiguity, would be an indispensible aspect of any new historicist program.

Loomer's signal reminder to today's new historicist is that there is every empirical reason to believe that our history and its general impetus are tragically ambiguous, and that they do not necessarily foster a good, a redemptive, a creative conversational community. In their utter ambiguity, our history and its God are as likely to engender conversations and interactions that are destructive as conversations and interactions that are creative. Loomer's point is that history, when seen without the dominating obsession for rational coherence, is invariably and valuationally ambiguous; and God is the expression for history's vector toward increasing ambiguity and stature. So Loomer abandons the hope for a benign context, the hope so characteristic of most Jewish and Christian institutions, and, apparently, of most fellowships of new historicists. The idea of God suggests that the conversation will grow richer aesthetically, but not that it will grow better morally.

The moral obligation rests in the hands of the persons who converse, just as James and Dewey had recognized, and not in the "will" of history or history's God. One theological implication for the new historicism is clear: in the words of Shirley Jackson Case, "The making of religious history is a heavy responsibility to place upon mankind."[74] Worse, to make this conversation and community creative a tendency inherent in history must be fought.

It is just such implications that are unexamined in a new historicism without an empirical epistemology, without a radical historicism, and without an American religious component. The introduction of an American religious historicism into the new historicism could contribute to its empirical adequacy and its valuational sophistication.

CHAPTER 6

Beyond Method:
Toward a Concept of God

We may regard the chase for truth as paramount, and the
avoidance of error as secondary; or we may, on the other hand,
treat the avoidance of error as more imperative, and let truth
take its chance. Clifford . . . exhorts us to the latter course.
Believe nothing, he tells us, keep your mind in suspense
forever, rather than by closing it on insufficient evidence incur
the awful risk of believing lies. You, on the other hand, may
think that the risk of being in error is a very small matter when
compared with the blessings of real knowledge, and be ready
to be duped many times in your investigation rather than
postpone indefinitely the chance of guessing true.

—William James, "The Will to Believe"[1]

For James, life is a struggle to evolve, not a procedure
for avoiding wounds. According to James, W. K. Clifford was so intent on
avoiding wounds that he effectively withdrew from real intellectual struggle.
This is what happens, James warned, when the skeptical preoccupation prevails,
as it has in the modern world.

In this one respect, today's new historicists, both outside and inside
religious thought, whatever their enormous strengths in advancing a new and
"postmodern" historicism, stand with Descartes, Hume, Kant, and W. K. Clifford. Although they break with the modernists by adopting a historicism that
is pluralistic and pragmatic, and by rejecting a foundationalism, realism, and
the transcendentalized subject, in this one respect their historicism is not a
break with modernism but its extension. Richard Rorty, Richard Bernstein,
Nelson Goodman, Hillary Putnam, Mark C. Taylor, Jeffrey Stout, and many
others tend to be so dominated by the skeptical question that the center of

their thought is method—where method is understood to be, more than anything else, the painstaking effort to say the way thought should proceed if false claims are to be avoided. Despite their innovative zest, sometimes their tone is quaintly stern, warning others that they must not believe what they are inclined to believe. This admonitory and methodological caution is implicit even in the titles of their best recent books: *Philosophy and the Mirror of Nature* (beware of false mirrors); *Beyond Objectivism and Relativism* (beware of false methods); *Flight from Authority* (beware of those who flee authority); *Erring* or *Against Method* (beware of the inerrant and the methodic). The primary mission is not to move positively toward new truths, but to avoid the historic mistakes. Even their rashness in rejecting traditions of thought smells chaste, untouched as they now are by the sins of realism, transcendental subjectivism, or foundationalism. In their strenuous rejection of past inerrancy they become inerrantly modest.

If, the point is, today's new historicists are too thin, too empty of claims for truth or, as we have said earlier, of ways of perceiving values in history, if they miss the historicism of the classical American philosophers and theologians, it is because they have come to their historicism by way of European thinkers who taught them that the real problem is making errors. Even as they have rejected most doctrines of their heroes, they have retained their heroic, error-hating methodological attitude.

By contrast, the classical American philosophers and theologians were more interested in knowing truth than in avoiding error, even if that meant getting duped repeatedly. When these philosophers and theologians turned away from modes of thought that centered on method, they turned toward a field of knowledge. For them, this field can be described best by the term *nature*. They replaced the prevailing and predominantly European methodologism with naturalism.

James and Dewey and (here I include) Whitehead and the Chicago School religious thinkers and the religious empiricists such as Meland and Loomer, were marked by a common trait: at some point in their lives they abandoned the modernist hope that confusion could be dispelled through the right method. James broke with the physiological materialism that dominated his medical studies; Dewey broke with Hegelian intellectualism; Whitehead broke with the *a priori* method of mathematical logic. The Chicago School theologians and the religious empiricists broke not only with biblical authoritarianism, but with the quest for universal theological truth. Meland broke with Henry Nelson Wieman's behaviorism; Loomer broke with Whitehead's, Wieman's, and Hartshorne's search for perfection.

They all appropriated a picture of the world as their starting point, but their world was not the supernaturalist order of the premodernists, nor was it the scientific or rationalistic orders of the modernist. It was a world in which, not intellectual order, but historical process was primary, and in which the course of that process was not metaphysically bounded, but simply was chosen—by the interpretations of the historical actors. Because this historical process included, particularly for Dewey and Whitehead, more than human, cultural history, because it centered on nonhuman history, it can be called a naturalistic historicism; or, technically, a neonaturalism; or, in this special sense, a naturalism. And, from this picture of the world, all else followed—even, but quite secondarily, method. The method that followed was a method of openness. It was not a freestanding method, which assumed that adherence to the right procedure assured the avoidance of error. It was a method that leaned on a worldview and aimed to test that worldview.

On the other hand, today's new historicists seem to stand with the main line of modern thinkers in believing that it is more important to know how to think than to know what to think; it is better to be wrong for the right reasons, than to be right for the wrong reasons. They may have thrown out Descarte's metaphysical bath water, but they kept his methodological baby. They may reject his particular anxiety, but they stand shoulder to shoulder with his attempt to avoid error by beginning again, this time the right way—that is, not with the opinions of authorities but with some new procedure. They may have denied Kant's effort to hang method on certain permanent and universal forms of sensing and knowing, but they kept his preoccupation with procedure, his effort to lay out a methodological route that avoids the dead ends of those who had tried before. With Hans-Georg Gadamer they may claim to reject the sufficiency of scientific methods and any preoccupation with "a problem of method at all."[2] But whether they are hermeneutical or neopragmatic, whether they are textual or conversational, they demonstrate their faith that in a procedure lies the answer to our problems. In this particular respect they are modernists—which is not to deny the postmodern novelty of so much else that they do.

The deconstructionists and neopragmatists, like sojourners, travel lightly through this world, concentrating on how best they might approach it—if they choose to approach it at all. Even in these desperate times, they seldom begin by asking, What is this world? Instead, they first don the right clothes and mount the right horse and only then seek whatever today might be the quarry. Methodological proprieties come first.

By comparison, the classical American philosophers and theologians were earth-creatures already embedded in a natural process. They were more interested in the fact that they were actually related to the world than in the many ways in which that fact systematically might be known, authorized, and tested.

They were naturalists first, seeking, more than anything, to interact effectively with a context. Method was primarily a device for elaborating and testing their naturalism. They called their context natural to distinguish it from a supernatural context on one side and from an exclusively human context on the other side. When, more specifically, they called themselves neonaturalists, they distinguished themselves from nineteenth-century, positivistic, deterministic, materialistic naturalists. Usually, they were not humanists who included nature; they were naturalists who included the human only because it was part of natural history. They were not modernists for whom avoiding error through foolproof techniques was primary, but postmodernists who began within the natural process, within what today is called the chain of signs or the conversation, but who included the nonhuman "signs" and "conversations" as well as the human. Method, then, became important only as a means of developing that interaction. Speaking religiously, because faith in the natural process was primary, for them it was simply sacreligious to put methodology first. To put first the "right" position on epistemology, tests for truth, or fine points of metaphysics was equivalent to worshipping the icon, the priest, the book.

Alternatively, today's new historicist tends still to believe that, if a procedure is followed undeviatingly, tracked to its very end, then the truth will be found; or, at the very least, the commitment to technique will have been so heroic that even to miss the truth and remain skeptical is not truly a defeat but somehow a victory. It is as though the methodologist deserves to control the world if he or she is serious enough about how to do it. Today's historicists tend to love lockerrooms, where they formulate the right plan of attack, where actually playing to know the truth is better ignored.

SOURCES OF METHODOLOGISM

For what historical reasons should today's deconstructionists have gravitated to methodologism? One explanation—but certainly not the only explanation—lies in their connection with modern European philosophers. Methodologism characterizes the mainstream of modern European thought, from Descartes to Derrida. (By methodologism I mean: (1) the belief that a previous intellectual failure can be traced to a failure, not in what to think, but in how to think, a failure to select, for example, the right authority, the right way of knowing, or in the right way of justifying claims to knowledge; and (2) the belief that the best cure for failure is to adopt a new procedure of thought.) The problem for Descartes came, primarily, to a problem of method. Confronted with the intellectual skepticism brought about by the demise of previously accepted church authorities, Descartes's answer was a new procedure of justification. He sought, first of all, not better knowledge, but a better *scientia,* a better mode of demonstration;[3] and in this Descartes set the pattern for modern philosophy. In seeking a better mode of demonstration, Descartes turned, then, from external authorities to procedures internal to the knower, and in this he was in strange accord with Martin Luther. (For the answer to religious confusion, according to Luther, really was not only *sola scriptura,* for scripture could err and was subject to conflicting interpretations; the final source of certainty for Luther was the method of faith, the capacity to discern the Word. Finally, Luther's method for reaching right religious conclusions, like Descartes's, was subjectivistic.) Now the modern problematique of skepticism and subjectivistic methods endured through the eighteenth century, even when subjectivistic justification took a beating at the hands of David Hume.

Immanuel Kant's methodologism is the most vivid reiteration of the Cartesian approach between the seventeenth century and the present. Kant attempted to circumvent modern objections to knowledge by responding, first, to David Hume's contention that all nonanalytic and nonsynthetic judgments are worthless. Kant believed that this would eliminate not only metaphysics, a loss Hume expected, but natural science and mathematics, a loss Hume had not expected. For Kant, this meant that science and mathematics must be justified on the basis of some third kind of judgment that Hume had missed: the synthetic *a priori.* That is, certain notions (e.g., causation) are synthetic and not analytic (e.g., because causation is not contained in such notions as "that which happens"); and yet they are *a priori* and not contingent because they are necessary to all possible experience. Kant's point here is methodological; his interest in the sciences had to do with "*how* they are possible," not with the fact that they are true, something obvious to everyone.[4] His emphasis is on methodology, on how we can know what we already know. And Kant's explanation is subjectivistic in that it explains how we know by introducing the synthetic *a priori,* which is a form of human thought. Equally, when explaining moral or practical reason, Kant's aim is not to set forth moral truths; in fact, he claims that his moral conclusions are purely formal. His problem is methodological: to explain how, given the chaos of empirically conditioned reason and the moral skepticism it introduces, moral judgments are possible.[5] And, again, his explanation is subjectivistic: that is, it refers to the will and the direction of the will by *a priori,* autonomous reason, rather than by any divine, social, or empirical causes.

It seems, then, that Kant accepted Descartes's problematic—namely, that we hold false opinions because we use wrong procedure. Kant focused on skepticism, not on the nature of the world. While he could have chosen to propound an alternative view of the world, he set forth instead a method—a procedure for answering skepticism, a dodge around that particular obstacle. To develop his methodological answer, he turned to the one thing even a skeptic would accept, the deliverances of the internal self. For Kant, then, as for Descartes, the progress was from skepticism about our knowledge, to a method establishing that knowledge is possible.

However, Kant had left open the question of solipsism, of whether the objective world, nature, the thing-in-itself, is known, or whether the self actually is talking only to itself. In the third critique, Kant attempts to answer this question by turning to the artistic genius, whose talent gives to art a rule taken from nature. "Since talent," says Kant, "as an innate productive faculty of the artist, belongs itself to nature, we may put it this way: *Genius* is the innate mental aptitude (*ingenium*) *through which* nature gives the rule to art."[6] However, Kant's solution was jeopardized, for even here his answer was subjectivistic. As Hegel noted, the genius's work of art remains abstract, a human artifact, and fails to be located concretely in space and time.

Hegel attempted to correct this subjectivism by rationally demonstrating how the spirit itself, the spirit in its purely subjective form, can be understood as the spirit for itself, the spirit as objective. "In this way," Hegel says, "it is in its existence aware of itself as an object in which its own self is reflected."[7] Hegel's aim was to move beyond Kant, from the implicit objectification to the explicit and rational demonstration of the objectification of the subjective spirit. And Hegel thought of his philosophy as "scientific" just to the degree that it succeeded in doing this. Hegel's work, however, is always haunted by the rejoinder that the so-called objectivity of spirit is merely a construct of the subjective self. And Hegel's own methodologism is found in the priority he gives in all his work to the task of simply being "scientific," of demonstrating that and how the translation from the subjective to the objective is possible.

An argument for how the methodologistic preoccupation has been sustained more recently on the Continent, particularly in France, can be taken from Mark C. Taylor's comprehensive "Introduction" to his anthology, *Deconstruction in Context.* Taylor's account begins with the assertion that "the Western philosophical project can be understood as the repeated effort to overcome plurality and establish unity by reducing the many to the one."[8] Taylor argues that this project has been countered by a succession of thinkers from Kierkegaard, Nietzsche, Husserl, Saussure, Heidegger, Wittgenstein, Sartre, Merleau-Ponty, Emmanuel Levinas, Georges Bataille, Maurice Blanchot, on down to Derrida. These philosophers, unlike Descartes and Kant and, to some extent, Hegel, aim not to reduce plurality to unity, difference to identity, or objectivity to subjectivity, but to do just the reverse. Taylor argues that in this process the subject has been "deconstructed"; and this is true in the technical sense that the unifying constructions of the ontologizing subject have been dismantled. Taylor does not note, however, that by no means has subjectivism itself been overcome.

If the major consequence of the deconstruction of the ontologizing self has been the recognition that unity has been reduced to plurality and identity has been reduced to difference, then the subject, living isolated from the world beyond itself, has no choice but to authorize its own solitary interpretation. Ironically, while the transcendental self may have been deconstructed, this led to a new, more intense subjectivism and methodologism, a preoccupation with understanding how one understands anything at all. It may be that Western thought was committed to projecting identities and unities, and that the Continental postmodernists have overcome these identities and unities by deconstructing them. Nevertheless, they have perpetuated the modernist love for method and the subject. Taylor's own brilliant and historicist *Erring* is a case in point, for it exhausts itself in metaphors concerning how we should proceed in this brave new historicist world, and says almost nothing about what for Taylor and his history the local truth might be.[9]

A similar preoccupation with methodology characterizes the neopragmatic thinkers in the United States, specifically Richard Rorty, Richard Bernstein, Nelson Goodman, and Hilary Putnam. Their methodologism is rather straightforward. As I noted repeatedly in earlier chapters, the neopragmatists argue that "conversation," the procedure of communicating without the comfort of ontological support, is the saving method.

Richard Bernstein, in *Beyond Objectivism and Relativism,* declares himself beyond the "Cartesian anxiety" that has driven us to methodologies and then to the equally problematic forms of nihilistic relativism. Nevertheless, Berstein's summary of Gadamer, Habermas, Rorty, and Arendt, and his own conclusions point, once again, toward the sufficiency of method—this time, to the method of "cultivating the types of dialogical communities in which *phronesis,* judgment, and practical discourse become concretely embodied in our everyday practices."[10]

Equally, Richard Rorty advances a methodology when he calls conversation hermeneutical and edifying. Hermeneutics replaces the "epistemological" claim "that man has an essence-namely, to discover essences";[11] and edifying philosophy replaces "systematic philosophy, " which contends that the entire culture will benefit if it emulates a particular philosophical practice. But hermeneutics and edifying philosophy are simply methods. So when Rorty claims that hermeneutics "is basically not a problem of method at all,"[12] he is merely denying that hermeneutics seeks essentialist epistemologies whereby one procedure becomes the key to commensurability. He would have us replace a fixation on essences with a fixation on methods. Rorty's actual and sustaining methodologism is best represented by his claim that "the way things are said is more important than the possession of truths" and "that the point of edifying philosophy is to keep the conversation going rather than to find objective truth."[13] Here, at least, conversation itself—simply the procedure itself—is supreme, and not the truth it finds or the action to which it leads.

Nelson Goodman's pragmatism also fits this general neopragmatic methodological paradigm. Goodman places himself in a line with Kant, who "exchanged the structure of the world for the structure of the mind" and with C.I. Lewis, who "exchanged the structure of the mind for the structure of concepts." Goodman, himself, exchanges "the structure of concepts for the structure of the several symbol systems."[14] The vital question, then, is the methodological question of whether a belief fits into the symbol system of a group of people. Goodman's *Ways of Worldmaking* is just that—a commentary on how right beliefs are constructed rather than on what they are.

Hilary Putnam seems to be the neopragmatist most likely to avoid a subjectivistic methodologism, given his impatience with the subjectivistic extremes of Thomas Kuhn, Paul Feyerabend, and Richard Rorty and his sense of the importance of making "transcendental arguments" that would describe general conditions.[15] Nevertheless, Putnam confesses to being a neo-Kantian "internalist,"[16] one who finds his mission largely in demonstrating how our claims to external truth in fact are comments on what is internal to our own thought— even if he is not an internalist who with Feyerabend will say, "Anything goes." In *Reason, Truth and History,* for example, he appears more interested in this methodological gambit, than with establishing anything true about the world.

SOURCES OF NATURALISM

The American deconstructionists and neopragmatists consistently refuse to move from their methodologism to some field of general knowledge, least of all to some kind of cosmology. Even though they may share the pragmatic method with the classical American pragmatists, the neopragmatists do not associate themselves with the cosmology of the classical American pragmatists. Presumably, they worry that to accept this cosmology would be to subvert their historicist methodology—this, despite the fact that the classical American pragmatists explicitly rejected the kinds of universal and eternal cosmological verities that would violate the historicism of the neopragmatists.

From the other side, the classical American philosophers and theologians share with the deconstructionists and the neopragmatists a fierce objection to extrahistorical claims. Their naturalism committed them to a procedure that avoids such commitments. They attempted to set forth a third position, beyond the metaphysical and epistemological search for essences later to be disparaged by both the Continental hermeneuticists and the American neopragmatists and beyond the simple relativistic denial of that search. When Richard Bernstein names the third option "beyond objectivism and relativism," he both does and does not name the effort of the classical American philosophers and theologians. He names it in that he points to a thirdness, but he does not name it when he leaves the naming of the thirdness at the level of methodology. The distinctiveness here of the classical American thinkers is that they named that world to which such a third methodology must point. They reappropriated the cosmological task; and from this, and this only, did their methodology follow.

The classical American philosophers and theologians approached the cosmological question by asking about the one and the many. Cosmologically, what lay behind the search for universal essences was the presumption, as Mark C. Taylor says, that plurality could be reduced to unity. The converse was a nihilistic contentment with sheer plurality, difference, and relativism. Now the classical American philosophers and theologians rejected extreme notions of both identity and difference, both monism and pluralism. In the first chapter of his *Pragmatism,* James flatly rejects both tender-minded, idealistic monism and tough-minded, materialistic pluralism. In the first chapter of his *Experience and Nature,* Dewey flatly rejects both idealistic unities and mechanistic pluralities, treating them as the unfortunate upshots of an ill-begotton spirit/body, self/world dualism. And in the particular area of cosmology Alfred North Whitehead can appropriately be called in to lend support to James and Dewey—if, that is, the less metaphysical, more historicist Whitehead is cited. Whitehead, in *Process and Reality,* rejected both "the subjectivist principle" with its monistic world pictures and "the sensationalistic principle" with its plurality of sense data.

These original new historicists sought a third cosmological position, one on which their historicism finally depended. It is a cosmology for which reality, itself, is the process of interpretation, or the living chain of interpretations. In this process, the individual is the interpreter of the world, whether that individual is a present self interpreting the past many or whether that individual is one among the past world's many—who once did interpret but now is interpreted. In this process, self and world are each both mind and body, both rational and physical, both faces of one reality that is better seen as an organic unity than as a two-layered duality. This position is not some third option which is an amalgam of extreme monism and extreme pluralism, an amalgam James called simply inconsistent.[17] It is a distinct, separate, and new position where, in the words of James, the world simply is "a rich and active commerce."[18]

Interpretation creates the world. For James, present truth, the currently successful decision about how to interpret the world, should be seen as itself constituting in part the future world's past. Consequently, "truth is *made,* just as health, wealth and strength are made, in the course of experience."[19] For Dewey, this means that the present act of interpretation "thus has a metaphysical implication"; it creates the deepest reality there is. Even thought, even imagination, contributes to the evolutionary process.

> Consequently reason, or thought, in its more general sense, has a real, though limited, function, a creative, constructive function. If we form general ideas and if we put them in action, consequences are produced which could not be produced otherwise. Under these conditions the world will be different from what it would have been if thought had not intervened.[20]

James, says Dewey, far from diminishing the importance of reason, gave reason a creative function. With his odd poetry, Whitehead claims that "any local agitation shakes the whole universe."[21] We have learned, says Whitehead in 1938, that nothing has a simple location at a point in space or time; field theory indicates that the only adequate outlook is to see all things related in process, the past always creating the present, the present always creating the future. No ostensible laws or universal principles escape this condition. Even "the laws of nature are merely all-pervading patterns of behaviour, of which the shift and discontinuance lie beyond our ken. Again, every science is an abstraction from the full concrete happenings of natures. But every abstraction neglects the influx of factors omitted into the factors retained."[22] For Whitehead, every event in the world, even the event in the mind of the person who composes a mathematical axiom, interprets the world it receives and contributes to the new world that follows. Every event is an interpretation, and every interpretation is an experience; and, Whitehead rants, "apart from the experiences of subjects there is nothing, nothing, nothing, bare nothingness."[23] And every subject feels, interprets, and constitutes the world in its distinct way.

James, Dewey, and Whitehead advance a cosmology in which the interpretive process is alone real, and in which that process is actualized and created only in the present subjective experience of interpretation. This is a third position. It is not a subjectivism, for subjective experience is understood to arise from past objects and to be validated or invalidated by reference to future objects. It is not an individualism, for in the most profound ways the self is social and historical in that it is internally related to and composed by its social past and externally related to and constitutive of the social future. Whitehead drew the fullest picture of a historical cosmology when he adopted a form of panpsychism, claiming that all present entities, from the present atom to the human thinker, are interpreting subjects. Yet his "reformed subjectivist principle" is thoroughly historicist as it embeds the subject in past and future societies.[24]

It is not as though this picture of the natural world is inconsistent with the methodologism of the deconstructionists and the neopragmatists. But they chose not to develop such a cosmology of interpretation or any other specific knowledge of the world. The effect of that choice is crucial for the notion of God to which it leads.

THE DOCTRINE OF GOD

The similarities and the differences between today's new historicists and the classical American philosophers and theologians, particularly as these impinge on the notion of God, can be illustrated by a chance occurrence. On June 13, 1907, William James wrote to congratulate Henri Bergson on his *Evolution Creatrice*. "To me at present," James said, "the vital achievement of the book is that it inflicts an irrecoverable death-wound upon Intellectualism. It can never resuscitate!" James did acknowledge that "the *élan vital*, all contentless and vague as you are obliged to leave it, will be an easy substitute to make fun of." But, yielding to his will to believe in the achievements of others, James went on to say: "But the beast *has* its death-wound now, and the manner in which you have inflicted it . . . is masterly in the extreme."[25]

James's antagonism for intellectualism is similar to the antagonism of today's new historicist, whether that be the Continental deconstructionist's antagonism for logocentrism or the American neopragmatist's antagonism for a correspondence theory of truth realism. In each case, the intellectualist is viewed as one who would invest supreme confidence in a scheme for reality, rather than recognize the historical change that renders all schemes temporary and local.

Furthermore, James's alternative to intellectualism is not altogether different from the alternative advanced by the deconstructionists and the neopragmatists. He went on to say to Bergson: "I feel that at bottom we are fighting the same fight, you a commander, I in the ranks. The position we are rescuing is 'Tychism' and a really growing world."[26] *Tychism* was a term used by Charles Sanders Peirce to depict the chance, unpredictable, indeterminate nature of some things, and by James to depict that nature in all things. When the deconstructionists and the neopragmatists picture the interpreter working without a metaphysical net, rendering the world a particular way without the assurance of a universal justification, they are Jamesean Tychists. There are these important congruences, then, that make the classical American philosophers and theologians forerunners of today's deconstructionist and neopragmatic new historicists.

There is, however, an important difference, a difference that explains how today's new historicists still stand with the intellectualists against whom James and Bergson revolted. Today's historicists continue to be so preoccupied with their (intellectual, schematic) method that they neglect the world this method was to help them know. Bernard Meland suggested this difference when he found in one respect no marked change from Enlightenment to present forms of thinking: they all tend to invest their confidence in their own fallible forms and symbols, in their own procedures for approaching the world. To Meland such self-assurance is demented because it tends to define reality in terms of methods and forgets that methods are only ways of reaching something beyond methods.[27]

An acute awareness of earlier forms of that category mistake led the classical American philosophers and theologians to subordinate their radical empiricism and pragmatism to " 'Tychism' and a really growing world." It was the world, after all, and not our methods of coping with the world, not even the empiricist epistemology, that fascinated James and Dewey and Whitehead and the Chicago School theologians. The absurdity of centering on human methods is enlarged when it is remembered that for naturalists like Dewey and Whitehead the world of human cognition occupied only a small place. It was this interpretation of the world they wanted pragmatically to test, not their pragmatic method itself. It was this world they wanted empirically to know, not that empiricism itself.

As I have noted in several ways now, the real difference between today's new historicists and yesterday's is the difference between methodologism and naturalism. They share a basically historicist method, where it is assumed that everything depends on transient, relative, and revisable interpretations of a transient and relational world, and where it is acknowledged that interpretations of history themselves constitute historical reality. And this joint membership in a new historicism places them generally in the same chain of thinkers. But when today's Continental hermeneuticists and American neopragmatists give primacy to method, they differentiate themselves from their American, historicist predecessors.

This difference might explain the otherwise confusing variety of new historicist efforts to talk about the nature of God. There are theologians whose thought about God works primarily out of a historicist methodology, and there are theologians whose thought about God works primarily out of a historicist naturalism. While the former tend to focus on a Continental and hermeneutical methodology or an American and neopragmatic methodology, the latter tend to focus on an American naturalism.

The clearest and most explicit embodiment of the Continental and deconstructionist new historicism is offered by Mark C. Taylor in his *Erring: A Postmodern A/theology.* There Taylor offers a Hegelian and a Derridian reconception of the world and of God. In the first part of the book, Taylor deconstructs or delogocentricizes the notions of God, the self, history, and the book. Taylor tends to treat nineteenth-century Continental idealism as though it had been true not only for European thinkers, but as thought it were simply the received opinion. Consequently, the deconstruction of this authoritative idealism appears simply catastrophic, as "the death of God," "the disappearance of the self," "the end of history," and "the closure of the book." But at the same time Taylor intends to avoid the simple alternative—that is, simply to treat God as an utterly meaningless term, the self as autonomous, history as hollow, and philosophy and theology as things of the past. Taylor sees himself as among those people who "constantly live on the border that both joins and separates belief and unbelief."[28] Abjuring both theology (seeing this as idealistic) and atheism (seeing this as a crass rejection of everything theological), Taylor sets forth a deconstructive, nonidealistic theology, an a/theology. He redefines God as writing, the self as a specific deconstructive trace through time, history as the whole temporal congeries of such traces, and the book as a text always recreated by reinterpretation and never grounded or founded ouside of history.

More specifically regarding the doctrine of God, Taylor seeks to move beyond modernism's humanistic atheism, to a postmodern notion of God as emptied into the historical process of deconstructive writing. *Writing,* used in the technical way Taylor uses it, acknowledges that no longer does the signified function as a standard and dominate the signifier, so that the signifier's task is simply to replicate the signified; instead, the signified and the signifier interact, so that the signified, or whatever once might have passed as the logos, is "as much invented as revealed, as much created as discovered."[29] Here God is "the complex web of such written interrelations," totally identified with a form of historical writing.

Now why should Taylor's notion of God be called methodologistic? Is not his picture as thoroughly naturalistic as that of the classical American philosophers and theologians? To put it in their terms, is not God now brought entirely into the natural process, so that we have a material notion God, as distinguished from a God who is nothing more than our talk of God? Taylor, after all, does say that

> The untotalizable totality of negativity becomes more comprehensible if approached through the notion of *force.* As I have emphasized, writing embodies a tissue of differences in which terms are sites of passage. This liminal passageway is the domain of force. Constantly in transition and perpetually transitory, force is absolute passage or passage as absolute.[30]

Here Taylor's language is thoroughly metaphysical, even if it is nonlogocentric. He does point, finally, to a universal and eternal condition that is the historical process itself. He apparently agrees with, say, Bernard Meland, for whom God may not be Taylor's "absolute passage" but is the virtually equivalent "creative passage." Taylor sounds like a process theologian when he elevates process and relationality to the status of a condition of everything, while avoiding process theology's typically logocentric metaphysics. God is the historical force or milieu that makes writing possible. This claim is by no means trivial, and seems to give to the notion of God a significant content.

But why does Taylor stop just shy of taking that next step taken by American naturalistic philosophers and theologians? He leaves his account at the level of a deconstructive negativity underlying historical process, a negativity that by itself is not ineluctably theological. Why does he not push through to a positive notion of God?

While on the surface it might appear plausible to call Taylor a shy process theologian or an unwitting American naturalistic theologian, he remains a methodologist. By characterizing his a/theology as *Erring*—in practice as well as title—Taylor disolves his notion of God into pure methodology. He not only refuses to offer any proposition about God at any moment and in any local world—as the classical American theologians did when they applied their theology to contemporary history to yield a Christ of faith, as opposed to a Jesus of history, or to yield a Christian social ethics for their time. Taylor refuses to discuss any specifically religious meaning to the historical process, even to ask what the word "God" might add to our understanding of that process. Apparently, he feels that this would illicitly reverse his own previous deconstruction, and reintroduce theology's ahistorical or logocentric nature. Taylor seems to conclude that the proper religious stance is purely playfully, that now the religious person is to go on forever erring, both deconstructing past logocentric constructions and wandering aimlessly, purposelessly, in the play of words.[31] Finally, then, Taylor advocates a form of behavior—which is to say, a pure (clean) form, nothing but a method. What is the theologian to do, but to abandon even any specific name for God or any religious interpretation for any time and place, and to talk simply about the method of erring itself? Taylor stops just at the threshhold of a theistic naturalism, and insists on play—the play that is concerned with nothing so much as with how you play.

Taylor's methodology is by no means trivial. Perhaps Taylor is a philosopher of religion, and I am asking him to perform as a theologian. Nevertheless, philosophers such as James, Dewey, and Whitehead went on to add some content to what Taylor has called a force, by claiming that that force has a tropism, a spin, something urging the growth of value in the historical process, and that it opens particular truths for their own times.

Jacques Derrida's characterization of God appears to be similar to Mark Taylor's, although it is far briefer and more circumspect. Derrida is most explicit when he discusses the poetry of Edmond Jabés. Derrida notes that Jabés echoes the Cabala when he repeats themes "of the question within God, of negativity within God as the liberation of historicity and human speech, of man's writing as the desire and question *of* God . . . , of history and discourse as the anger of God emerging himself, etc., etc."[32] For Jabés and, apparently, for Derrida, the meaning of God resides in the process of writing, in the chain of acts wherein history reflects on itself. Derrida's nonlogocentric theism is adequately described by Taylor's words: "Scripture *is* the divine milieu, and the divine milieu *is* writing."[33] Naturally, Derrida rejects Levi-Strauss's wish for a restoration of the primal, preprocessive divine condition. But Derrida acts as though there are only the two options— either the preprocessive or the sheer process of writing itself. Derrida advocates "the Nietzschean *affirmation,* that is the joyous affirmation of the play of the world and of the innocence of becoming, the affirmation of a world of signs without fault, without truth, and without origin which is offered to an active interpretation."[34] It makes no sense to ask how the term *God* indicates anything more than the process, anything in the process added to what it would be without God. God must be, then, the pure form of play, elaborated through endless commentaries on how to play. That is, Derrida on God (admittedly, not a large part of Derrida) is not Derrida writing on some distinct content within the process, but is Derrida writing as a methodologist pure and simple. This is not an insignificant achievement, but it is a methodologism nevertheless.

As I will argue later, Taylor's and Derrida's methodologism is a function of how they approach the problem of God. They begin with human discourse or human interpretations (so that the metaphor of "writing" is not accidental), whereas the classical American philosophers and theologians begin, not with human discourse or even with human experience, but with what they regard nature to be—and only thereby get beyond method to a specific theological content. Taylor's and Derrida's deconstructionist methodologism can be found in muted forms in Susan Handelman's insightful *The Slayers of Moses* and in José Faur's *Golden Doves with Silver Dots,* and in their very sketchy comments on what God would mean to the people they study. The same approach can be found in the deconstructionists writing in *Deconstruction and Theology,* particularly in the work of Thomas Altizer, Charles Winquist, Robert Scharlemann, and Carl Raschke. My concern here is not to object to the deconstructionist's methodologism itself, but to ask whether it leaves to the term *God* any significant use at all.

If the Continental deconstructionism of Taylor and Derrida ends in theological methodologism, is the same true of current American theological neopragmatism and historicism? Jeffrey Stout, in *The Flight from Authority*, suggests the theological implications of neopragmatism and its historicism. Like Taylor, he seeks to avoid the simple alternatives between foundationalism and the despairing rejection of foundationalism. Focusing on ethics, he rejects foundationalism as an unsustainable basis for ethics; yet he rejects just as strenuously the typical reversion to ethical relativism. He argues on pragmatic and historicist grounds for a third option: an ethics based on historical community. Creative interaction with a historical community can provide a continuity that is meaningful without requiring an extrahistorical foundation. We can reach the ethical conclusions we need if we converse with others and pragmatically test our conclusions through reference to history.

Although Stout works out of a theological heritage of moral language, he appears to abandon theology—including, apparently, any notion of God. Theology has either retained its distinctness from secularity but become culturally irrelevant (the situation of the followers of Barth and Kiekegaard) or has retained its relevance but lost any theological specificity (the situation of the followers of Tillich and Bultmann). In a 1983 article, he initially hopes for a third option, a "hermeneutical theology," that would "work out a conception of *situated freedom*." Stout quotes Mark C. Taylor's version of situated freedom approvingly, and suggests that "to be human is to be situated in nature, history, culture, and society—to have a particular location."[35] Stout shows how James Gustafson's theocentric ethics might fill this particular bill. However, Stout concludes that on this point Gustafson finally is puzzling. Why, given his thorough grounding in history, does Gustafson need God? The earlier dilemma opens again: either Gustafson's notion of God pushes his work to the point of cultural irrelevance or his adoption of critical cultural standards has rendered his theology no longer distinctly Christian. In either case, Stout is willing to argue "that no one has struggled more valiantly or more honestly" to write a hermeneutical theology than Gustafson.[36] The third option is unfilled and, apparently for the time being, unfillable (even the most valiant have failed). It follows that we are left in this article and in *The Flight from Authority* merely with the hope for "communities and institutions in which the virtues of good people and good conversation can flourish."[37] That is, he leaves his readers conversing, and in that conversation they are attentive not to any sort of God, but only to a stout-hearted method.

In his 1983 review of *The Flight from Authority*, Edmund Santurri suggests that Stout may have abandoned the notion of God prematurely. Santurri suggests that Stout abandons theism because it conflicts "with fundamental rules of inference governing the 'modern academic disciplines'." Santurri suggests that Stout's loyalty to the disciplinary rules is based on their pragmatic success in promoting common social interests. But, Santurri responds, "might one not also contend that theistic constructions of the world recommend themselves on equally compelling pragmatic grounds?"[38] Santurri argues that liberation theology may be making just such a pragmatic case for theism today. To lend credence to this contention, he cites Cornel West, who combines Rortian pragmatism and liberation theology.

In his 1985 "The Historicist Turn in Philosophy of Religion," West allies himself with the historicism that flows from the tradition Stout has used, the Port Royal probabilists. Like Stout, West repeatedly rejects the forced option between "transcendental objectivism" and the "subjectivistic nihilism" sometimes advanced by those who reject transcendental objectivism. On the one hand, West accepts the denials of Willard Quine, Nelson Goodman, and Wilfred Sellars, contending that they have effectively overcome the transcendentalized subject as a sphere of inquiry, realism (or, conventionalism) in ontology, and the Myth of the Given (or, foundationalism) in epistemology.[39] On the other hand, West rejects what he feels is their moral nihilism, their neglect of the coming historical, political, and cultural struggle in favor of socially innocuous, subjective, and academic preoccupations.[40] But then, unlike Stout, West turns to theology.

West does not discount theology as either culturally irrelevant or religiously indistinct. Rather, he looks to religion as a way to advance the struggles of history by tapping into a specific set of communal norms. Furthermore, West unlike those we have just examined, recognizes that his location within a religious history requires him, where possible, to utilize that history. Consequently, he uses not only his Afro-American cultural heritage, but also the classically American philosophies of Peirce, James, and Dewey. However, when West looks specifically at current theologies that attend to isues of the oppressed and of social practice (such as those of Gustavo Gutierrez, Mary Daly, and James Cone), he finds in them a obsolete transcendental objectivism. And while West will cite approvingly the White-headian liberationist efforts of Schubert Ogden or John B. Cobb, Jr., he seems not to adopt their theism. And this is where Cornel West stops: with a yearning for theology, but with no specific notion of God—in fact, the idea is barely mentioned. Whether or not that amounts to methodologism, I cannot say. West does commit himself far more firmly on the way one should proceed theologically than on what, materially, God might be and what such a God might imply for specific action. On the other hand, West's critiques do not seem to preclude for reasons of methodological purity the possibility of a notion of God relevant to a community's own time and place, as do those we have considered heretofore.

If Taylor and Derrida are rooted in a Continental, hermeneutical tradition and Stout and West are rooted in an American, pragmatic tradition, Gordon Kaufman may be the figure who is moving from the former to the latter. More important, he may be moving from a more methodological historicism to a more naturalistic historicism. This is not to argue that Kaufman has contradicted himself, but only that his emphasis appears to be changing. One key to understanding Kaufman's movement is to watch his use of the word *history*. In his 1960 *Relativism, Knowledge, and Faith*, where he gives primary acknowledgements to Dilthey, Collingwood, and Tillich, *history* is virtually an anthropological or cultural term, having to do with subjective constructions of cultural realities. In his 1975 *An Essay on Theological Method*, Kaufman retains that neo-Kantian emphasis, but augments it with pragmatic checks; however, the checks refer only to the cultural realities of the way people are humanized and relativized within the religious process. Kaufman's 1980 *The Theological Imagination* is more complex; while at points it endorses a neo-Kantian dualism and by implication merely subjective and cultural notions of history, it also introduces strong criticisms of the dualism.[41] Finally, in his 1985 *Theology for a Nuclear Age*, Kaufman moves further toward abandoning that dualism when he refers to "empirical historical changes."[42] This last book was occasioned, in part, by a change in physical history—that for the first time nature itself is contingent on an arbitrary physical possibility, nuclear war. This change, particularly because it involved human use of physical power, made the notion of the sovereignty of God pragmatically unacceptable. Here, history clearly referred to and was pragmatically tested by reference to nature, as well as to culture. By implication Kaufman also took a long step from a preoccupation with method to a preoccupation with the world. Kaufman makes his naturalism explicit in his vigorous attack on those often neo-Kantian theologians who have separated the spiritual from the physical and have argued, consequently, that "empirical disconfirmation" of theological claims is impossible "in principle."[43]

Certainly, Kaufman's notion of the "imaginative construction" gives witness to his continuing appreciation for the Continental tradition where the subject is dominant in the configuration of history. I am not aware that he ever acknowledges that a notion of history can be empirically induced, discerned, or generalized. Nevertheless, his growing interest in the empirical adequacy of concepts of history to the facts of nature represents a movement of his thought toward a more naturalistic historicism.

The consequence of Kaufman's new naturalism is that he has become more, not less, embedded in history A neo-Kantian subjectivism provides a formal and methodological safehaven from the inescapable perils and accidents of physical history. When Kaufman emphasizes the way cultural symbols and the cultural imagination itself can be obliterated by a natural history that includes a nuclear war, he becomes more, not less attentive to the power of history.

Kaufman's more naturalistic historicism has effects on his notion of God. Kaufman appears now to be a postmodern realist. He is postmodern in that he does not accept what Jeffrey Stout calls "epistemological realism," where there is "the hopeless attempt to make correspondence to *undescribed* reality serve as a criterion." But he has become, it seems to me, a realist, nevertheless, when he accepts what Stout calls a "correspondence between theoretical statements and the facts as they are described."[44] With this realism Kaufman can contend that God is not only a human construct, but also a "hidden creativity" that functions as "a reality, an ultimate tendency or power, which is working itself out in an evolutionary process."[45] It is this natural reality that humanizes and relativizes humans in culture. Here then, is a naturalistic historicism that ventures a God functioning not entirely in cultural and linguistic imaginative constructs, but also in natural events that could override any and all such contructions.

Kaufman's recent effort, while it represents a significant move from a purely Continental historicism toward a more naturalistic understanding of God, was in some ways clearly anticipated by the Chicago School theologians. The scholarship of George Burman Foster, Gerald Birney Smith, Shailer Mathews, and Shirley Jackson Case in the first five decades of this century was guided always by the sociohistorical method, which made theological truth a function and construct of historical situations. First, they examined a people's social situation in a particular historical era; then they explained how and to what extent a people's notion of church, Christ, or God could be understood as a function of and an answer to those situations.

However, a fully naturalistic historicism is found neither in Kaufman nor in the Chicago School theologians, but in the writings of the classical American philosophers and of those theologians who were explicit in their attention to these philosophers. These philosophers began to concentrate on what God is, rather than on how God might be known. Further, their naturalism not only applied to nature, as well as to culture, but was empirically derived from nature, as well as from culture.

John Dewey and Henry Nelson Wieman, despite their mixed feelings about organized religion, may have undertaken a more direct search for

knowledge of God than anyone. Dewey, in particular, is cognizant of the subjectivity of religious knowledge when he calls it an act of imagination. In *A
Common Faith*, he argues that the notion of " 'God' represents a unification
of ideal values that is essentially imaginative in orgin."[46] But Dewey's construc-
tivism is also in part empirically derived as Kaufman's is not. The imagined
ideal, Dewey says, is not "wholly without roots in existence and without support from existence";[47] rather, "the ideal itself has its roots in natural conditions; it emerges when the imagination idealizes existence by laying hold of
the possibilities offered to thought and action."[48] It is this absolutely crucial
extension of his notion of imagination that carries Dewey's notion of God clearly
into the realm beyond a methodological historicism to a naturalistic historicism,
where the idea of God not only is pragmatically applied to nature but, in part,
empirically derived from nature.

And here Dewey speaks for William James, Alfred North Whitehead,
Bernard Meland, and Bernard Loomer in identifying an interpretive imagination—an imagination that, to put it in evolutionary terms, is both free to
construct subjective variations and is derived from and determined by
environmental possibilities outside the subject. Their position is beyond
objectivism and subjectivism, but in more ways than Bernstein suggests in his
Beyond Objectivism and Relativism. Not only do they recognize that the subject
reaches cosmic conclusions that must be tested through pragmatic analysis, as
Kaufman and the early Chicago School theologians do when they reach a
historicist notion of God. But also with a radical empiricism they can explain,
as the deconstructionists, the neopragmatists, Kaufman, and the early Chicago
School theologians cannot, *how it is that the religious person is able to arrive
at a theistic hypothesis that has even the remotest chance of pragmatic confirmation.* James, Dewey, and Whitehead recognized the awkwardness of the neo-
Kantian subjectivist: the inability to explain how subjects can imagine notions
that are more than stabs in the dark awaiting pragmatic lights to show whether
they have hit anything; that imagined notions, in fact, can be pregnant with
insight, awaiting a likely pragmatic confirmation. Their radically empirical
epistemology allows them to contend that the religious person may have a
vague, indistinct, unclear, groping sort of empiricist apprehension of the
"whole," to use Dewey's term, of the "more," to use James's term, of the divine
"lure," to use Whitehead's term, of the "creative event," to use Wieman's term,
or of the "creative advance," to use Meland's term. Their radical empiricism,
in short, allows them to do work that today's new historicism cannot do.

Lacking even this vague and weak sense of religious knowledge, the
deconstructionists and neopragmatists and even Kaufman can see no more in
the concept of God than a heritage of lucky and unlucky guesses—lucky when

they turned out to have some utility, unlucky when they did not. They offer no explanation for how those guesses were reached. Nor do they account for the religious person's crucial claim that, when they know God, they know something. Like Thomas Kuhn and Paul Feyerabend before them, today's new historicist would claim that theological research would have nothing to do with religious experience and everything to do with pragmatic tests of what must be subjective fantasies. There would be no point in attempting to look at past history for insight about what God means.

[handwritten margin note: where is the epistemology behind the pragmatism?]

I do not mean to suggest, however, that the truth will be reached if postmodernism will simply turn back to the theological followers of James, Dewey, and Whitehead. With the possible exception of Meland, who consistently emphasized anthropology and cultural theory, these empirical and process theologians were inclined to trust too simply their capacity to intuit universal truths about God. Even the empiricists had an unwarranted confidence that their empirical generalizations about the creative process were somehow generally valid; and they had this confidence even while arguing that the rationalistic and dogmatic theologians were too trusting of their *a priori* rationality. Consequently, even Bernard Loomer and Henry Nelson Wieman tended to ignore the kind of cultural relativity that the deconstructionists, the neopragmatists, and that Taylor, Stout, West, and Kaufman appropriately have urged on us in recent years.

American religious historicism would be foolish to ignore the achievement of Continental deconstructionism and the strange American neopragmatism that has grown up in the last three decades out of the European influences of Willard Quine, Heidegger, and Wittgenstein. American religious historicism might be even more foolish to ignore the recent achievement of Michel Foucault, whose historicism extends the best in American new historicism perhaps more adequately than Derrida's, but whose impact on American religious thought is now minimal (and, thus, has been neglected in this descriptive study); this wave too of European thought must be more completely and integrally absorbed. Clearly, the tortuous philosophical mainstreams of nineteenth- and twentieth-century Continental Europe, particularly the heavy emphasis on the constructive role of imagination and language, can serve as a corrective of the hermeneutical naivete of the empirical and process theologians—of their tendency to indulge in "the hopeless attempt to make correspondence to *undescribed* reality serve as a criterion." While Continental hermeneutics and deconstructionism, in particular, should not drown American new historicism, they should be seen as the great and unexpected contributions by today's new historicists to any American religious historicism.

   If in America the hermeneutical modesty of Continental methodological historicism were included within the American empirical and naturalistic historicism, this might lead to a notion of God that was more genuinely American than anything earlier. First, tempered with such methodological historicism an American theology would abandon efforts to state the *a priori*, metaphysical, or context-independent truths about God. It would abandon Whitehead's primordial nature of God and Hartshorne's absolute side of God, as well as the extrahistorical generalizations about God offered by American theological empiricists. It would recognize the extent to which American thought about God is really the thought of a national community and that it can attain little more than a "correspondence between theoretical statements and the facts as they are described" from an American context. Second, this theology would recognize the extent to which the American context and its God are recurringly radically empirical, radically historicist, and naturalistic; and it would develop that tradition in its new context. Third, it would recognize that the American context is clearly and obviously Jewish and Christian in ways we have not described here, but which must be recognized in any historically adequate account of American theology.

   This acknowledged, an American religious historicism must freely exercise in practical and historical arenas the pragmatic test. Although it is not the first question, the last question is, "To what extent will an American historicist concept of God make a practical difference in the lives of those who accept it?"

   Thus, this history of an American method issues naturally in a call to move beyond method, beyond even the philosophy of religion, to an American historicist theology within the Jewish and Christian traditions.

NOTES

Preface

1. Paul Ricoeur, *The Symbolism of Evil*, trans. by Emerson Buchanan (Boston: Beacon Press, 1969), p. 350.
2. Richard Niebuhr, *The Meaning of Revelation* (New York: The Macmillan Co., 1941), p. 50.

Acknowledgments

1. *The Letters of William James*, two volumes, ed. by Henry James (Boston: The Atlantic Monthly Press, 1920), I, p. 127.

Chapter 1

1. Langdon Gilkey, *Reaping the Whirlwind: A Christian Interpretation of History* (New York: Seabury Press, 1981), p. 358.
2. Ibid., p. 121.
3. Richard Rorty, *Consequences of Pragmatism (Essays: 1972-1980)*. Minneapolis: University of Minnesota Press, 1982), p. 172.
4. Gilkey, p. 188.
5. Richard Rorty, *Philosophy and the Mirror of Nature* (Princeton, N. J.: Princeton University Press, 1979), chaps. 7, 8.
6. Rorty, *Consequences of Pragmatism*, p. xxxv.
7. See, e.g., ibid., pp. xxxvii–xliv.
8. Ibid., pp. xviii, 207.
9. Nelson Goodman, *Ways of Worldmaking* (Indianapolis, Ind. and Cambridge: Hackett Publishing Co., 1978), p. 6. Goodman briefly reviews the themes of this book in "Notes on the Well-Made World," *Partisan Review* 51 (1984): 276–88.
10. Goodman, *Ways of Worldmaking*, p. 3.
11. Ibid., p. 2.

12. Ibid., p. 110.

13. See, e.g., the essays by Miller, de Man, and Hartman in Harold Bloom et al., *Deconstructionism and Criticism* (New York: Seabury Press, 1979).

14. Frank Lentricchia, *After the New Criticism* (Chicago: University of Chicago Press, 1980), p. 175.

15. Ibid., p. 180.

16. Ibid., p. 186.

17. Ibid., p. 177.

18. Wlad Godzich, "Afterword: Religion, the State, and Post(al) Modernism," in Samuel Weber, *Institution and Interpretation* (Minneapolis: University of Minnesota Press, 1987), pp. 153–64.

19. Hilary Putnam, *Reason, Truth and History* (Cambridge: Cambridge University Press, 1981), pp. 201–03, 215–16.

20. Ibid., p. 216.

21. Ibid., p. 104.

22. Ibid., pp. 111, 117.

23. Richard J. Bernstein, *Beyond Objectivism and Relativism: Science, Hermeneutics, and Praxis* (Philadelphia: University of Pennsylvania Press, 1983), p. 224.

24. Ibid., p. 231.

25. Rorty, *Consequences of Pragmatism*, p. 158.

26. Goodman, *Ways of Worldmaking*, pp. 138ff.

27. Putnam, p. 216.

28. Frank Lentricchia, *Criticism and Social Change* (Chicago: University of Chicago Press, 1983), p. 1.

29. Ibid., p. vii.

30. For accounts of Hayden White's historicism, see his *Tropics of Discourse: Essays in Cultural Criticism* (Baltimore, Md.: The Johns Hopkins University Press, 1978), and his *Metahistory: The Historical Imagination in Nineteenth-Century Europe* (Baltimore, Md.: Johns Hopkins University Press, 1973).

31. See also Frank Lentricchia, "Reading History with Kenneth Burke," in *Representing Kenneth Burke*, ed. Hayden White and Margaret Brose (Baltimore, Md.: Johns Hopkins University Press, 1982), pp. 119–49.

32. Lentricchia, *Criticism and Social Change*, p. 16.

33. Ibid., pp. 17–19.

34. Cornel West, "Nietzsche's Prefiguration of Postmodern American Philosophy," *Boundary 2* 9 and 10 (Spring/Fall 1981): 265.

35. Cornel West, book review of *Philosophy and the Mirror of Nature*, by Richard Rorty in *Union Seminary Quarterly Review* 37 (Fall/Winter 1981–82): 184.

36. Cornel West, *Prophesy Deliverance! An Afro-American Revolutionary Christianity* (Philadelphia: The Westminister Press, 1982), p. 11.

37. Ibid., p. 145.

38. Ibid., p. 16.

39. Ibid., p. 15.

40. Cornel West, "The Historicist Turn in Philosophy of Religion," *Knowing Religiously,* ed. Leroy S. Rouner (Notre Dame, Ind.: University of Notre Dame Press, 1985), p. 38.

41. Ibid., p. 47.

42. Jeffrey Stout, *The Flight from Authority: Religion, Morality, and the Quest for Autonomy* (Notre Dame, Ind.: University of Notre Dame Press, 1981), p. 264.

43. Roger Scruton, *From Descartes to Wittgenstein: A Short History of Modern Philosophy* (New York: Harper & Row, 1982), p. 132.

44. For an analysis of the neo-Kantian dualism of Bultmann's theology, see Anthony C. Thistelton, *The Two Horizons: New Testament Hermeneutics and Philosophical Description with Special Reference to Heidegger, Bultmann, Gadamer, and Wittgenstein* (Grand Rapids, Mich.: Wm. B. Eerdmans Publishing Co., 1980), chap. 8.

45. See, e.g., his coauthors of *Deconstruction and Theology* (New York: Crossroad, 1982): Thomas J. J. Altizer, Max A. Myers, Carl A. Raschke, Robert P. Schalemann, Charles E. Winquist.

Chapter 2

1. Richard Rorty, "Idealism and Textualism," in Richard Rorty, *Consequences of Pragmatism* (Minneapolis: University of Minnesota Press, 1982), p. 140.

2. Richard Rorty, "Introduction," in Rorty, *Consequences,* p. xli. Here Rorty distinguishes *Philosophy* from the *philosophy* which is the humbler and pragmatic enterprise of coping.

3. See David W. Noble, *The End of American History: Democracy, Capitalism, and the Metaphor of Two Worlds in Anglo-American Historical Writing, 1880-1980* (Minneapolis: The University of Minnesota Press, 1985).

4. Sacvan Bercovitch, *The American Jeremiad* (Madison: The University of Wisconsin Press, 1987).

5. Richard J. Bernstein, *Beyond Objectivism and Relativism: Science, Hermeneutics, and Praxis* (Philadelphia: University of Pennsylvania Press, 1983), pp. 109–15.

6. Ibid., p. 111.

7. Ibid., p. 112.

8. Cornel West, *Prophesy Deliverance! An Afro-American Revolutionary Christianity* (Philadelphia: The Westminster Press, 1982), pp. 15–24.

9. Bernstein, *Beyond Objectivism,* p. 175.

10. Ibid., p. 185.

11. Ibid., p. 197.

12. Hans-Georg Gadamer, *Truth and Method* (New York: The Seabury Press, 1975), p. 447.

13. Ibid., p. 446.

14. Bernstein, *Beyond Objectivism,* pp. 199–200.

15. Rorty, *Consequences*, pp. 152–53.

16. Ibid., p. 52.

17. William James, *Pragmatism*, (Cambridge: Harvard University Press, 1979), p. 42.

18. A community which Rorty, reverting to his odd geneology, designates the conversation of "Europe." Rorty, *Consequences*, 172–73.

19. Ibid., p. 172.

20. Ibid., p. 54.

21. Richard Rorty, "Solidarity or Objectivity?" in *Post-Analytic Philosophy*, ed. by John Rajchman and Cornel West (New York: Columbia University Press, 1985), p. 3. Reprinted by permission of *Nanzan Review of American Studies*.

22. Ibid., pp. 3–4.

23. Ibid., p. 5.

24. Richard J. Bernstein, "Philosophy in the Conversation of Mankind," a "critical study" of Richard Rorty, *Philosophy and the Mirror of Nature*, in *The Review of Metaphysics* 33 (June 1980): 772; Cornel West, a book review of Richard Rorty, *Philosophy and the Mirror of Nature* in *Union Seminary Quarterly Review* 37 (Fall/Winter 1981–82): 184; Frank Lentricchia, *Criticism and Social Change* (Chicago: The University of Chicago Press, 1984), p. 160. See also Mark Lilla, "On Goodman, Putnam, and Rorty: The Return to the 'Given'," *Partisan Review* 55 (1984/2): 220–235.

25. Richard Rorty, "A Reply to Dreyfus and Taylor," *The Review of Metaphysics* 34 (1980): 39. Inconsistently with the position he took in the passages cited above, Rorty here associates Gadamer and Heidegger with the hermeneutics of attitude.

26. Ibid.

27. In one respect this characterization of the Pharisees is particularly unfair and ironic, for the Pharisees established an evolving oral tradition (the Mishnah), allowing it to move beyond the static tradition (the Torah) and pragmatically and continually to redefine the faith. See Ellis Rivkin, *The Hidden Revolution* (Nashville, Tenn.: Abingdon, 1978).

28. Rorty, *Consequences*, p. 166.

29. Rorty, "Solidarity or Objectivity?," p. 13.

30. Ibid., p. 12.

31. Ibid., p. 14.

32. See Chapter 4 herein for my accounts of his implicit metaphysics, which enables him to posit a morality and to use that as a basis for objecting to his objectivist opponents.

33. Putnam, *Reason, Truth and History* (Cambridge: Cambridge University Press, 1981), p. 216.

34. Goodman, *Ways of Worldmaking* (Indianapolis, Ind. and Cambridge: Hackett Publishing Co., 1978), pp. 138–40.

35. Martin E. Marty, "A Sort of Republican Banquet," *The Journal of Religion* 59 (October 1979): 387.

36. William James, *A Pluralistic Universe* (Cambridge, Mass.: Harvard University Press, 1977), p. 25.

37. John Dewey, *Experience and Nature* (New York: Dover Publications, Inc., 1958). p. 71.

38. Ibid., p. 49.

39. Wolfhart Pannenberg, "Preface to the American Edition," *Revelation as History,* ed. by Wolfhart Pannenberg, trans. by David Granskou (New York: The Macmillan Company, 1968). p. ix.

40. Ibid., p. 5.

41. Wolfhart Pannenberg, *Jesus–God and Man,* second ed., trans. by Lewis L. Wilkins and Duane A Priebe (Philadelphia: Westminster Press, 1977), p. 33.

42. Pannenberg, "Introduction," *Revelation as History,* p. 6.

43. Ibid., p. 13.

44. Pannenberg, *Jesus,* p. 28.

45. Ibid., p. 34.

46. Pannenberg, "Introduction," *Revelation as History,* p. 19.

47. Pannenberg, "Dogmatic Theses on the Doctrine of Revelation," ibid., p. 133.

48. Ibid., p. 142.

49. Wolfhart Pannenberg, *Basic Questions in Theology,* trans. by George H. Kehm, vol. 1 (London: SCM Press, Ltd., 1970), pp. 134–35.

50. For an introductory history of tradition history see, Bernhard W. Anderson, "Tradition and Scripture in the Community of Faith," *Journal of Biblical Literature* 100 (1981): 5–21.

51. Gerhard von Rad, *The Problem of the Hexateuch and Other Essays,* (New York: McGraw-Hill Book Company, 1955), p. 3.

52. Gerhard von Rad, *Old Testament Theology* (2 vols; New York: Harper and Brothers, 1962) vol 1, pp. v, vi.

53. Ibid., p. 119.

54. Martin Noth, "The Laws in the Pentateuch: Their Assumptions and Meaning," in *The Laws in the Pentateuch and Other Studies,* trans. by D. R. Ap-Thomas (London: SCM Press, Ltd., 1984).

55. Douglas A. Knight, "Revelation through Tradition," *Tradition and Theology in the Old Testament,* ed. by Douglas A. Knight (Philadelphia: Fortress Press, 1977), p. 169.

56. Ibid., p. 149.

57. Robert A. Laurin, "Tradition and Canon," *Tradition and Theology,* ed. by Knight.

58. "Tradition and Biblical Theology," *Tradition and Theology,* ed. by Knight, p. 306.

59. Bernhard Anderson notes Sanders's *Torah and Canon* (1972) and Hanson's *Dynamic Transcendence* (1978) in his "Tradition and Scripture in the Community of Faith," p. 9.

60. Scroggs, "Sociological Introduction of the New Testament: The Present State of Research," *The Bible and Liberation: Political and Social Hermeneutics,* ed. by Norman K. Gottwald, rev. ed. (Maryknoll, N. Y.: Orbis Books, 1983), pp. 341–43.

61. Norman K. Gottwald, "Introduction: The Bible and Liberation: Deeper Roots and Wider Horizons," *The Bible and Liberation,* ed. by Gottwald, p. 2.

62. Joseph L. Hardegree, Jr., "Bible Study for Marxist Christians: The Book of Hosea," *The Bible and Liberation*, ed. by Gottwald, p. 106.

63. Scroggs, "Sociological Introduction," p. 338.

64. Norman K. Gottwald, *The Tribes of Yahweh: A Sociology of the Religion of Liberated Israel, 1250-1050 B. C. E.* (Maryknoll, N. Y.: Orbis Books, 1979), p. 701; emphasis in original.

65. Norman K. Gottwald, "The Theological Task after the *Tribes of Yahweh*," *The Bible and Liberation*, ed. by Gottwald, p. 194.

66. Jacques Derrida, "Edmond Jabès and the Question of the Book," trans. by Alan Bass, *Writing and Difference* (Chicago: The University of Chicago Press, 1978), p. 64.

67. Ibid., 68.

68. Ibid; emphasis in original.

69. Ibid., p. 71; emphasis in original.

70. Ibid., p. 70; emphasis in original.

71. Ibid., pp. 78-71.

72. Susan A. Handelman, *The Slayers of Moses: The Emergence of Rabbinic Interpretation in Modern Literary Theory* (Albany: State University of New York Press, 1982), p. 22.

73. Ibid., p. 28.

74. Ibid., pp. 24–25.

75. José Faur, *Golden Doves with Silver Dots:Semiotics and Textuality in Rabbinic Tradition* (Bloomington: Indiana University Press, 1986). p. xxvi.

76. Ibid., p. xiii. Faur does argue that for the Hebrews "'writing' is intrinsic to nature" (p. 25) and elaborates by reference to Maimonides, attempting thereby to relate semiology to a nature. However, this effort simply does not fit the generally linguistic orientation of Faur's study as a whole. See also my argument that Derrida neglects nature in my *American Religious Empiricism* (Albany: State University of New York Press, 1986), Chapter 2.

77. Von Rad, *Old Testament Theology*, I, p. 138. see also Gerhard von Rad, *Wisdom in Israel* (Nashville, Tenn.: Abingdon Press, 1977), especially chap. 9, "The Self-Revelation of Creation."

Chapter 3

1. See, e.g., Roger A. Johnson, "American Empiricism in German Theology: William James' Impact Upon Ernst Troeltsch," *Harvard Theological Review* 80 (October 1987).

2. See Darnell Rucker, *The Chicago Pragmatists* (Minneapolis: University of Minnesota Press, 1969); Charles Morris, "The Chicago School, "*The Pragmatic Movement in American Philosophy* (New York: George Braziller, 1970), pp. 174–91.

3. See, e.g., William Hynes, "The Hidden Nexus between Catholic and Protestant Modernism: C. A. Briggs in Correspondence with Loisy, von Huegel, and Genocchi," *Downside Review* (July 1987).

4. See, e.g., Walter Marshall Horton's 1934 "The Decline of Liberalism" in *American Protestant Thought in the Liberal Era*, ed. by William R. Hutchison (Lanham, Md.: University Press of America, 1986), pp. 190–96. Trutz Rendtorff in "The Modern Age as a Chapter in the History of Christianity; or, the Legacy of Historical Consciousness in Present Theology" (*The Journal of Religion* 65 [October 1985]) recognizes that neo-orthodoxy and liberalism, including The Chicago School, have been opponents; but he also argues that they are allies, particularly in sharing a fundamental historical realism.

5. William W. Fenn raises this distinction in a lecture given in 1918. See William W. Fenn, "War and the Thought of God," *American Protestant Thought in the Liberal Era*, ed. by Hutchison, pp. 149–54.

6. P. Joseph Cahill, " 'Theological Studies, Where Are You?' " *Journal of the American Academy of Religion* 52/4 (December 1984): 745–46.

7. Reinhold Niebuhr, *The Nature and Destiny of Man: A Christian Interpretation*, 2 volumes in 1 (New York: Charles Scribner's Sons, 1949), I, chap. 10, sec. 4.

8. Arthur O. Lovejoy, *The Great Chain of Being: A Study of the History of an Idea* (Cambridge, Mass.: Harvard University Press, 1982), pp. 329–32.

9. Henry Nelson Wieman, *The Organization of Interests*, ed. by Cedric Lambreth Helper (Lanham, Md., University Press of America, 1985), p. 79.

10. Thomas Kuhn, *The Structure of Scientific Revolutions* (Chicago: The University of Chicago Press, 1962) and Paul Feyerabend, *Against Method: Outline of an Anarchistic Theory of Knowledge* (London: Verso, 1984).

11. See, e.g., J. Hillis Miller, Geoffrey Hartman, Paul de Man, et al, *Deconstruction and Criticism* (New York: The Seabury Press, 1979).

12. Lovejoy, *The Great Chain of Being*, p. 329.

13. Shirley Jackson Case, "Education in Liberalism," *Contemporary American Theology*, ed. by Vergillius Ferm (New York: Round Table Press, Inc., 1932), p. 112.

14. Ibid., pp. 115–16.

15. Shailer Mathews, *New Faith for Old: An Autobiography* (New York: The Macmillan Co., 1936), chap. 1.

16. Shailer Mathews, "Theology as Group Belief," *Contemporary American Theology: Theological Autobiographies*, Second Series, ed. by Vergilius Ferm (Freeport, N. Y.: Books for Libraries Press, 1969), p. 166.

17. Ibid., p. 167.

18. Ibid., p. 169.

19. Norman Gottwald, "The Theological Task after *The Tribes of Yahweh*," *The Bible and Liberation: Political and Social Hermeneutics* (rev. ed.), ed. by Norman K. Gottwald (Maryknoll, N. Y.: Orbis Books, 1983), p. 191; emphasis in original.

20. Mathews, "Theology as Group Belief," p. 172.

21. See also, Shirley Jackson Case, "Whither Historicism in Theology," *The Process of Religions: Essays in Honor of Dean Shailer Mathews*, ed. by M. H. Krumbine (New York: The Macmillan Co.), 1933, pp. 52–71.

22. Shirley Jackson Case, *The Christian Philosophy of History* (Chicago: The University of Chicago Press, 1943), p. 92.

23. Ibid.

24. Ibid., p. 93.

25. Ibid., p. 77.

26. Ibid., p. 80.

27. Ibid.

28. Ibid.

29. Ibid. Case did not draw, but could have drawn, a damaging implication for his own conclusions—that neo-orthodox theologians, despite their distaste for the optimism implicit in all notions of progress, retain a subjective sense of progress themselves. They, after all, did believe that their writings represented progress beyond liberal theology. Could neo-orthodoxy deny liberalism without, at least in this small way, implicitly accepting it?

30. Ibid., p. 164

31. Ibid., p. 176.

32. Ibid., p. 177.

33. Ibid., p. 179.

34. Richard Rorty, *Consequences of Pragmatism (Essays: 1972-1980)* (Minneapolis: University of Minnesota Press, 1982), p. 166.

35. See Case, *Christian Philosophy of History*, chap. 6.

36. Shirley Jackson Case, *Jesus: A New Biography* (New York: Greenwood Press, 1968), p. 109.

37. Shirley Jackson Case, *The Social Origins of Christianity* (New York: Cooper Square Publishers, Inc., 1975), p. 253.

38. Shirley Jackson Case, *The Origins of Christian Supernaturalism* (Chicago: The University of Chicago Press, 1946), p. 234.

39. Case, *The Christian Philosophy of History*, p. 195–97.

40. Ibid., p. 206.

41. Ibid., p. 86.

42. Ibid., p. 210. But Case proceeds to say that "God is within, as well as above, his universe." How, saying this, can Case avoid the appearance of reverting to just that Hellenistic dualism he had said was no longer acceptable?

43. For a general study of Case, as well as an introduction to the Chicago School, see William J. Hynes's excellent *Shirley Jackson Case and the Chicago School: the Socio-Historical Method* (Chico, Calif.: Scholars Press, 1981).

44. Shailer Mathews, *The Atonement and the Social Process* (New York: The Macmillan Co., 1930), p. 11.

45. Ibid.

46. Ibid., p. 16.

47. "Mathews, "Theology as Group Belief," p. 168.

48. Shailer Mathews, *Jesus on Social Institutions* (Philadelphia: Fortress Press, 1971), p. 13.

49. Mathews, *The Atonement and the Social Process*, p. 16.

50. Ibid., p. 32–33.

51. Ibid., pp. 146–51.

52. Ibid., p. 185; see also pp. 22 and 150.

53. Ibid., p. 180.

54. Ibid., p. 181.

55. Mathews, *Jesus on Social Institutions,* p. 13.

56. Shailer Mathews, *The Faith of Modernism* (New York: AMS Press, 1969), p., 82.

57. Ibid.

58. Feyerabend, *Against Method.* For example, the scientific rationalist "will be quite unable to discover that the appeal to reason to which he succumbs so readily is nothing but a *political manoeuvre."* Equally, science uses "interests, forces, propaganda and brainwashing techniques." p. 25.

59. Benjamin B. Warfield, William Adams Brown, and Gerald B. Smith, "The Task and Method of Systematic Theology," *The American Journal of Theology* 14 (April 1910): 217. See also Gerald Birney Smith, "Systematic Theology and Ministerial Efficiency," *The American Journal of Theology* 16 (October 1912): 594–95.

60. Smith, "The Task and Method of Systematic Theology," p. 221.

61. Ibid., p. 224.

62. Smith, "Systematic Theology and Ministerial Efficiency," p. 605.

63. Gerald Birney Smith "The Christ of Faith and the Jesus of History," *The American Journal of Theology* 18 (October 1914): 523.

64. Smith, "Systematic Theology and Ministerial Efficiency," 597.

65. Gerald Birney Smith, "Christianity and the Spirit of Democracy," *The American Journal of Theology:* 21/3 (July 1917): 349.

66. Ibid., p. 346.

67. Smith, *Social Idealism and the Changing Theology* (New York: The Macmillan Co., 1912), p. 201.

68. See, e.g., Hynes, *Case and The Chicago School,* p. 12.

69. Charles Harvey Arnold, *God Before You and Behind You: The Hyde Park Union Church Through a Century 1874–1974* (Chicago: The Hyde Park Union Church, 1974), p. 154; Charles Harvey Arnold, *Near the Edge of Battle: A Short History of the Divinity School and the "Chicago School of Theology" 1866–1966* (Chicago: The Divinity School Association, The University of Chicago, 1966), p. 29.

70. George Burman Foster, *The Finality of the Christian Religion,* Part 1 (Chicago: The University of Chicago Press, 1909), p. 315.

71. Ibid., pp. 311–12.

72. Ibid., p. 323.

73. Ibid., p. 324.

74. W. Creighton Peden, "The Radical Tradition: Paine and Foster," *The American Journal of Theology and Philosophy* 5 (January 1984): 30.

75. Foster, *The Finality of the Christian Religion,* p. 312.

76. George Burman Foster, *The Function of Religion in Man's Struggle for Existence* (Chicago: The University of Chicago Press, 1909), pp. 114–15.

77. Ibid., p. 64.

78. Ibid., p. 63.

79. Ibid., pp. 107–08.

80. George Burman Foster, "Pragmatism and Knowledge," *The American Journal of Theology* 11 (October 1907): 591–92.

81. Arnold, *God Before You, pp. 154–57.*

82. Foster, *The Function of Religion*, p. 596.

83. John B. Cobb, Jr., "Process Theology and the Doctrine of God," *Bijdragen* 41 (1980): 351.

84. See Edward Scribner Ames, *The Psychology of Religious Experience* (Boston: Houghton-Mifflin Company, 1910); and Edward Scribner Ames, *Religion* (Chicago: John O. Pyle, 1949, first published in 1929).

85. John B. Cobb, Jr., *Process Theology as Political Theology* (Philadelphia: Westminster Press, 1982), p. 39.

86. This and preceding quotations from Bernard E. Meland, "Reflections on the Early Chicago School of Modernism," *The American Journal of Theology and Philosophy* 5/1 (January 1984): 11.

87. Larry E. Axel, "Process and Religion: The History of a Tradition at Chicago," *Process Studies* 8 (Winter 1978): 238; Axel quotes from Kenneth Smith and Leonard Sweet, "Shailer Mathews: A Chapter in the Social Gospel Movement," *Foundations* 18 (1975): 311.

88. David Tracy, *Plurality and Ambiguity: Hermeneutics, Religion, Hope* (San Francisco: Harper & Row, 1987), p. 77. See, however, conflicting endnote 40, where Tracy argues that this does not require him to abandon the "transcendental analysis" of his *Blessed Rage for Order.*

89. Ibid., p. 62.

90. Ibid., pp. 36, 113.

91. Jerald C. Brauer, "Changing Perspectives on Religion in America," *Reinterpretation in American Church History,* ed. by Jerald C. Brauer (Chicago: University of Chicago Press, 1968), pp. 1–28.

92. Jerald C. Brauer, "Introduction," *The Impact of the Church Upon Its Culture,* ed. by Jerald C. Brauer (Chicago: The University of Chicago Press, 1968), p. 2.

93. Brauer, "Changing Perspectives," p. 11.

94. Martin E. Marty, "Reinterpreting American Religious History in Context," *Reinterpretation,* ed. by Brauer, pp. 195–18.

95. "Despite [Frank Hugh] Foster's enthusiasm for what seemed epoch-making and what looked like greatness, not a single first-rate intellect was remembered to have been a part of the [early liberal] movement . . . . Was there, one speculates, a brain drain from seminaries? . . . Was the choice by theologians to be adaptive a sign of limited genius or did it limit genius and thus drive it to other fields?" Martin E. Marty, *Modern American Religion,* Volume I, *The Irony of It All, 1893–1919* (Chicago: The University of Chicago Press, 1986), pp. 27–28.

96. Martin E. Marty, *A Nation of Behavers* (Chicago: The University of Chicago Press, 1976), p. 30.

97. Ibid., p, 3,

98. Martin E. Marty, "Two Integrities: An Address to the Crisis in Mormon Historiography," *Journal of Mormon History* 10 (1983): 4–5.

99. Ibid., pp. 15–16.

100. Ibid., p. 18

101. Robert W. Funk, "The Watershed of the American Biblical Tradition: The Chicago School, First Phase, 1892–1920," *Journal of Biblical Literature* 95/1 (March 1976): 13.

102. Ibid.

103. Ibid.; Funk quotes from Ernest Dewitt Burton, "The Place of the New Testament in a Theological Curriculum," *The American Journal of Theology* 16 (1912), pp. 191–192.

104. Ibid., p. 20. Funk seems at places to argue that the 1892–1920 period was a watershed because the sociohistorical method had dealt with the questions of the authority of scripture and the literary critical method had not (e.g., pp. 7, 13); at other places he seems to argue that the sociohistorical method resolved the authority of scripture no more effectively than the literary critical method of Harper and others (e.g., pp. 6, 20). I have attempted to explain Funk's approach in a way most congenial to his general concern for the irony in the loss of the sociohistorical method of criticism.

105. Funk, "The Watershed," pp. 19, 9, 7.

Chapter 4

1. Joseph Haroutunian, "Theology and American Experience," *Criterion* (Alumni Quarterly, The Divinity School, The University of Chicago) 3 (Winter, 1964): 7.

2. Ibid., p. 8.

3. Ibid., p. 4.

4. See my Chapter 3 herein.

5. Haroutunian, "Theology," p. 4.

6. Ibid., p. 5.

7. Ibid., p. 6.

8. Ibid., p. 7.

9. Ibid.

10. Ibid., p. 8.

11. Ibid., p. 11.

12. Ibid.

13. Joseph Haroutunian, *Piety versus Moralism: The Passing of the New England Theology* (Hamden, Conn.: Archon Books, 1964), p. 281.

14. Ibid., p. xxi.

156 History Making History

15. Edwards participated in the first Great Awakening, a revivalistic movement which swept New England from 1740 to 1743, and imbibed an evangelical piety from his grandfather, Solomon Stoddard; but Haroutunian does not claim that that had much to do with the development of Edwards's own pietistic sensibility. Nor does Haroutunian make much of John Locke's influence on Edwards's empiricism, although Haroutunian does say that Edwards's formal psychology takes a cue from Locke's psychology. Ibid., pp. 220–21.

16. Ibid., p. xxii.

17. Ibid., pp. 78–82, 91, 94.

18. Ibid., p. xxv.

19. For my account of the priority of radical empiricism to pragmatism in the work of the classical American pragmatists, see chap. 5 herein.

20. Richard Rorty, *Consequences of Pragmatism (Essays: 1972–1980)*. (Minneapolis: University of Minnesota Press, 1982), p. xviii.

21. Ibid., p. 150.

22. Ibid., chap. 5, "Dewey's Metaphysics."

23. Ibid., pp. xvii–xviii; see also p. 175.

24. Ibid., p. xxxv.

25. John E. Smith, *The Spirit of American Philosophy: Revised Edition* (Albany: State University of New York Press, 1983), p. 235.

26. William James, *Pragmatism* (Cambridge, Mass.: Harvard University Press, 1975), p. 136.

27. Rorty, *Consequences,* pp. 165–66.

28. James, *Pragmatism,* p. 125.

29. Rorty, *Consequences,* xv; see also pp. 90–92.

30. Ibid., p. 70.

31. Ibid., p. 175.

32. Rorty, *Consequences,* pp. 52, 166.

33. See my chapter 2 herein and Richard Rorty, "Solidarity or Objectivity?" in *Postanalytic Philosophy,* ed. by John Rajchman and Cornel West (New York: Columbia University Press, 1983).

34. See my Chapters 1 and 2 herein.

35. Shailer Mathews, *The Faith of Modernism* (New York: AMS Press, 1969), p. 23; emphasis in original.

36. Shailer Mathews, *Jesus on Social Institutions* (Philadelphia: Fortress Press, 1971), p. 97.

37. Bernard E. Meland, "A Post-Retreat Comment to Professor Haroutunian," *Criterion* 3: 12.

38. George Burman Foster, "Pragmatism and Knowledge," *The American Journal of Theology* 5 (October 1907): 594. This characterization applies as well to more recent pragmatists. Willard Quine, for example, in his landmark 1951 essay inaugurating neopragmatism said, "As an empiricist I continue to think of the conceptual scheme of science as a tool, ultimately, for predicting future experience in the light of past

experience" (Willard Van Orman Quine, "Two Dogmas of Empiricism," from Willard Van Orman Quine, *From a Logical Point of View: Nine Logico-Philosophical Essays* [Cambridge, Mass.: Harvard University Press, 1953] p. 44).

39. Foster, "Pragmatism and Knowledge," p. 595; emphasis in original. See my discussion of Foster in Chapter 3 herein.

40. Ibid., p. 596; emphasis in original.

41. Richard Rorty, *Philosophy and the Mirror of Nature* (Princeton, N. J.: Princeton University Press, 1979), p. 315.

42. Ibid., p. 316.

43. Jeffrey Stout, "The Voice of Theology in Contemporary Culture," *Religion and America: Spiritual Life in a Secular Age,* eds. Mary Douglas and Steven Tipton (Boston: Beacon Press, 1982, 1983), p. 261. Stout quotes from Ian Hacking, "Is the End in Sight for Epistemology?" *Journal of Philosophy* 77 (1980): 579–88.

44. Jeffrey Stout, *The Flight from Authority: Religion, Morality, and the Quest for Autonomy* (Notre Dame, Ind.: University of Notre Dame Press, 1981), p. xi.

45. Ibid., p. 257.

46. Ibid., p. 63

47. Ibid., p. 256.

48. Ibid., p. 194.

49. Ibid., p. 125.

50. Nancy Frankenberry develops this point at the end of Chapter 2 in her *Religion and Radical Empiricism* (Albany, N. Y.: The State University of New York Press, 1987).

51. Stout, *Flight from Authority,* especially chapters 8 and 12.

52. Ibid., p. 4.

53. Ibid., p. 12.

54. Ibid., pp. 202–203.

55. Ibid., p. 218.

56. Ibid., pp. 258–259, emphasis in original.

57. Ibid., p. 272.

58. For a critique more insistent than my own of the negative implications of Stout's project for religious meaning see, Edmund N. Santurri, "The Flight to Pragmatism," *Religious Studies Review* 9 (October 1983): 330–38.

59. See Ralph Barton Perry, *The Thought and Character of William James: Briefer Version* (New York: George Braziller, 1954), pp. 119–126; and Jacques Barzun, *A Stroll with William James* (New York: Harper & Row, 1983), pp. 16–19.

60. Stout, *Flight from Authority,* p. 5–6.

61. Ibid., p. 5; emphasis in original.

62. Ibid., p. 97.

63. Ibid., p. 103.

64. Ibid., p. 165.

65. Ibid., p. 163.

66. Ibid., p. 264.

67. Ibid., p. 163.

68. Rorty, "Solidarity or Objectivity," p. 12.

69. Conrad Hilberry, *The Moon Seen as a Slice of Pineapple* (Athens: University of Georgia Press, 1984), p. 20. Reprinted by permission of *Poetry Northwest* and the poet.

70. William Carlos Williams, *Paterson*, (New York: New Directions, 1963), p. 144.

71. Charles Olson, *Selected Writings of Charles Olson*, ed. by Robert Greeley (New York: New Directions, 1976), p. 16.

72. For an amplification of this point see my *American Religious Empiricism* (Albany: The State University of New York Press, 1986), chap. 4.

73. Stout, *Flight from Authority, p. 247; emphasis in original.*

Chapter 5

1. "A Vision of Ourselves," *Time* 126 (July 29, 1985): 58. Reprinted by permission from TIME.

2. In John Dewey, *The Influence of Darwin on Philosophy: And Other Essays in Contemporary Thought* (Bloomington: Indiana University Press, 1965).

3. William James, *The Will to Believe and other Essays in Popular Philosophy* (Cambridge, Mass.: Harvard University Press, 1979), p. 189.

4. William James, *Pragmatism* (Cambridge, Mass.: Harvard University Press, 1979), p. 142.

5. William James, "Is Life Worth Living?" in *The Will to Believe*, p. 55; emphasis in original.

6. William James, "A Pluralistic Mystic," *Essays in Philosophy* (Cambridge, Mass.: Harvard University Press, 1978), p. 189.

7. Charles Sanders Peirce, *Collected Papers of Charles Sanders Peirce*, vols. 1–6, ed. by Charles Hartshorne and Paul Weiss (Cambridge, Mass.: The Belknap Press of Harvard University Press, 1978), 5, p. 323. See also Murray G. Murphey, "Kant's Children: The Cambridge Pragmatists," *Transactions of the Charles S. Peirce Society*, 4 (Winter 1968): 11.

8. Peirce, *Collected Papers*, 5, p. 318.

9. Ibid., p. 40.

10. William James, "Remarks on Spencer's Definition of Mind as Correspondence," in William James, *Essays in Philosophy*, p. 8; emphasis in original.

11. Ibid., p. 18.

12. In William James, *Essays in Radical Empiricism* (Cambridge, Mass.: Harvard University Press, 1976.

13. William James, "On Some Omissions of Introspective Psychology," *Mind* (January 1884) in John J. McDermott, "Forward," in Charlene Haddock Seigfried, *Chaos and Context: A Study of William James* (Athens, Ohio: Ohio University Press, 1978), p. x.

14. William James, "The Experience of Activity," *Essays in Radical Empiricism*, p. 93; emphasis in original.

15. William James, *The Varieties of Religious Experience* (Cambridge: Harvard University Press, 1985), pp. 36–37.

16. James, "A World of Pure Experience," *Essays in Radical Empiricism*, p. 35.

17. James, "Spencer's Definition," p. 21.

18. William James, "The Function of Cognition," *The Meaning of Truth* (Cambridge, Mass.: Harvard University Press, 1975), p. 23.

19. This crucial sentence is included in the text of "A World of Pure Experience" included in *The Writings of William James: A Comprehensive Edition*, ed. by John J. McDermott (New York: The Modern Library, 1968), p. 207 and in *Essays in Radical Empiricism and A Pluralistic Universe* (New York: Longmans, Green and Co., 1947), p. 73; it is omitted in "A World of Pure Experience," *Essays in Radical Empiricism*, (Cambridge, Mass.: Harvard University Press, 1976), p. 36.

20. William James, "Does 'Consciousness' Exist?" in *Essays in Radical Empiricism*, p. 13.

21. James, "Spencer's Definition," p. 21; emphasis in original.

22. John Dewey, "From Absolutism to Experimentalism," *The Philosophy of John Dewey*, Volume I, *The Structure of Experience*, ed. by John J. McDermott (New York: G. P. Putnam's Sons, 1973), p. 2.

23. Ibid., pp. 5–8.

24. Ibid., p. 10.

25. Ibid., p. 12.

26. John Dewey, "The Postulate of Immediate Empiricism," in Dewey, *The Influence of Darwin on Philosophy*, pp. 226n–27n.

27. John Dewey, *Experience and Nature* (New York: Dover Publications, Inc., 1958), p. 28.

28. John Dewey, *Art as Experience* (New York: Capricorn Books, 1958), p. 15.

29. Ibid., p. 16.

30. John Dewey, *A Common Faith* (New Haven, Conn.: Yale University Press, 1952), p. 19.

31. Ibid., p. 13.

32. Dewey, *Art as Experience*, pp. 192–95.

33. Dewey, *A Common Faith*, p. 18.

34. Ibid., p. 19.

35. Ibid., p. 14; emphasis in original.

36. Ibid., p. 49.

37. Ibid., p. 46.

38. Ibid.

39. Ibid., p. 47; emphasis in original.

40. See my *American Religious Empiricism* (Albany: State University of New York Press, 1986), pp. 19–27.

41. John E. Smith, *The Spirit of American Philosophy*, rev. ed. (Albany: State University of New York Press, 1983), 173.

42. Bernard Eugene Meland, *Seeds of Redemption* (New York: The Macmillan Co., 1947), p. vii; emphasis in original. (The lectures were postponed; consequently, the actual delivery did not occur during the weeks of the bombing.)

43. Ibid., p. 7.

44. Bernard Eugene Meland, *Reawakening of the Christian Faith* (Freeport N. Y.: Books for Libraries Press, 1972), p. ix.

45. Meland, *The Seeds of Redemption*, p. ix.

46. Meland, *The Reawakening of the Christian Faith*, p. viii.

47. Bernard E. Meland, *Higher Education and the Human Spirit* (Chicago: Seminary Cooperative Bookstore, Inc., 1966), pp. 11–12, 40–41.

48. Ibid., p. 48.

49. Ibid., p. 54,

50. Ibid., p. 64.

51. Ibid., p. 156.

52. Ibid., pp. 157–58.

53. Bernard E. Meland, *Faith and Culture* (New York: Oxford University Press, 1953), chap. X, "The Problem of Human Goodness."

54. Ibid., p. 162.

55. Bernard E. Meland, *Fallible Forms and Symbols: Discourses on Method in a Theology of Culture* (Philadelphia: Fortress Press, 1976), p. 24.

56. Ibid., pp. vii–viii.

57. Bernard M. Loomer, "An Atomic Energy Proposal," *The Chicago Magazine* 73 (1979): 22.

58. Ibid., p. 25.

59. Ibid., p. 24.

60. Bernard M. Loomer, "Religion and the Mind of the University," in *Liberal Learning and Religion*, ed. by Amos N. Wilder (Port Washington, N. Y.: Kennikat Press, 1969), p. 155.

61. Ibid., p. 165.

62. Ibid.

63. Ibid., p. 167.

64. Bernard M. Loomer, "Reflections on Theological Education," *Criterion* 4 (Autumn 1965): 5.

65. *The Size of God: The Theology of Bernard Loomer in Context*, ed. by William Dean and Larry Axel (Macon, Ga.: Mercer University Press, 1987).

66. Ibid., p. 21.

67. Ibid., p. 23; emphasis in original.

68. Ibid., p. 51.

69. Ibid., p. 23.

70. Ibid., p. 41.

71. Ibid., p. 34.

72. Ibid., p. 31.

73. Ibid., p. 41.

74. Shirley Jackson Case, *The Christian Philosophy of History* (Chicago: The University of Chicago Press, 1943), p. 176.

Chapter 6

1. William James, *The Will to Believe and Other Essays in Popular Philosophy* (Cambridge, Mass.: Harvard University Press, 1979), pp. 24–25.

2. Hans-Georg Gadamer, *Truth and Method* (New York: The Seabury Press, 1975), p. xi.

3. See Jeffrey Stout, *The Flight from Authority: Religion, Morality, and the Quest for Autonomy* (Notre Dame, Ind.: University of Notre Dame Press, 1981), p. 37.

4. Immanuel Kant, *Critique of Pure Reason*, trans. by J. M. D. Meiklejohn (New York: E. P. Dutton & Co., Inc., 1940), pp. 35–36; emphasis in original.

5. Immanuel Kant, *Critique of Practical Reason*, trans. by Lewis White Beck (Indianapolis: Bobbs-Merrill Educational Publishing, 1956), p. 16.

6. Immanuel Kant, *Critique of Judgment*, trans. by J. C. Meredith (London: Oxford University Press, 1964), p. 168; emphasis in original.

7. G. W. F. Hegel, *The Phenomenology of Mind*, trans. by J. B. Baillie (New York: The Macmillan Co., 1961), p. 86.

8. Mark C. Taylor, "Introduction: System . . . Structure . . . Difference . . . Other," in *Deconstruction in Context: Literature and Philosophy*, ed. by Mark C. Taylor (Chicago: University of Chicago Press, 1986), p. 8.

9. Frank Lentricchia makes a similar point as he accepts deconstructionism's elimination of the logocentric but argues that the Yale deconstructionists have fallen into a new subjectivisim and formalism, and neglected what should be the social and political aspects of historicism. See Lentricchia, *After the New Criticism* (Chicago: University of Chicago Press, 1980), Chapter 5; and *Criticism and Social Change* (Chicago: University of Chicago Press, 1983). See also Giles Gunn's critique of post-structuralism from a standpoint closer to the one I support, *The Culture of Criticism and the Criticism of Culture* (New York: Oxford University Press, 1987). (Had I been able to read Gunn's book while this book was being written, its insights would have been used.)

10. Richard J. Bernstein, *Beyond Objectivism and Relativism: Science, Hermeneutics, and Praxis* (Philadelphia: University of Pennsylvania Press, 1983), p. 223.

11. Richard Rorty, *Philosophy and the Mirror of Nature* (Princeton, N. J.: Princeton University Press, 1979), p. 357.

12. Ibid., pp. 357–58.

13. Ibid., p. 359, 377.

14. Nelson Goodman, *Ways of Worldmaking* (Indianapolis: Hackett Publishing Co., 1978), p. x.

15. Hilary Putnam, *Reason, Truth and History* (New York: Cambridge University Press, 1982), pp. 113, 216, 119.

16. Ibid., p. 52, 60.

17. William James, *Pragmatism* (Cambridge, Mass.: Harvard University Press, 1979), p. 14.

18. Ibid., p. 39.

19. Ibid., p. 104, emphasis in original.

20. J. Dewey, *Philosophy and Civilization* (Glouster, Mass.: Peter Smith, 1968), p. 25.

21. Alfred North Whitehead, *Modes of Thought* (New York: The Free Press, 1966), p. 138.

22. Ibid., p. 143.

23. Alfred North Whitehead, *Process and Reality: An Essay in Cosmology*, corr. ed., ed. by David Ray Griffin and Donald W. Sherburne (New York: The Free Press, 1978), p. 167.

24. Ibid., pp. 166–67.

25. *The Letters of William James*, ed. by Henry James (2 vols; Boston: The Atlantic Monthly Press, 1920), vol 2, pp. 291–292; emphasis in original.

26. Ibid., p. 292.

27. Bernard E. Meland, *Fallible Forms and Symbols: Discourses on Method in a Theology of Culture* (Philadelphia: Fortress Press, 1976), p. 24.

28. Mark C. Taylor, *Erring: A Postmodern A/theology* (Chicago: University of Chicago Press, 1984), p. 5.

29. Ibid., p. 68.

30. Ibid., p. 111; emphasis in original.

31. Ibid., pp. 11–12, 150.

32. Jacques Derrida, "Edmond Jabès and the Question of the Book," in *Writing and Difference*, trans. by Alan Bass (Chicago: University of Chicago Press, 1978), p. 74; emphasis in original.

33. Taylor, *Erring*, p. 116.

34. Jacques Derrida, "Structure, Sign and Play in the Discourse of the Human Sciences," in *Writing and Difference*, p. 292; emphasis in original.

35. Jeffrey Stout, "The Voice of Theology in Contemporary Culture," in *Religion and America: Spiritual Life in a Secular Age*, ed. by Mary Douglas and Steven Tipton, (Boston: Beacon Press, 1982, 1983), p. 253; emphasis in original.

36. Ibid., p. 259.

37. Stout, *The Flight from Authority*, p. 272.

38. Edmund N. Santurri, "The Flight to Pragmatism," *Religious Studies Review* 9 (October 1983): 334.

39. Cornel West, "Nietzsche's Prefiguration of Postmodern American Philosophy," *Boundary 2*, 9 and 10 (Spring/Fall 1981).

40. Ibid., p. 265.

41. In a 1978 article eventually published in *The Theological Imagination*, Kaufman was willing to say that the metaphysical and theological imagination is a Kantian notion, referring to the necessity to construct subjective worlds. Nevertheless, in

that same volume Kaufman acknowledges that clear Kantian distinctions between the free, spiritual meanings of humans and the necessities of the natural world have been eroded by new developments. It happens, he says, that "nature no longer appears as a static and immovable lawful structure" and that we now know that "all human functions are rooted in and presuppose our bodiliness," (See, Gordon D. Kaufman, *The Theological Imagination* (Philadelphia: The Westminster Press, 1980), pp. 244, 237.

42. Gordon D. Kaufman, *Theology for a Nuclear Age* (Philadelphia: Westminster Press, 1985), p. 9.

43. Ibid.

44. Jeffrey Stout, "A Lexicon of Postmodern Philosophy," *Religious Studies Review* 13 (January 1987): 21; emphasis in original.

45. Kaufman, *Theology for a Nuclear Age,* pp. 41, 43.

46. John Dewey, *A Common Faith* (New Haven, Conn.: Yale University Press, 1952), p. 43.

47. Ibid., p. 47.

48. Ibid., p. 48.

INDEX

aesthetic experience: 109; empiricist
and historical (Dewey), 109; and
religious acts, 109; unity in diversity
(Loomer), 120
After the New Criticism: 9, 161 n 9
*Against Method: Outline of an
Anarchistic Theory of Knowledge:* 124
Altizer, Thomas: 137
*American Christianity: An Historical
Interpretation with Representative
Documents,* 69
American Religious Empiricism: xi
Ames, Edward Scribner: 66
*The Analogical Imagination: Christian
Theology and the Culture of
Pluralism:* 68
Anglo-American positivists, see:
Positivism
Aristotle: 33
Arnold, Charles Harvey: 60
Aron, Raymond: 19
Art as Experience: xii, 107, 108, 109
The Atonement and the Social Process:
54, 55
Augustine and history: 2
Axel, Larry: 65, 67; Dewey, 67;
Mathews, 67; Smith, 67, Sweet, 67
Ayer, A. J.: 4

Bacon, Francis: 4, 6
Barth, Karl: 16, 47, 64
Beard, Charles: 24
Belo, F.: 39
Bercovitch, Sacvan: 24
Berger, Peter: 23

Bergson, Henri: 133
Bernstein, Richard: ix, 1, 12, 20–21, 23,
24, 25, 26, 27, 28, 31, 86, 123, 131,
142; Arendt, 11, 27, 129; *Beyond
Objectivism and Relativism: Science,
Hermeneutics and Praxis,* 11, 20, 24,
26, 31, 124, 129, 142; Bultmann, 26;
Cartesian anxiety, 11, 18, 21, 129;
contemporary forces preventing com-
munity, 11; Derrida, 24; dialogic
communities, 27, 31, 129; Dilthey,
26; Feyerabend, 11; Gadamer, 26–7;
Habermas, 27; Hegel, 11, 24;
Heidegger, 24, 26, Husserl, 24; Kant,
24; Kuhn, 11; Lakatos, 11; Marx, 11;
phronesis, 11, 129; pragmatism, 31;
Rorty, 11, 26, 30, 129, critique of
Habermas and Gadamer, 27; Winch, 11
*Beyond Objectivism and Relativism:
Science, Hermeneutics and Praxis:* 11,
20, 24, 26, 31, 124, 129
*Beyond Preference: Liberal Theories of
Independent Association:* 67
*The Bible and Liberation: Political and
Social Hermeneutics:* 38
*Blessed Rage for Order: The New
Pluralism in Theology:* 68
Brauer, Jerold C.: 69, 76; Baird, 68;
Garrison, 69; Handy, Loetscher and
H. S. Smith, 69, *American Chris-
tianity: An Historical Interpretation
with Representative Documents,* 69;
Hudson, 69; McNeill, 69; Mead, S.,
68, 69, *The Lively Experiment,* 69;
Mode, 68, 69; Spinka, 69; Sweet, 68;
Willoughby, 69

165